Windows NT™ for the Technical Professional

Louis Columbus and Nik Simpson

Windows NT™ for the Technical Professional

By Louis Columbus and Nik Simpson

Published by

OnWord Press
2530 Camino Entrada
Santa Fe, NM 87505-4835 USA

SAN 694-0269
First Edition, 1995
10 9 8 7 6 5 4 3 2 1
Printed in the United States of America

Cataloging-in-Publication Data
Columbus, Louis and Nik Simpson
Windows NT for the Technical Professional
Includes index.
1. Windows NT (computer operating system) 2. Engineering 3. CAD I. Title
94-66165
ISBN 1-56690-064-6

Trademarks

Windows NT, Windows NT Workstation, MS-DOS, Windows NT Server, and other products are trademarks or registered trademarks of Microsoft Corporation. OnWord Press is a registered trademark of High Mountain Press, Inc. Other products and services, including AutoCAD, MicroStation, Pro/ENGINEER, MGE, and ArcView, are mentioned in this book that are either trademarks or registered trademarks of their respective companies. OnWord Press and the authors make no claim to these marks.

Warning and Disclaimer

This book is designed to provide information about Windows NT. Every effort has been made to make this book complete and as accurate as possible; however, no warranty or fitness is implied.

The information is provided on an "as-is" basis. OnWord Press shall have neither liability nor responsibility to any person or entity with respect to any loss or damages in connection with or rising from the information contained in this book.

About the Authors

Louis Columbus

After graduating from the University of Arizona with a double-major in Marketing and Management Systems, Louis began working for Printronix as a Market Analyst. While working for Printronix, Louis completed a Masters in Business Administration from Pepperdine University. Louis has also worked for Toshiba America and CalComp as a Product Manager. At Toshiba, Louis was Product Manager for the P Series printers, in addition to the MK Series of disk drives. At CalComp, Louis was responsible for the PlotMaster, ColorMaster, and ColorMaster Plus series of color thermal transfer printers. Interested in learning more about the systems side of computing, Louis joined Intergraph in 1992 as a Systems Consultant. His daily activities include providing pre-sales support and assistance to Intergraph customers, the Intergraph sales force, and the resellers now actively selling Intergraph's line of plotting solutions. In addition, Louis hosts customer visits to Huntsville and completes many sales and product training sessions each year.

As a beta site for the first Windows NT releases from Microsoft, Louis has first-hand knowledge of how to install and use this operating system. Prior to completing *Windows NT for the Technical Professional*, Louis has had two other books published on Windows NT. The first is *Learn Windows NT In A Day*, which has been translated into both Chinese and Japanese, and is used within these countries as a textbook for students studying this operating system. The second book, *Networking with Windows NT* defines the networking aspects of this powerful operating system. In total, Louis had had seven other books published.

Nik Simpson

Nik started his working life in the United Kingdom as a teacher. After completing his post-degree qualification in teaching, he went to work for Intergraph UK in the training group. In 1987 Nik left Intergraph to work for 18 months with AT&T, both in the United Kingdom and the United States. In 1988 Nik rejoined Intergraph UK and now works as a Systems Consultant for Intergraph Computer Systems in Huntsville, Alabama. In the two periods working for Intergraph, Nik has been involved in many areas including: training on Intergraph products; support for CLIX (Intergraph UNIX) customers; application developer support for CLIX; systems software presales support and marketing; and server systems presales support and marketing.

As part of his duties at Intergraph, Nik has had access to the very early betas of Windows NT and has been a user for almost three years. With more than 10 years of UNIX experience combined with almost 3 years of NT experience, Nik has an excellent understanding NT-UNIX interoperability as well as general use of Windows NT.

Acknowledgments

Without the assistance, commitment and determination of Margaret Burns this book would still be just an outline, waiting to be assembled and written. She is one of the best editors I have had the pleasure to work with and can literally make an author drop what they are doing and complete a task just through sheer guilt! Her doggedness to see this book through is commendable. Thank you to Dan Raker for continuing to believe in this project and keeping it moving through over a year of development. I appreciate your patience and willingness to hold on until this book was ready. Thanks to Frank Conforti for taking the initial idea, refining it, being patient, and shepherding the early chapters through the review process. Thanks to Matt Ragen at Microsoft for the timely reviews of the manuscript and the assistance in getting the perspective of the developers.

I'd like to thank Jeff Pugh for providing excellent support during the transition period from Windows NT 3.1 to 3.51, and the outstanding level of support he provided for this book. Making systems available for the specific screens, ensuring systems would be available, and being flexible enough to respond to the many demands of this book really makes Jeff a member of this book's team. I'd also like to thank John Simmons for helping me to understand the intricacies of Windows NT's Print Manager and his willingness to answer time-consuming questions during the process of creating this book. Thank you Greg Kessloff for your willingness to spend extra hours with me, giving me the opportunity to fully understand MicroStation Version 5's many features. You are a true asset to any organization you are a member of. Thanks for the great screen captures too. Special thanks to Brigitte Sinton for her patience and team-oriented attitude in sharing the workload, making it possible for me to have evenings free to write this book. Thank you Tobin Gilman for your interest in this project, and your flexibility in giving me the time I needed to complete it. Thanks to Dennis Sanders for giving me the support I needed to complete this book as well. I thoroughly enjoy being a member of your organization. Thanks to Richard Malm for his technical review. Thanks to Intergraph for the loan of a TD2 workstation.

Book Production

This book was produced in Ventura Publisher 4.1.1. The cover design is by David Rohr, using QuarkXpress 3.11 and Aldus FreeHand 3.0.

OnWord Press

OnWord Press is dedicated to the fine art of professional documentation.

In addition to the author who developed the material for this book, many members of the OnWord Press team contribute to the book that ends up in your hands. In addition to those listed below, other members who contributed to the production and distribution of this book include Joe Adams, James Bridge, Roxsan Meyer, Jean Nichols, Robin Ortiz, and Bob Leyba.

Dan Raker, President
Kate Hayward, Publisher
Gary Lange, Associate Publisher
David Talbott, Acquisitions Editor
Carol Leyba, Production Manager
Janet Leigh Dick, Marketing Director
Margaret Burns, Project Editor
Carol Leyba, Production Editor
David Rohr, Cover designer
Margaret Burns, Indexer

Conventions Used in this Book

The following conventions were used throughout this book:

✦ ***NOTE:*** *Notes present important information or concepts that might otherwise be overlooked.*

✔ ***TIP:*** *Tips show shortcuts and hints that help you to be more productive.*

✘ ***WARNING:*** *Warnings point out functions and procedures that could get you in trouble if you are not careful.*

Dedications

To my wife Cheryl for her constant love, encouragement, and understanding. Without her support this book would not have been possible.

Louis Columbus

This book is dedicated to Eliza, my cat who died in January, a great companion, but a lousy typist.

Nik Simpson

Contents

Introduction

With the advent of personal computers, the entire scope of computing has changed. Desktop-based systems have continually brought new and more powerful solutions to engineers, designers, and individuals involved in all facets of engineering. Never before have the fields of product development, engineering, and manufacturing been transformed by a shift in computing power from the mainframe to the desktop. Operating systems have led this shift in computing power from centralized mainframes to decentralized, distributed networks. Windows NT Workstation exemplifies the progression of operating systems away from centralized resources to distributed files, printers, and resources for workgroups.

The goal of this book is to give you a solid understanding of how the Windows NT operating system works, how its features can make you more productive in an engineering environment, and how to integrate Windows NT into an existing computer network. Included within this book are hands-on examples and case studies illustrating how engineering, design, and consulting companies have integrated Windows NT into their existing system configurations and increased overall productivity.

An Overview of Windows NT Workstation 3.51

Getting to know how Windows NT works first involves understanding the role it plays in the Microsoft Windows product line. Here's a quick overview of the Windows product family:

Windows 3.1: This is a graphical user environment based on the MS-DOS operating system, which was designed primarily as a tool for single-user computing sessions. The Microsoft Windows 3.1 interface has become a market standard for desktop computing. Over 40 million copies of Microsoft Windows 3.1 have been sold worldwide.

Windows NT 3.1: Windows NT is a highly versatile, 32-bit multitasking operating system based on a series of subsystems that ensure compatibility with a wide variety of application programs. Specifically, these subsystems ensure compatibility with MS-DOS, 16- and 32-bit applications programs. Key features of the Microsoft Windows NT operating system include the following:

- ❑ Easy-to-use graphical user interface for navigating through the variety of file groups located throughout the Desktop.

- ❑ Support for preemptive multitasking, making it possible to complete several tasks simultaneously.

- ❑ Support for MS-DOS File Access Table (FAT), OS/2, HPFS, and Windows NT System file structures.

- ❑ Built-in networking and electronic mail capabilities.

- ❑ Compatibility with 32-bit based applications, ensuring high performance of CAD, engineering, and mechanical programs.

- ❑ Programs created for MS-DOS and Microsoft Windows can be used with Windows NT Workstation.

- ❑ Support for Microsoft OS/2 version 1.X application programs.

Windows NT Server: The Microsoft Windows NT operating system is based on a client/server architecture, where Windows NT 3.1 is the client interface and Windows NT Server (NTS) is the server-based component. The key features of Windows NTS are:

- ❑ Like Windows NT 3.1, NTS is a 32-bit preemptive multitasking operating system that has been ported to Intel-based, RISC-based, and multi-processor–based workstations.

- ❑ NTS is based on a microkernel design that integrates security and manageability, providing a reliable platform for mission-critical application programs.

❒ Included within NTS is built-in file sharing capabilities for workgroup computing, and an open network system that includes built-in support for NETBEUI, TCP/IP, and other popular network transport mechanisms or protocols. NTS also provides resources to ensure Novell Netware and Banyan Vines clients can interact on a Windows NT–based network.

❒ NTS, like its client counterpart, is based on a series of subsystems that ensure compatibility with MS-DOS, 16-bit Windows, and OS/2 application programs.

❒ A single network logon lets users access network resources, including client-server applications, using one user account and one password per user.

❒ Advanced data protection features such as disk mirroring, disk striping with parity (RAID 5), and like Windows NT 3.1, support for uninterruptable power supplies.

❒ Remote Access Service that makes it possible to dial up to the NTS-based server from home or while traveling. The Remote Access Service supports asynchronous telephone communications, including ISDN and X.25 compatibility.

❒ Services for Macintosh that enables Macintoshes and PCs to work together on the same Windows NT–based network. Macintosh users can access NTS resources just as they would connect to any other AppleShare server to share files, printers, and client/server applications.

How Windows NT and Windows NT Server Differ

Windows NT 3.51 is the client interface of the client/server architecture on which the Windows NT operating system is based. Windows NT's client capabilities are actually a subset of NTS' full range of functionality, because the former includes client-oriented commands and tools that make server-based resources possible to a diverse set of clients. The major difference between Windows NT and NTS is the ability of the latter to use domains and trust relationships between domains. These domains are composed of client/server relationships between workstations and servers.

Windows NTS differs from Windows NT by offering superior fault-tolerance capabilities, such as disk mirroring (RAID level 1) and disk striping with parity (RAID level 5) on network servers. RAID is used for ensuring reliability on a file server. There are six levels of RAID capability, each having a progressively higher level of system redundancy and reliability. At level 1, disk mirroring is used for writing identical series of data sets to two separate hard disks. Disk striping with parity is a more advanced technique where several physical disks share a common set of logical data, making it less likely a single disk will impact the availability of data. You can use options within Windows NTS for completing RAID-oriented fault tolerance and data reliability tasks.

Using options in NTS, you can also define user profiles for trust domains and interrelationships throughout the network of which your server is a member. This makes transferring files from one domain to another seamless. You can also define anonymous FTP accounts on an NTS-based system, making it possible for others throughout the network to download files from the server you are using. In addition to file transfer capability, NTS also includes Services for Macintosh, which gives Macintosh users' access to resources located on the Windows NTS. Also included in NTS is support for Banyan VINES and Novell NetWare clients.

System Requirements

Windows NT Workstation 3.51

Here's the minimum hardware prerequisites that need to be met in order to install and use Windows NT 3.51:

- ❏ **Hardware:** 32-bit x86-based microprocessor (such as Intel 80386/33 MHz or higher) or supported RISC-based microprocessor such as MIPS R4000 or DEC Alpha.

- ❏ **Video:** VGA or higher resolution display adapter.

- ❏ **Hard disks:** One or more hard disks with a minimum of 75MB free hard disk space on the partition that will contain the Windows NT system files. Approximately 92MB of free disk space is required for RISC-based systems.

- ❏ **Floppy drive:** For x86-based systems, a SCSI CD-ROM is required to load the software; it is optional on x86-based systems.

❐ **CD-ROM drive:** On RISC-based systems, a SCSI CD-ROM is required for loading software; it is optional on x86-based systems.

❐ **Network Adapter Cards:** One or more is required for use in conjunction with Windows NTS.

❐ **Memory:** A minimum of 12MB of RAM is recommended, with 16MB suggested for x86-based systems; 16MB of RAM on RISC-based systems is a minimum requirement.

✔ *TIP: If you're planning to use high-performance CAD software in conjunction with Windows NT, install at least 32MB of RAM in your workstation before installing the operating system.*

❐ **Optional Components:** A mouse or other pointing device is optional, but highly recommended, as are additional SCSI CD-ROM drives.

Windows NT Server

Here are the prerequisites for installing and using Windows NT Server:

❐ **Hardware:** 32-bit x86-based microprocessor (such as Intel 80386/33 MHz or higher) or supported RISC-based microprocessor such as MIPS R4000 or DEC Alpha.

❐ **Video:** VGA or higher resolution display adapter.

❐ **Hard disk:** One or more hard disks with a minimum of 90MB free hard disk space on the partition that will contain the Windows NTS system files. Approximately 100MB of free disk space is required for RISC-based systems.

❐ **Floppy drive:** For x86-based systems, you'll need to have one high-density floppy disk drive available.

❐ **CD-ROM drive:** On RISC-based systems, a SCSI CD-ROM is required in order to load the software; it is optional on x86-based systems.

❐ **Network Adapter Cards:** One or more is required for use in conjunction with Windows NTS.

❐ **Memory:** A minimum of 16MB of RAM is recommended, with 32MB suggested for x86-based systems; 16MB of RAM on RISC-based systems is a minimum requirement.

❏   **Optional Components:** A mouse or other pointing device is optional, but highly recommended, as are additional SCSI CD-ROM drives.

Who Should Read this Book

This book is for technical professionals interested in learning more about how Windows NT can help them accomplish their tasks. Many engineers spend over 70% of their time completing tasks that communicate their ideas. This leaves 30% of their time for design tasks. Windows NT is complementary to each of these roles. Using the multitasking capabilities of Windows NT, an engineer can be completing a report describing a development project, and then switch to a CAD program such as Intergraph's MicroStation Version 5.0 to complete design tasks. This flexibility that engineers have in designing and documenting their efforts makes the Windows NT operating system ideal for technical professionals. This book is organized to give the technical professional the opportunity to learn how to use the Windows NT operating system.

The first-time user of Windows NT will also find this book valuable as a learning tool. This book begins with an overview of the Windows NT operating system applets or small applications, then proceeds to a complete section describing how to use engineering applications in conjunction with the Windows NT operating system. The final third of the book explains how Windows NT plays a complementary role within an organization. The first-time Windows NT user will find this section particularly useful for understanding how interoperability is available with third-party operating systems, including UNIX-based clients and servers. There's also a chapter for the first-time Windows NT user considerations for using Windows for Workgroups.

The CAD administrator will also find this book useful as both a teaching tool and troubleshooting guide. For CAD administrators evaluating Windows NT for their organization's use, the chapters describing how Windows NT can be optimized for organizations will prove helpful. The beginning chapters of this book will assist the CAD administrator in describing to beginning users how they can become more productive with technical tasks by using the Windows NT operating system.

Windows NT for the Technical Professional is an ideal book for anyone interested in learning how Windows NT can be effectively used for completing technical tasks. From the beginning Windows NT user, who has a complete series of step-by-step instructions showing how to complete tasks to the hints and tips for CAD administrators for managing interoperability of their existing hardware configurations, *Windows NT for the Technical Professional* is an ideal tutorial as well as reference book you'll want to refer to again and again.

How this Book Is Organized

Windows NT for the Technical Professional is organized to give you a complete picture of how Windows NT Workstation works, and how you can use it for completing technical tasks more efficiently. The goals of this book are to give you:

❏ A hands-on knowledge of how to use the applets, options, and applications included within Windows NT to make you more productive in your work.

❏ How to install, use, and switch between applications once they are installed in Windows NT.

❏ A thorough understanding of how to use MS-DOS based technical applications within the Windows NT environment.

❏ Knowledge of how the subsystems included within Windows NT provide you with the necessary interoperability with existing investments in software.

❏ Gain an understanding of how object linking and embedding are included within Windows NT, and how this feature can be used for streamlining both design and documentation tasks when using Windows NT.

If you're familiar with the Control Panel and Print Manager from Windows 3.1, you'll notice quite a difference in Windows NT Workstation. Both of these commonly used tools are now strengthened to accentuate NT's networking orientation. Where Windows 3.1 had fewer than ten applets in the Control Panel, Windows NT has 17. The Print Manager in Windows 3.1 was designed primarily for a single-user workstation environment, where the Print Manager in Windows NT is designed to give you more flexibility in using network-based printing and plotting resources.

Getting in Touch with the Authors

Throughout this book, we will strive to give you the most accurate and timely descriptions of the Windows NT operating system as they relate to the technical professional. If you have any comments or questions, or are interested in finding additional information on a subject, you can reach us via Internet at lecolumb@ingr.com.

The Importance of Microsoft Windows NT

Introduction

With every new generation of operating system there's the promise of increased performance, better and more efficient functionality, and the best promise of all, interoperability with existing systems. Microsoft's Windows NT operating system provides the necessary tools for migrating from UNIX or IBM's OS/2 operating systems, giving technical users the opportunity to streamline existing operations with Windows NT while retaining investments in existing software and hardware.

The intent of this book is to provide you with a comprehensive framework you can use for evaluating the Microsoft Windows NT operating system. The book moves from general to specific features of Windows NT Workstation. This chapter begins by giving you insights into why Microsoft decided to pursue the Windows NT operating system strategy, then continues through an overview of the benefits this operating system provides technical users.

The History of Microsoft Windows NT

In the 1950s a prominent researcher stated that America would need no more than five computers for all the computing needs of the country. Today this statement sounds absurd, there are some *people* with that many computers! Computers are no longer the preserve of large organizations, most people doing any sort of technical work have a computer on the desk.

There are many factors that have influenced the widespread adoption of desktop computers, chief among these are:

❑ Applications

❑ Simpler operating environments

❑ CPU power

It is hard to pick one of these factors as the most important because they are largely interdependent. For example, by the early eighties it was clear that the command line was a clumsy way of working with a computer and intimidating to many potential users. The answer was a graphical user interface or GUI; this required much more CPU power, so early efforts such as the work done by Xerox PARC never got much further than the research laboratory. In 1984 Apple introduced the Macintosh and brought the advantages of the GUI interface to the world. Unfortunately for Apple, the rest of the world wanted to use IBM-compatible machines because they where cheaper and had more applications. The popularity of the Macintosh GUI prompted several companies to develop GUI environments for the IBM PC. Of these, the Microsoft Windows system quickly became the de facto standard.

Windows has one major fault, it requires the presence of MS-DOS, DOS is a very limited operating system. The limitations of DOS have resulted in several unfortunate side effects:

❑ **Limited use of new more powerful hardware:** DOS has to live in 640KB of memory. In 1982 this was not a limitation, because 640KB represented a large system. In 1995, many systems have 16MB or more of memory.

❑ **Stability:** Modern operating systems such as UNIX protect the hardware from rogue programs. DOS has no such protection, meaning that a single application can crash the system.

❑ **Portability:** DOS is written for the Intel x86 family of processors. It is not portable to other processors, being inextricably entwined with the IBM PC architecture. Applications written for DOS also tend to be hard to port because of the many system dependencies and poorly defined operating system interfaces.

Despite these limitations, the combination of DOS and Windows has dominated the desktop for several years. For a new operating system to capture the desktop it needs several features:

❏ **Windows GUI:** Users don't wish to relearn the interface.

❏ **Compatibility:** The new operating system has to be able to run many existing applications as a way to protect investment.

❏ **Modern design:** The new operating system has to overcome the design limitations of DOS.

Windows NT is the first operating system to do this.

❏ **OS and application portability:** The operating system and applications written for it should be easily portable to any processor architecture.

Windows NT's Roots

Prior to the era of personal workstations that have the processing power to simultaneously handle concurrent tasks, there was the minicomputer. Many of the features found in the Microsoft Windows NT operating system were first seen on operating systems developed for minicomputers such as the DEC VAX series of machines. Features common to Windows NT and these minicomputer operating systems include the following:

❏ The operating system is protected from applications.

❏ Applications run in a virtual environment so that they cannot accidentally affect another application.

❏ Applications and the operating system share resources such as CPU time under the control of the operating system.

❏ Operating system allows resources to be assigned to different users and prevent unauthorized access to applications, services, and data.

These features first appeared on the desktop in the form of workstations running the UNIX operating system, another minicomputer operating system that migrated to the desktop. These older minicomputer operating systems turned desktop environments have undergone many changes to try to bring them into the GUI era. Unfortunately they fall short in several areas:

❏ No Windows 3.1 GUI

❑   Lack of applications

❑   Cost

Windows NT represents a merging of the Windows 3.1 GUI with a fully featured 32-bit operating systems to provide a platform for desktop computing.

The Thin Line Between PC and Workstation

Personal computers have quickly grown in both performance and market dominance. Originally, the term *workstation* was reserved for specific high-performance (and high price) graphic intensive computers. This moniker was worn by a small number of vendors, which included Sun Microsystems, Hewlett Packard, and Silicon Graphics. Today, however, with PCs sporting 32- and 64-bit microprocessors, the term *workstation* has become somewhat blurred. Now a workstation is considered any computer capable of completing several tasks at the same time. With this new definition, it became apparent that an operating system capable of providing technical users with the benefits of UNIX and the ease of use of Microsoft Windows desktops was needed.

In 1988, Microsoft hired Dave Cutler from Digital Equipment Corporation to begin development of what would eventually become Microsoft Windows NT. Mr. Cutler had been with Digital Equipment Corporation for 17 years and had made contributions to RSX-11M as well as being the chief architect of the VMS operating systems. Mr. Cutler began assembling teams of developers to complete the project, which had as its goal the development of an operating system that was capable of handling mission-critical applications in large, disperse computing environments. Deciding to pursue the Microsoft Windows NT operating system strategy made it possible for Microsoft to reap the benefits of Mr. Cutler's knowledge of the VMS operating system and Mach Kernel, two projects he had been involved in with, as par of Digital Equipment's operating system product line. The need for an operating system that was truly scaleable, portable, compatible with existing applications, and had the necessary support for internationalization drove the initial development efforts of Microsoft Windows NT.

From these goals and others described later in this book, this innovative approach to managing resources, applications, and data in a diverse environment grew to become what Microsoft Windows NT is today.

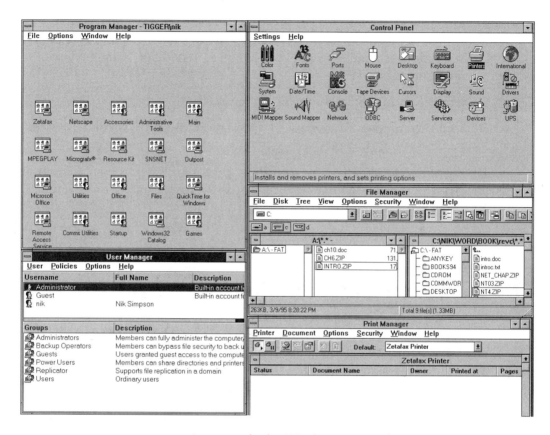

An example the Windows NT Desktop.

An Overview of Windows NT Workstation

The combination of features offered in Windows NT makes it a very attractive solution for new desktop and server systems being installed. The following are included in the basic package:

❑ Multithreaded, multitasking, multiprocessing, 32-bit operating system kernel

❑ Networking

❑ Windows 3.1 GUI

❑ Support for Intel x86, MIPS R4***, DEC Alpha processors, with others to follow

❑ File and printer sharing

❑ Network-based meeting and appointment scheduler integrated with a electronic mail system

❑ Security up to U.S. government C2 standards

❑ Ability to run most Windows 3.1 applications, even on non-Intel processors

This feature set is unrivaled by any other operating system. A combination of the merits of NT and the marketing savvy of Microsoft, makes the success of NT a sure bet.

Choosing Windows NT for Your Operation

Before Windows NT, UNIX was the only choice for developers and users of such technical applications as CAD and CASE. Widely available for every processor type known to humanity, UNIX suffers from a plethora of standards. Almost every vendor takes the UNIX operating system and enhances or modifies it in some way so that it is no longer quite compatible with other versions. The diversity of UNIX implementations means that developers face a daunting task of making applications run under a seemingly infinite variety of operating systems. For the user, every system presents subtle differences in user interface and operation, not to mention a limited choice of applications.

Windows NT, on the other hand, offers potential gains for both the developer and the user of software. For the developer Windows NT promises a common operating system across all of the important 32-bit processors. For the user, this means consistent operation and a larger availability of applications. Currently, Windows NT can be found on the following systems:

For good or ill, Microsoft intends to keep a strict control on the implementation of Windows NT so that "evolution by committee," which has so damaged UNIX, does not occur. The diagram below shows the basic structure of Windows NT. The only part that contains machine-specific code is the hardware abstraction layer (HAL).

Windows NT Status on Various Processors

Processors	Status
Intel x86 (486, Pentium etc.)	Windows NT 3.5 shipping today
Digital Alpha	Windows NT 3.5 shipping today
MIPS R4000 Family	Windows NT 3.5 shipping today
IBM/Motorola PowerPC	Windows NT 3.5 available in 1995
Sun SPARC	Under consideration
HP-PA RISC	Under consideration

Vendors are not allowed to modify very much else; this ensures true source code compatibility from one platform to the next. The dictation of a common operating system interface allows application programmers to concentrate on solving the problem, not coding round differences between one implementation of the operating system and another.

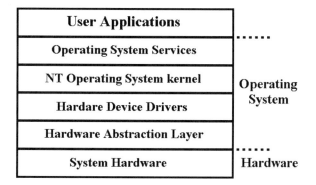

WINDOWS NT operating system structure.

Multiplatform Support

In the past, supporting multiple platforms was a complex and expensive task, requiring significant porting effort to overcome differences in processor architectures and operating environments. Windows NT offers the first completely identical environment on every important processor family. A port for an application becomes a recompile and recertification, making multiplatform support a reality. As a comparison, the UNIX operating system is different in some ways on practically every platform, the developer must face the following:

❏ Some recoding/porting of the application.

❏ Rewrite of documentation.

❏ Expense of providing multiple platforms to support and development staff.

For the technical user, Windows NT offers a choice of platforms to fit application needs. If a user needs maximum software compatibility, he or she can choose the Intel platform. If maximum performance of native Windows NT applications is the goal, the user can choose almost any RISC processor. With identical operating environments, Windows NT ensures the user has applications with a common look and feel across all platforms, thus protecting investment in hardware, software, and application training.

Windows NT's Coexistence with Existing Environments

In theory it is possible to implement a complete Windows NT operating environment for an entire company. In practice Windows NT has to interoperate with existing resources because few companies can afford the cost or take the risk of changing overnight. One major vendor of systems, Sequent Corporation, faced the problem of integrating Windows NT into an existing environment and produced a seamless mix of UNIX, Windows NT, and Windows for Workgroups with a minimum of disruption. The problems faced and solutions found are instructive.

How Sequent Computer Integrates Windows NT and UNIX

Sequent, one of the leading manufacturers of UNIX-based servers in the world, decided to introduce a new server family running Microsoft Windows NT. In addition, Sequent was able to integrate Windows NT into their existing UNIX environment without any interruption to the operation. The advantages of adopting Windows NT became clear as the company reaped the benefit of simple printer, mail, and file sharing throughout the organization. Sequent's previous reliance on a mixed UNIX and Windows-based local area network had made this level of integration difficult, if not impossible to achieve.

Integrating new technology, especially in the realm of operating systems, is a challenging task. It was an even more challenging task for Sequent, because the barriers to change were more cultural than technological. Sequent was founded in 1983 with the mission of being a major vendor of symmetric multiprocessing (SMP) computer systems for the UNIX marketplace. Sequent was the first company to offer a UNIX-based SMP server, and as a result, won many customers, including worldwide telecommunication companies, airlines, and financial services companies.

After growing to the $350 million mark in sales by 1993, Sequent was looking for a direction to further expand its sales opportunities. The company decided that Windows NT offered the best growth path for both their product line and the internal work and process flows within its own business. In 1993 Sequent announced a line of SMP-based servers based on the Windows NT operating system. These servers were called the Sequent *WinServer*™ family.

The cultural bias toward UNIX had been perpetuated by Sequent using its own UNIX servers throughout all departments of its company. When WinServer was introduced, departments that had formerly been using the UNIX-based servers were converted to Windows NT. Mark Anastas, Senior Manager for Windows NT Systems at Sequent says that, "The real benefit to customers is for the vendor who is providing a product to have a deep understanding of how it will be used in a production environment. Consequently, it always has been an important part of Sequent's culture to use the products we market." Sequent adopted Windows NT throughout its 1600-employee workforce. The excellent client-server environment offered by a combination of Windows NT Workstation 3.5 and its close cousin, Windows NT Server 3.5, has enabled the company to deploy new management systems and productivity tools throughout the organization.

Setting the Wheels in Motion

Including Windows NT into the daily activities inside Sequent was a long-term project, requiring a team of six people. Two were from the newly created Windows NT business unit and four members of the UNIX technical staff. Together, the team had to devise a plan for making sure the end users could have access to everything they had in the UNIX environment, in addition to the added benefits of the Windows GUI. In designing a solution to this problem, the Sequent team focused on several problems:

❑   Providing terminal access to existing UNIX character-based applications.

❑   Integrating UNIX and Microsoft Mail environments.

❑   Enabling transparent file and print sharing.

❑   Providing remote access services.

In keeping with the strong cultural value within Sequent of using their own technology, the team decided on a client-server module that could be replicated at any Sequent office in the world. This modular approach made it possible to take workgroups of Sequent employees and move them from UNIX-based workstation to Windows NT without interruption of day-to-day tasks. Because each module was also easily integrated into the existing UNIX network resources, the phase-in could be done either gradually so that individual department's needs could be accommodated, or all at once. The choice of switching from UNIX to Windows NT was up to each group. This allowed them to decide when would be the best time given the group's current schedules and commitments.

Maintaining Connectivity

Each module consists of a Sequent WinServer running the Windows NT Server operating system. Client systems consist of Intel-based 80486 PCs and notebooks running Windows for Workgroups. Because Windows NT shares a common networking environment with Windows for Workgroups, this provided the necessary connectivity between client and server.

For access to command line–based UNIX applications, Windows NT clients could use the built-in "telnet" client. On WFWG seats, users could use the Telnet client supplied in the TCP/IP utilities package they were using. Using the Telnet client, users could login to a UNIX host and run existing UNIX applications.

Email: A Key Resource

Electronic mail has become an essential tool in large organizations. Using today's worldwide electronic mail networks, global companies like Sequent can provide a level of communication undreamed of 10 years ago. To ensure that electronic mail wouldn't be interrupted, a mail gateway was constructed to interconnect Microsoft Mail with Sequent UNIX-based servers running in an SMTP mail network. This combination of Microsoft Mail's friendly user interface and UNIX's ability to route mail throughout the global electronic network resulted in improved service, with a minimum of interruptions. Using Windows NT *Remote Access Services* (RAS), any user with access to a phone line at home or on the road could send electronic mail to any Sequent office anywhere in the world.

Sharing Files and Printers

No network is complete without the ability to share files between machines and to print to devices on the network. Windows NT offers both of these features, but Sequent also needed to share resources with UNIX systems, so some third-party products for both UNIX and Windows NT where required. For a more detailed discussion on this topic, see Chapter 7, "Networking and Windows NT."

The Benefits of Windows NT Workstation

So what are the benefits of going to the Microsoft Windows NT operating system? The main benefits of moving to Windows NT parallel the design objectives Microsoft had in mind when it created Windows NT. Here's a brief tour of the major benefits of moving to Windows NT in the context of the design goals that this revolutionary operating system was created to fulfill.

Windows NT and Symmetric Multiprocessors

Instead of being limited by an operating system capable of only using the functionality in a single microprocessor, Windows NT was developed to take advantage of multiple microprocessors within a workstation or server. No longer do applications running under Windows NT need to wait for a microprocessor's time when more than one processor is available in the system. This design goal is particularly relevant for people involved with high-end applications such as Autodesk's AutoCAD, Intergraph's MicroStation Version 5, as well as mainstream office automation applications provided by many companies, including Microsoft and Lotus. Being able to have both a spreadsheet and MicroStation Version 5 completing tasks at the same time, at the highest performance possible, is profiled in later chapters of this book. The ability of Windows NT to take advantage of more than one microprocessor contributes to higher performance when completing concurrent tasks, such as using office automation programs and CAD programs at the same time.

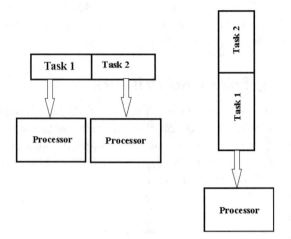

Symmetric multiprocessor.

In the past, the design of a symmetric multiprocessor (SMP) hardware platform required a manufacturer to invest large amounts of R&D in the following areas:

❏ Memory bus architecture

❏ Cache and memory management unit (CAMMU)

❏ Operating system

The proprietary design of each SMP product made these systems very expensive. Their market was generally limited to large corporate server environments like enterprise-wide database servers. In an effort to broaden the acceptance of SMP hardware, several vendors, like Intel and Corollary, introduced chip sets that allow a system designer to choose "off-the-shelf" components to implement both the memory bus and the CAMMU.

The design of the operating system has continued to be one of the biggest challenges and costs to developing SMP platforms. The most common operating systems currently in use, UNIX, MS-DOS, Netware, OS/2, and Apple System 7 are either incapable of supporting SMP hardware or require major redesigns. In the past, UNIX has been the chosen platform for modification due to both industry available expertise and easier portability for application designers. Unfortunately, there has not been an accepted standard for SMP kernels or threaded application programming interfaces. A plethora of incompatible UNIX SMP implementations have been created by NCR, Sequent, Sun, SGI, Pyramid, and many others. This lack of a common standard has created numerous disadvantages:

❏ The hardware vendor is required to invest large amounts of R&D in modifying a UNIX implementation to support SMP hardware. This is a very complex task. Some vendors have spent years designing and tuning their implementations.

❏ Independent software vendors must do a separate port to each platform, which increases cost and limits software availability. A second problem for an independent software vendor is whether to exploit any threading features in the operating system. This support requires greater work and leads to more support problems due to the differences between each operating system. Therefore, many vendors have not exploited the benefits of SMP designs, which has limited acceptance and usefulness.

❏ Peripheral card vendors have to write device drivers for each brand of operating system they support. These separate designs are expensive and limit the availability of peripherals on each platform.

❏ End-users carry the burden of the previously mentioned disadvantages in both exorbitant costs and poor availability of hardware and software solutions.

The solution to this problem is a standard, SMP-capable operating system like Windows NT. Windows NT allows a system designer to use standard components and design a hardware platform to run a readily available operating system. Independent software vendors and peripheral vendors are able to support this system with standard product offerings, thus keeping costs to a minimum while increasing availability. Currently there are two widely available operating systems that support SMP hardware:

With problems of hardware design and operating system availability solved, SMP systems are set to become an important part of computing solutions from the desktop to the enterprise-wide server. Now that independent software vendors are able to focus design of their products toward a few widely accepted standards, the performance benefits of SMP architectures will be realized. Already, applications such as Adobe PhotoShop for Windows NT have been threaded to make the best use of the SMP desktop machines available from several vendors.

Windows NT's Multiplatform Compatibility

Microsoft wanted to create an operating system that could be quickly moved from one hardware platform to another, without having to completely rewrite essential portions of the operating system. This is sometimes referred to as the *portability of an operating system*. Being able to further the level of compatibility available to you is the end result of the goal Microsoft had in designing this feature into Windows NT.

Security

Existing PC operating systems such MS-DOS and IBM's OS/2 have no concept of file protection or ownership. This inability to protect important files rules out these operating systems for use in many corporate and governmental operations. Realizing this, Microsoft included extensive security features in Windows NT.

Windows NT meets the U.S. government security standards outlined in the Department of Defense C2 security standard. Foremost in this is file ownership, with the ability to grant or deny access rights to files based on user name, group, or any combination. The combination of a rich set of security levels and a simple GUI gives Windows NT an advantage over the majority of competing operating environments.

In many environments, monitoring attempts to access files is as important as preventing unauthorized access. Windows NT provides a detailed audit trail of attempts to access files. This is essential when tracing unauthorized use of corporate or government networks.

To help a system administrator monitor the network, Windows NT records a variety of events from users logging in, to application usage and even hardware errors. This is known as *logging events*.

In many UNIX-based networks, passwords and other sensitive information are transmitted in clear text over the network. This makes break-ins simple for a skilled operator with the ability to read information packets on the network. Windows NT encrypts any sensitive information transmitted around the network, adding an extra level of security.

This powerful combination of features in Windows NT makes it perfectly suited to the rapidly developing networks of computers that are forming the new information superhighway.

Comparing Operating Systems: How Windows NT Stacks Up

How does Windows NT compare with UNIX and OS/2? Why is Windows NT the best operating system for you? Throughout this section you'll find out how Windows NT stacks up relative to the other popular operating systems. Windows NT in general builds on the lessons learned from UNIX and OS/2. Let's take a look at how Windows NT compares with UNIX, then profile the differences between Windows NT and OS/2.

Comparing Windows NT and UNIX

UNIX and Windows NT have much in common, not surprising because they have evolved to perform similar tasks, to some extent, both share the following features:

UNIX Versus Windows NT: A Comparison of Features

Feature	UNIX	Windows NT
Processor support	UNIX in a variety of forms is available on all major processor architectures. As yet no standard implementation exists.	Windows NT runs on Intel, DEC Alpha, MIPS R4000, and PowerPC. Ports for SPARC and HP-PA RISC are under development.
Multiuser abilities	Each user has an account that they must use to access the system. Many users can access the system simultaneously via character-based logins.	Each user has an account he or she must use to access the system. Only one user can login to a system at a time
Multitasking abilities	UNIX allows many programs to run simultaneously with complete protection from each other.	Windows NT allows many programs to run simultaneously, with complete protection from each other.

UNIX Versus Windows NT: A Comparison of Features

Feature	UNIX	Windows NT
Virtual memory	UNIX allows programs to run even if they take more memory than the system has. This done by shuffling portions of a program between memory and disk as they are needed.	Windows NT also manages user programs so that they can run even if there is insufficient memory. The techniques used are basically the same as in UNIX.
Multiplatform support	Different versions of UNIX are available to run on many different processors. As yet there is no standard UNIX implementation.	Windows NT runs on the majority of microprocessors. Unlike UNIX, the implementation is identical to the user or programmer.
Robust filesystem	UNIX filesystems are designed to prevent data loss and provide protection of user data from misuse or system failure.	Windows NT has a filesystem referred to as NTFS. NTFS has all the features of a typical UNIX filesystem, as well more flexible file protection schemes such as Access Control Lists (ACL).
High Availability	Support for uninterruptable power supply (UPS) systems is common in UNIX; some even support a software implementation of RAID technology to protect data from disk failure. At the most expensive end of the spectrum are systems that approach true fault tolerance, with the operating system hardened to withstand many hardware failures.	Windows NT includes UPS support as standard, while RAID is supported in the server version of Windows NT. When Windows NT systems are clustered in a network, files can be replicated across the network to provide access to data even if the originating system for the data is shut down. Another important feature is the ability to create backup controllers for groups of Windows NT systems. If the primary controller fails, it can be repaired without interrupting user access to the systems.

UNIX Versus Windows NT: A Comparison of Features

Feature	UNIX	Windows NT
Architecture	Most UNIX kernels consist of a single system with all services integrated. This makes adding or modifying the kernel complex. Many UNIX vendors are trying to reimplement UNIX in modular microkernel design. In this design the kernel is very simple, with services each being a separate module.	Windows NT was designed some 20 years after UNIX and benefits from the experience gained in that time. Designed as a microkernel architecture, it divides system services in separate, easily replaceable modules. This design makes adding new functionality simpler.
Symmetric Multiprocessor Support (SMP)	Most UNIX implementations can only use a single processor. Implementations that are SMP capable vary widely from vendor to vendor. Writing applications for UNIX SMP systems is difficult because of this lack of standardization.	Windows NT was designed to be SMP capable from the outset. As a result, its implementation is identical across all platforms. This is already paying dividends as application developers take full use of extra processors on any platform running Windows NT.
Networking	Most UNIX systems can be networked to provide services such as email, file sharing, and printer access. While the underlying protocols such as NFS are standard, the user interface remains obscure and inconsistent.	Windows NT is *network ready* out of the box. With a simple GUI, even nontechnical users find file and print sharing simple. Also included are many services to make interoperation with existing UNIX networks simple. Facilities not included in the standard operating system are rapidly being provided by third parties. Third-party services include NFS client and Server and X Windows Server.

UNIX Versus Windows NT: A Comparison of Features

Feature	UNIX	Windows NT
PC Network Support	UNIX has several add-on applications such as LAN Manager and NetWare for UNIX. These allow a UNIX host to share resources with PC clients. These tools are usually not included in the system.	Windows NT Server includes support for several PC networking systems straight out of the box.
Graphical User Interface (GUI)	Many UNIX systems come with a GUI. Like many UNIX facilities there is no complete standard so the *desktop* looks and functions differently from system to system.	Windows NT on all platforms uses the GUI first introduced in Microsoft Windows. The Windows GUI is the most prolific and widely used desktop interface in the world.
3D Graphics Environment	Most UNIX workstation vendors include tools and libraries for 3D graphics. Most prevalent is the OpenGL system pioneered by Silicon Graphics.	Windows NT 3.5 includes support for OpenGL. This will bring 3D applications such as visualization and rendering to the Windows NT desktop. In the past such applications only ran on expensive workstations.
Support for standard peripherals	Most UNIX systems have hardware that is supplied by a single vendor. These systems have limited support for peripherals because they use proprietary technology to interface between the system and peripherals.	Designed to run on standard PC architectures, Windows NT has the ability to use standard peripherals. RISC systems running NT are also designed around the PC standards such as EISA to ensure maximum compatibility.
Run PC productivity applications	Several attempts have been made to run Windows and DOS applications from a UNIX system. None have been really satisfactory, being slow and limited in support of the thousands of applications available.	Windows NT can run the majority of Windows and DOS programs even on RISC processors where performance is reduced because so much has to be emulated.

Windows NT Versus OS/2

Both the Microsoft Windows NT operating system and IBM's OS/2 share the same design goals, yet take fundamentally different approaches to accomplish them. Throughout this section you'll learn how the similarities and differences show how the Windows NT operating system meets many of the same requirements OS/2 meets for integration into a computing environment.

OS/2 Versus Windows NT: A Comparison of Features

Feature	OS/2	Windows NT
Processor support	Intel only. PowerPC is due in 1995.	Windows NT runs on Intel, DEC Alpha, MIPS R4000, and PowerPC. Ports for SPARC and HP-PA RISC are under development.
Multiuser abilities	No	Each user has an account he or she must use to access the system. Only one user can login to a system at a time.
Multitasking abilities	Yes	Yes
Virtual memory	Yes	Yes
Robust filesystem	Uses HPFS, lacks the advanced security features of NTFS.	Windows NT has a filesystem referred to as NTFS. NTFS has all the features of a typical OS/2 filesystem as well more flexible file protection schemes such as Access Control Lists (ACL).
High Availability	Yes	Yes
Architecture	Current kernel architecture is similar to most UNIX systems. The replacement called Workplace OS will have a microkernel architecture.	Microkernel architecture.
Symmetric Multiprocessor Support (SMP)	Yes	Yes

OS/2 Versus Windows NT: A Comparison of Features

Feature	OS/2	Windows NT
Networking	None built-in in standard version.	TCP/IP, NETBEUI, and NetWare.
PC Network Support	LanServer version has NETBEUI support.	Windows NT Server includes support for all the major PC networking systems straight out of the box.
Graphical User Interface (GUI)	Yes	Yes
3D Graphics Environment	None	OpenGL
Support for standard peripherals	Standard PC hardware design, well supported by OS/2 device drivers.	Designed to run on standard PC architectures, Windows NT has the ability to use standard peripherals. RISC systems running Windows NT are also designed around the PC standards such as EISA to ensure maximum compatibility.
Run PC productivity applications	Good compatibility with Windows 3.1 and DOS applications. Compatibility bought at the expense of stability to a degree. Cannot run Windows NT or Windows 95 applications.	Windows NT can run the majority of Windows and DOS programs even on RISC processors where performance is reduced because so much has to be emulated.

Major Omissions from OS/2 When Compared with Windows NT

One of the major missing features in OS/2 is security. Windows NT meets the U.S. Government C2 security criteria. OS/2 uses either the DOS FAT or HPFS filesystems. Neither of these file systems support any scheme of protection by ownership. Without this fundamental feature, it is not possible to have a secure environment.

Windows NT is network ready. OS/2, even in its latest versions, still makes networking an option in the entry level package. In order to integrate OS/2 into a network, it is necessary to add extra software packages. Both systems connect to dial-up services including Internet SLIP and PPP protocols.

The Windows NT operating system supports applications developed for the MS-DOS, OS/2 1.x, and Windows-16 and Windows-32 environments. This makes it possible to take existing MS-DOS, OS/2, Windows 3.1 (16-bit), and Windows 32-bit (Windows NT–based) applications and use them within Windows NT. Certain DOS and Windows applications will not be able to run because they try to directly access hardware, something a real operating system like Windows NT cannot allow. The Windows NT POSIX subsystem is there largely for standards conformance, no existing off-the-shelf applications will run in it. OS/2 offers better compatibility with Windows 16-bit applications and DOS because it does not protect hardware to the same degree as Windows NT.

Currently OS/2 supports many of the same environments as Windows NT, notably DOS and Win16. The designers of OS/2 have taken a different approach for supporting older DOS and Win16 applications. In Windows NT, the emphasis is on security and robustness at the expense of compatibility with packages that need to access the hardware directly. In contrast, OS/2 trades some stability and security for better support of DOS and Win16 applications.

The biggest problem for OS/2 is its support for future Microsoft programmer interfaces such as Win32. As the operating system and its interface becomes more powerful and sophisticated, the task of supporting it on top of another operating system gets progressively more difficult. As yet there are no known plans for support of Win32 applications for OS/2. This is important because all new Windows95 applications or new versions of existing applications are likely to be Win32 applications, making them unusable on OS/2.

A Day in the Life of a Windows NT User

You can get a glimpse into how powerful the day-to-day features of Windows NT are by following along with a design engineer as a typical day starts in the office. The ease of sharing data between applications highlights how easily Windows NT is included into an existing design and drafting environment.

Decreasing the Time to Change a Design File

Imagine you are a designer working for StarFleet Flyers, makers of high-performance bicycles. In this position you use MicroStation as your primary CAD design tool. MicroStation is a CAD product developed and marketed by Bentley Systems, Inc., of Exton, Pennsylvania. You are responsible for the design of a new series of competition frames and have completed the initial design. Follow along to see how Windows NT helps you perform your job.

The Start of Another Day

Your company is in the middle of a transition in product designs, moving from one product generation to the next. Working at a bicycle company would never be this hectic, you thought. But at StarFleet Flyers, sales have continued to grow rapidly, and as a result your company is getting increased market share and competition around the world. Because of this, you need to completely revise the product line quickly. This used to happen every 3 years, but now happens every 18 months or less.

At first, you and everybody else worked overtime to meet the demand, with only limited success. In an effort to shorten development time and alleviate some of the pressures, management decided to install Windows NT–equipped workstations. You love a challenge, so you plunge into another workday and tackle incoming assignments. We pick up the story as another day starts.

"Good morning." Your boss walks through the entrance of your cubicle, greeting you.

She finds you busily reading through your Microsoft Mail messages. You notice there's one such message from her that you haven't had time to read yet. Of course, that becomes the topic of discussion.

"Read my email yet?"

"I haven't had a chance yet." Your voice trails off as you quickly pounce on the mouse to open the message. There's a design file included as an attachment. You can tell by way of the paper clip on the outside of the message. Scanning the message, you notice that there's a major redesign needed of the new bicycle parts you've been working on.

"We need to have you make changes to your existing bike design frame."

You think to yourself that all the parts that rely on the frame now need to be changed. You're instantly thinking you could use the overtime for the new boat you want to buy.

"You'll also need to change the related parts." Your manager's voice trails off, as she continues looking through the design sketches in her hand. She pulls out an Excel spreadsheet from the stack of drawings, and lets it drift down onto your desk.

"What's this?" You've seen spreadsheets before from the initial design engineering sessions you've been involved in.

"It's a copy of the Excel spreadsheet with the measurements for the new frame."

"I'll take these and key them into the frame file, and stretch the existing frame design. I've attached a few of the related parts and I can also change them."

"Why don't you just get the Excel file to drive MicroStation to make the changes automatically?" Your boss sets down the papers she's carrying and hands you a diskette.

"How can I do that?" you ask.

"Frank over in Engineering can show you how to get the Excel spreadsheet to drive MicroStation." Your boss gathers up her papers and begins walking out of your cubicle. "You probably thought you'd have to work all weekend to complete this project. Right?"

"Yeah. I'll get with Frank."

Whew! Well, at least you don't have to key in hundreds of coordinates to create an entirely new bicycle. Instead, you'll get this whole series of steps from Frank and bang right through this design change.

On the way over to Frank's office you run into Bill.

Bill asks, "Do you have Bonsai 2000 street racer design on a floppy? I need the frame outlines for final check and approval for the Japanese market." Bill always looks like he's going 100 miles per hour.

"I'll have to get that for your today." You stop and think that under Windows NT you could create a shared directory of your design files, making it possible for Bill to get right to the necessary files he needs. "Bill, just connect to my network drive under File Manager and go to the Bonsai shared directory."

"OK. Under File Manager?"

"Yes." You start out again for Frank's office. Windows NT just made it possible for you to share all the files needed for the Bonsai project and not have to manage a series of floppies with various design file levels.

KNOCK, KNOCK.

"Come in." You walk into Frank's office (how'd he get an office with a real door?) and sit down. Frank is the resident systems guru and is captivated with the latest CAD program running on his Windows NT workstation.

"What's up?" he asks.

"Jennifer says you can make this Excel spreadsheet drive the necessary changes in a MicroStation design. How?" You hold up the diskette and the spreadsheet. You can tell by the puppy dog look on Frank's face that he wants to show you his newest creation.

"Come over here, I'll show you." Frank opens up the same Excel spreadsheet you're holding in your hands, and then proceeds to switch through the Windows NT Program Manager to MicroStation, which is already up and running.

"See, I wrote this short program to link our Excel spreadsheets with Micro-Station so that when you change anything in the spreadsheet it gets changed in the design file," Frank says. "Now watch...."

Frank proceeds to change the active coordinates for the new bicycle design in Excel. The design file begins to change in the background of Frank's screen. To get a better view, Frank splits the Excel spreadsheet on the left side of the screen, with MicroStation running on the right side. As the new coordinates are highlighted in Excel, the bicycle design changes.

"See, that's all there is to it." Frank continues demonstrating the program. "I'll mail you the instructions and the necessary files. That's it. It'll make changing the other associated parts easy as well."

"Thanks, Frank. I guess I won't need this floppy after all."

"Nah, I'll either email it to you or put it in your project directory. Either way, you won't need that floppy."

As you walk out of his office you can know the weekend is yours again.

Back in your office the email from Frank has already arrived. You get the files saved to the appropriate subdirectories per Frank's instructions and get to work changing the bicycle design.

Summarizing What Just Happened

This scenario shows how you can quickly change entire designs using the inherent capabilities included in the Windows NT operating system. Instead of having to manually key in hundreds of coordinates for the new design, the Excel spreadsheet "drove" the complete changes necessary to create a new part for the bicycle. This saves the designer literally hundreds of hours over the long-term.

The previous example also shows how files can be quickly shared among various workers in a workgroup without having to shuffle diskettes up and down the hallways. Instead, the *Connect To Network Drive* command in Windows NT's File Manager makes it easy to share files across any distance. This scenario also illustrates the concept of sharing messages and files through electronic mail. Instead of having to shuffle sets of memos and diskettes, and trying to keep them together, electronic mail makes it possible to keep entire projects organized using mail folders. These concepts are discussed in greater detail throughout this book.

Summary

From this chapter you should have learned the following:

❑ Why Windows NT is important.

❑ How Windows NT compares with its major competitors.

❑ How Windows NT will be a benefit to both application developers and users of computers.

❑ How Windows NT protects your investment in Windows 3.1 applications and training.

❑ How Windows NT could streamline your use of computers.

A Quick Tour of Windows NT Workstation

Introduction

Throughout this chapter, you'll learn how Windows NT Workstation works, including useful tips on getting started. If Windows NT hasn't been installed on your machine we will cover this issue as well, at least as an overview. Next, we'll walk you through starting up Windows NT, logging in, and using applications once you're in. Finally, we'll cover what to do when it is time to go home (aka shutting down). But, before we cover these topics let's see what a typical day looks like to a Windows NT user.

A Day in the Life: Drawing on Your Experience

Meanwhile, Back at Starfleet Flyers...

Let's return to our beleaguered hero diligently working away in his cubicle...

"Bob, can I see you for a minute?"

You think to yourself, "What now?" and walk over to your manager's desk. You notice there are several windows open on her workstation as she is completing both an Excel spreadsheet and a new part design. In the background there's an open document.

"I've been working up next year's manufacturing plans, and I'd like you to get them all included into the next operations review." Your boss looks at you over her glasses as she swivels around. She's really searching for her coffee you think, but instead, grabs last year's plan and plunks it down in front of you.

THUD.

"Use this as a model. I want to include the new StratoCruiser line as well."

"Do you want one master product illustration?" you ask, hoping a simple drawing file included in this massive document will do the trick.

"No, use renderings of each design and then roll them into the document." Your boss grabs for the book and starts flipping through it, showing you pictures. "Like this... and this." She continues to thumb through the document. "Marketing is taking this document over to our new plant in Louisville for a dog-and-pony show for WalShop. They need next year's line because WalShop wants to buy a year in advance."

You think you're about to enter word processing hell when your boss reads your face, and smirks a little bit.

"You're thinking about our old word processor—if you could call it that—the one on the network?" Your boss says, looking through her glasses instead of over them.

"Yeah, IP/Snail." You try to act depressed but are elated your boss knows about the old word processor/desktop publishing program affectionately called IP/Snail because it is excruciatingly slow and very unintuitive; a real pain to use.

"Well, don't think about it. I've set up a share on my Windows NT box and you can grab last year's report and simply cut and paste the new images." Your boss twirls around in her seat, staring point-blank into her workstation's screen.

"See, just use MicroStation to complete the rendered images and then take them to the Clipboard and paste them into your Word document. I want the latest designs plotted with pen tables."

"Word?" you ask.

"Yeah, Word. I've had all the documents from IP/Snail turned into Word documents so we can use them on our new workstations." Your boss straightens herself in her chair. You know she always feels proud when she has the latest technical advances.

"Great! I'll just get those files from you over the network. What about the design files?"

"Use OASIS to get the design files. You can find them in the Strato subdirectory. Also, be sure to use IPLOT to plot them to the screen."

You review in your mind that OASIS is the central file server with the design files for all projects, and IPLOT is the CAD plotting software our company is standardizing on.

"How do I plot to the screen with pen tables?" Before the question is out of your mouth you know the answer. So much for attending meetings after drinking only two cups of coffee; gotta get that third cup down soon.

"Ask Frank. He understands all that MicroStation and Intergraph stuff." Your boss is already onto the next task, nearly waving you out of her office.

"What's the deadline?"

"This Friday," your boss says, looking at her calendar. "I know it's tight but the WalShop account could send our StratoCruiser sales into space!" Your manager laughs. The puns about space and Star Trek are really beginning to wear thin. Your force a smile and walk down to see Frank.

"Good morning, Frank." You walk into Frank's office and take a seat. Just how *did* he get an office with a door?

"Morning." Frank is the CAD administrator and knows this stuff cold. You wonder if he absorbs information in his sleep. Frank has two monitors running with the Windows NT Performance Monitor in his office and he's tracking the network performance of the Windows NT network.

"How do you plot to the screen with IPLOT?" you ask, peering over Frank's shoulder at the constantly sliding bars of Windows NT's Performance Monitor.

"This Windows NT stuff is wild; look at this profile of our network. The Performance Monitor shows there's a bottleneck at the server." Frank's voice trails off as he opens the Print Manager on the screen. You watch over his shoulder as he opens up the NTWIN queue.

"Here, you just use this queue. I set this up on your workstation already. Just select the NTWIN queue from the IPLOT dialog box. That's it." Frank swirls around and looks at you as he gulps down the rest of his coffee. "Here, I'll show you now. Let's get some more coffee."

Frank walks down to your office, explaining the NTWIN queue and how you'll be able to get the plots you need down directly from within MicroStation using IPLOT.

"Thanks, Frank."

"Don't sweat it; this is easy stuff. And you can even use your existing pen tables from IPLOT."

You begin to realize why Frank has that office.

What Just Happened?

The above scenario shows how existing projects can be easily streamlined when the Microsoft Windows NT operating system is used. Instead of taking months to create the report showing next year's designs, it only will take a week's time. The older documents are going to be updated with the latest design files from manufacturing, making it easy to finish what would have otherwise taken months in a matter of weeks.

Using the full capabilities of more than one application program at a time is possible with Windows NT. Throughout the preceding slice-of-life story you saw how you can get the most out of the Windows NT operating system, while at the same time drawing from your own experience with existing programs. Take Microsoft Excel, Word, or MicroStation; no doubt you've learned quite a bit about the programs you need to use for doing your job.

The Microsoft Windows NT operating system has the ability to handle multiple tasks at the same time, making you more productive than if you had to complete a series of tasks in one application, close it, then open another application to complete another part of your job. The combination of DOS/Windows has offered a crude version of this ability for some time. The major differences are:

❏ **Stability:** DOS/Windows provides no protection; a rogue application can bring the system down completely and frequently does.

❑ **True multitasking:** In DOS/Windows, the application is in control, other applications only get serviced if the controlling application lets them. In Windows NT the multitasking is preemptive. In this model, the operating system is in control and allocates CPU and resources fairly so that many applications can coexist.

Installing Windows NT

With the entertainment out of the way, let's return to business. Many readers of this book probably already have Windows NT up and running on their system. After all, isn't that the job of Frank, the systems administrator (and the reason he gets a *real* office)? However, it doesn't hurt to know a little something about how its done.

Getting the workstation up and running with the Windows NT operating system is explained here. In this section you'll learn what the minimum hardware configuration needs to be for Windows NT to successfully run your applications, what considerations you need to take into account when installing Windows NT, how to install networking support within Windows NT, and how to customize Windows NT for your specific needs after it has been installed. You can get up and running quickly after reviewing the key points provided here.

Minimum Hardware Configuration

Getting Windows NT successfully installed, networked, and up and running is all based on selecting the best possible hardware configuration.

Processor Requirements

When looking at an Intel processor–based system, consider only an Intel Pentium or RISC-based computer or higher. While the Intel 80386 microprocessor is listed as the minimum one needed for running Windows NT, if you're going to be doing computing intensive tasks like running AutoCAD, Micro-Station, Pro/ ENGINEER, Intergraph's ModelView, I/RAS C, ArcView, or MGE products, then an Intel 80486-based computer is in order. The more powerful the processor, the better. Pentium- or RISC-based workstations deliver excellent performance for most engineering-intensive applications, computer-aided design and drafting being one of the prime examples. With more and more design programs becoming multi-threaded (the ability to process using more than a single 32-bit processing thread), performance of Windows NT–based applications on SMP workstations will increase dramatically. In light of this, it's a good idea to get the highest performance workstation you can afford for running Windows NT and its associated applications.

Disk Requirements

What about disk space? You'll want to have at least 540MB of hard disk space for the Windows NT operating system, your engineering applications (e.g., AutoCAD, MicroStation, or Pro/ENGINEER), and your office applications (e.g., Microsoft Office). With 540MB, you'll have enough disk space for all these applications and a few more. You'll also be able to save several large design files and be able to even use your NT workstation as a plot server. The more the hard disk space available, the better. With more hard disk space available, you'll be able to increase the virtual memory size used by the Windows NT operating system.

What types of hard disk should you use? Because there are a great variety of IDE and SCSI-based disk drives you can use on your Windows NT workstation. If you have a choice, always use a SCSI-based disk drive because the Windows NT operating system has excellent support for this interface.

In terms of memory needed for your Windows NT workstation, you should have a minimum of 16MB of RAM. While the Windows NT minimum configuration states that this operating system can work within 12MB of RAM, actual performance is pretty slow in this amount of memory. Larger applications such as AutoCAD will run much more happily in 32MB of memory; as a general rule, get all the memory you can.

Windows NT is network ready to fully use this ability. You'll need a networking card. For best performance use a 32-bit card (either EISA or PCI) if your machine can accept these cards. If you are not on a network but will be using a dial-up connection, then start with a 14.4K modem as a minimum; these are cheap and simple to use.

Installing Windows NT or any other large applications from floppy disk is a good way to waste half a day. CD-ROMs are increasingly used as a software distribution mechanism; if you don't already have one, get one.

In getting a complete Windows NT workstation built, it's a good idea to check and see whether all the components will work together within the Windows

NT environment. Outside of building the workstation and then trying to load NT, you can get a copy of the Microsoft Windows NT Hardware Compatibility List (HCL; email to ftp.microsoft.com). This list shows all the computers, SCSI disk drive adapters, CD-ROM disk drives, mice, video graphics display adapters, and even printers that have been tested with the Windows NT operating system. It's a good idea to use this list as a "shopping guide" when you're purchasing various components for your Windows NT workstation because Microsoft has already completed testing on each item listed. If you have a machine or components that are not on the HCL, all is not lost; many machines and components still work. You'll just have to use the Custom install and a little intelligence.

Getting Windows NT Installed

Increasingly, software companies are making their applications easier and less time consuming to install. This also holds true for the Microsoft Windows NT operating system. With a hardware configuration that is completely compatible, the installation routines supplied with NT make installation painless. If you have ever installed Microsoft Word, Excel, or any other Microsoft application, then you know what to expect. You can select between Express and Custom Setup. For purposes of this discussion, let's first look at Express Setup, and then look at the approaches you can take for Customized Setup later in this section. Once the installation routine searches through the hardware components of your workstation, a blue screen appears, showing the percentage of files installed. From a CD-ROM disk drive on an Intel 80486-based computer with 32MB of RAM, the entire installation process takes less than 35 minutes. Because the installation script will already have determined your system's hardware configuration, there are only a few selections to be made during Express Setup.

In Custom Setup, you tell NT which components are on your workstation, and how you want each installed. Using the Custom Setup you can load customized network device drivers, for example, if your company has standardized on a specific protocol. One instance where you will most likely use the Custom Setup is when you're working within a larger workgroup that has a customized device driver for using a network interface card. The Customized Setup also has to be used when you're installing device drivers not included in the baseline of Windows NT.

When deciding between Express versus Customized Setup, it's a good idea to first check and see if the existing network configuration you're using can use a standard device driver or needs a customized one. The same applies to SCSI adapters and other peripherals that may work with NT, but are not in the standard distribution. If you're unsure of this, check with your system administrator. If you're beginning with an entirely new network, you'll most likely want to complete an Express Setup, because this approach will get your network up and running quickly. Then after the entire Windows NT network is up and running, you can customize the network for your specific needs.

One choice you have to make when installing NT is what type of filesystem to use for the C: drive. NT can be installed on DOS FAT or on NTFS. If the machine will not boot DOS, then making the filesystem NTFS has many advantages:

❏ **Security:** FAT filesystem cannot be made secure.

❏ **Virus protection:** Because of the security of NTFS, many PC virus programs cannot be operated.

❏ **Robustness:** FAT is a very simple design. Power failures or hard reboots can cause irreparable damage to the structures on the disk. NTFS is much more robust and difficult to corrupt.

If you need to run DOS/Windows from the same disk, then you must use FAT as the filesystem because DOS cannot read NTFS format filesystems.

Networking Considerations: Making UNIX and Windows NT Work Together

Microsoft estimates that 20% to 25% of all Windows NT customers are users of UNIX and OS/2 operating systems who have decided to include NT in their work flows. These technical users need to be able to retain investments in their existing UNIX hardware on the one hand, while using the increasingly powerful features of applications built specifically for the Windows NT environment. Fortunately for technical professionals who are considering integrating Windows NT into their environments, the right tools and connections are already there. The strength of Windows NT is primarily in its networking features. But how does this work? How can you configure Windows NT to work in conjunction with UNIX-based workstations and servers? Follow along as a CAD administrator gets a Windows NT workstation up and running on a TCP/IP network. The Administrator starts by first opening the Main group located on the Windows NT Desktop. The Control Panel contains many utilities and applications supplied by Microsoft for installing networking support for a Windows NT workstation. The following figure shows the contents of Windows NT's Control Panel.

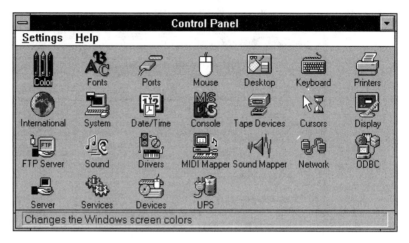

Windows NT's Control Panel.

Double-clicking on the Network icon shows the Network Settings dialog box, which is shown in the following figure.

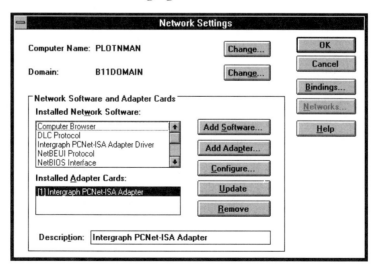

The Network Settings dialog box.

The Network Settings dialog box is the first in a series of dialog boxes designed to guide Windows NT users with Administrator or Power User status through the necessary steps of getting a Windows NT workstation up and running on a TCP/IP network. The CAD administrator selects the TCP/IP Protocol from the list of Installed Network Software, then clicks once on Configure.... The TCP/IP Configuration dialog box appears.

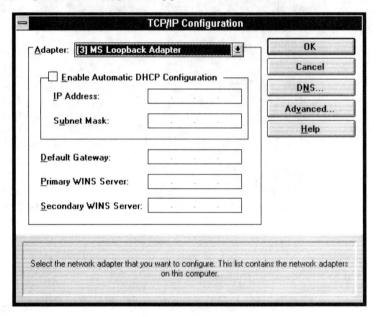

Configuring Windows NT workstations for TCP/IP is all menu-driven.

With the default gateway, Internet or IP address, and subnet mask figures already known, the CAD administrator types in each of these values, and then checks to make sure the correct Windows network adapter card is shown in the lower portion of the dialog box. The network adapter value shown in this dialog box reflects the network adapter device driver installed during Windows NT installation. If the adapter shown doesn't match the actual one installed in the Windows NT workstation, then the CAD administrator can use the options in the Network Settings dialog box to install a new network adapter card device driver. As with any peripheral, there has to be compatibility between the network adapter card device driver and actual network interface card installed.

With all the necessary values entered into the TCP/IP Configuration dialog box, the CAD administrator next double-clicks on the Connectivity... button, which leads to the TCP/IP Connectivity Configuration dialog box.

The CAD administrator in this instance selects the option DNS (Domain Naming Service) First, Then Hosts Files for the Name Resolution Search order. The Domain Naming Service is typically used in UNIX-based networks for associating IP or Internet addresses with specific workstations' names. The Domain Naming Service makes it possible for Internet addresses like *wrkstn. ingr.com* to work instead of listing the IP address (129.135.260.200). To complete the TCP/IP configuration, the CAD administrator clicks once on the TCP Domain Name and types in the TCP/IP registered domain name if you have one. For example, you might enter *mydomain.com.*Your machine would then be recognized on TCP/IP networks as *mymachine.mydomain.com*. If your company does not have a registered TCP/IP domain, leave this field blank.

With all the options set, the administrator clicks once on OK. The Connectivity dialog box closes, showing the TCP/IP Configuration dialog box. Clicking once on OK through the remainder of the dialog boxes brings the administrator back to the Windows NT Control Panel. After rebooting the Windows NT workstation in order to have the network options just selected written to the Registry file, the workstation is now ready for use as a design seat on a UNIX network.

Sharing Files

With Windows NT installed, the designers working on a project can quickly share files from a central library in much the same way files are shared between UNIX-based workstations and servers today. The designer using MicroStation Version 5 on an NT-based workstation could, for example, open the Command Prompt window and use the FTP and TELNET commands just as they are used on a UNIX workstation or server for getting files across the network.

In the example of the CAD administrator getting Windows NT and MicroStation Version 5 installed on a workstation, when it is time to load the necessary symbol libraries and reference files for a design project, the CAD administrator opens the Command Prompt window and types the command needed to gain access to the department server and get the necessary files loaded on the Windows NT workstation. The following figure shows an example of the

Command Prompt window being used for completing file transfers from a UNIX server using the FTP command. This is possible due to the Windows NT operating system's built-in support for the TCP/IP protocol.

```
(C) Copyright 1985-1995 Microsoft Corp.

c:\nik>ftp foo.garply.com
Connected to foo.garply.com.
220 foo.garply.com FTP server (OSF/1 Version 5.60) ready.
User (foo.garply.com:(none)): nik
331 Password required for nik.
Password:
230 User nik logged in.
ftp> ls -C
200 PORT command successful.
150 Opening ASCII mode data connection for /bin/ls (165.113.188.20,1125).
.profile             n16e11b3.exe            t1
.rhosts              n32e11b3.exe            winvn_93_14_intel.zip
.sh_history          netscape-1.1b3.hqx      ws_ftp32.zip
eudor144.exe         psp30.zip               wsg-12.exe
ewan1052.zip         setshell.zip            wsping32.zip
html.zip             t                       wtalk121.zip
226 Transfer complete.
357 bytes received in 0.11 seconds (3.22 Kbytes/sec)
ftp> get eudor144.exe
200 PORT command successful.
150 Opening ASCII mode data connection for eudor144.exe (165.113.188.20,1126) (2
93763 bytes).
```

Windows NT's Command Prompt being used for network file transfers.

Teams of designers who are all working on NT-based workstations can also share design files, reference files, even plotting files such as iparms, aparms, and metafiles using Microsoft Mail. Included as standard with both Microsoft Windows for Workgroups and Windows NT 3.1, Microsoft Mail uses an intuitive, easy-to-use interface for making it possible to share files as attachments to email messages.ail;See electronic mail

In the example of the company adopting Windows NT for several design seats, the designers and engineers using Windows NT workstations no longer need to use command-line file transfers from the Command Prompt window; they can simply mail the needed files to each other. The following figure shows an example of how this would be done. Notice from this figure how the MicroStation icon appears in the context of the email message. The file itself will be sent along with the beginning text at the top of the message. Mail messages may have an icon of a paper clip in the Microsoft Mail message, which denotes that a message with an attachment has arrived.

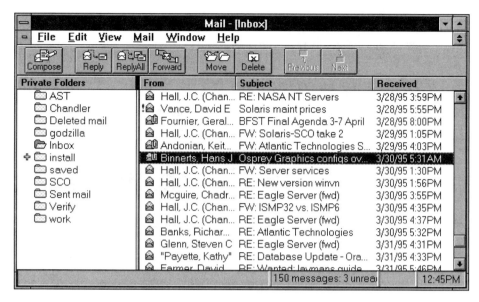

Using Microsoft Mail to share MicroStation documents.

Windows NT is equally adaptable to UNIX, other Windows NT, MS-DOS, and even Apple Macintosh computers that have TCP/IP protocol support installed on them. With TCP/IP network connectivity, Windows NT can quickly transfer files from a UNIX workstation and back again without taking any additional steps. As far as the UNIX workstations are concerned, the Windows NT workstation with TCP/IP network support installed is another UNIX workstation or server. The only missing piece in the standard NT product is support for the UNIX NFS file-sharing protocol. NFS client products are available from a number of vendors.

Starting Windows NT

The Flexboot option that is shown on your computer's screen when your system boots gives you the chance to select which operating system to run. On a Windows NT system there will always be at least two options: Windows NT Workstation Version 3.5 and Windows NT Workstation Version 3.5 (Standard VGS). On Intel systems you will also see a DOS option if the machine has DOS loaded. If you want to change the operating system that your computer boots into by default, see the System Services description in Chapter 3, "Up and Running with Windows NT."

After selecting Windows NT from the Flexboot option, the Welcome dialog box appears as shown below.

Welcome to Windows NT

Once all of that mysterious activity concludes you are presented with the Welcome message box. Think of this as Window's Marquee. To enter Windows NT proper you need to log in.

Windows NT's Welcome dialog box.

Press CTRL+ALT+DEL to log on. Pressing these keys brings up the proper Welcome dialog box that asks you to type in your Username, Domain (the workgroup you are a member of), and the password for the username account selected.

➦ *NOTE: Windows NT uses the CTRL+ALT+DEL sequence as a method for ensuring the security of your system. It is known that there are pirate screen templates that have been developed that capture your user name and password for NT, giving someone else access to your account. If such an illegal template is running, pressing the CTRL+ALT+DEL sequence will reboot your system.*

✔ *TIP: Always press the three keys, CTRL+ALT+DEL, before logging onto your system, even if a secondary dialog box already appears.*

Setting Up User Accounts and Passwords

As new personal computers and workstations are added to your Windows NT network, you'll want to set up accounts on the new systems for the users needing to access applications. Here's how you can set up user accounts and passwords under Windows NT:

1. Double-click on the *Administrative Tools* icon on the Desktop. The figure below shows the contents of the Administrative Tools group.

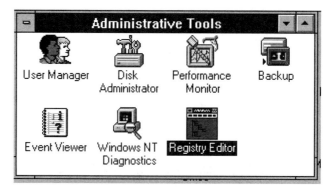

The Administrative Tools group.

2. Double-click on the User Manager icon. The *User Manager* dialog box is shown below.

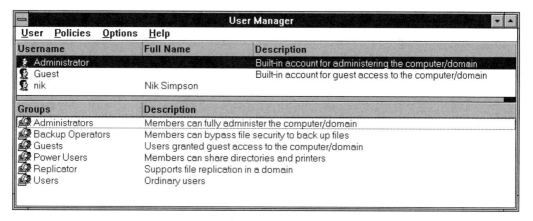

The User Manager.

3. Select New User from the User Menu to use the New User dialog box. The figure below shows the *New User* dialog box.

Using the options in this dialog box, you can create new user accounts.

1. Click once in the *Username:* entry field. Type the name of the new account you want to create.

2. Click once in the *Full Name:* entry, then type in the full name of the user you are adding the new account for. The name you enter here is displayed in several of the dialog boxes used for managing the Windows NT network.

3. Click once in the *Description:* entry and type a line of text that explains who this account is for. You could for example, type in the name of the organization or department the person is a member of.

4. Click once on the *Password:* entry, and type the password you want associated with the account you are creating.

5. Click once on the *Confirm Password:* entry. Type in the same password you had entered in the previous field titled Password:. After completing these steps, the New User dialog box appears as shown below.

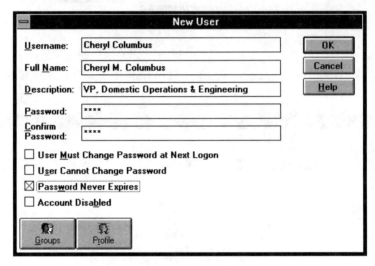

New User dialog box.

6. Click once on one of the following options that appear next within the New User dialog box. The options are briefly described here:

❑ **User Must Change Password At Next Logon:** Selecting this option prompts the user to change the password for this account during the next logon session.

❑ **User Cannot Change Password:** Selecting this option prevents the user from changing the assigned password. Use this option when you are creating an account that will be used by multiple users. For example, you'd probably want to use this option when you're creating a guest account.

❑ **Password Never Expires:** Selecting this option prevents the password you have entered earlier in the dialog box from ever being overwritten. An administrator is the only person who can change the password.

❏ **Account Disabled:** Select this option to disable the use of the account.

7. Click once on one of the options for specifying how the system will define how the password is going to be used in conjunction with the account.

8. Click once on OK. The new account is created.

Changing User Names and Passwords

The process of changing a user's account name and password is accomplished using the options included in the User Manager applet located in the Administrative Tools group. The steps provided here show how to change or modify a single user account. Keep in mind that the changes you make to your own or another user's account take effect the next time a logon is made to the account.

1. Double-click on the Administrative Tools group to show its contents. The figure below shows the applets, or small applications, that comprise the Administrative Tools group. These applets are represented as icons.

The User Manager icon is included within the Administrative Tools group and is used for managing accounts on workstations throughout your Windows NT system's domain or workgroup. With the User Manager, you can create and manage user accounts and workgroups, manage a specific workstation's account, define user rights for resources that are being shared, and set auditing policies. On a domain, you can only create local accounts unless you have the privileges necessary to manage the domain.

2. Double-click on the User Manager icon located in the Administrative Tools group. The User Manager is shown below.

The User Manager icon.

3. Click once on the user account for which you want to change the password. This highlights the account within the User Manager window.

4. Select User Properties from the User Menu in User Manager. The User Properties dialog box appears, and is shown below.

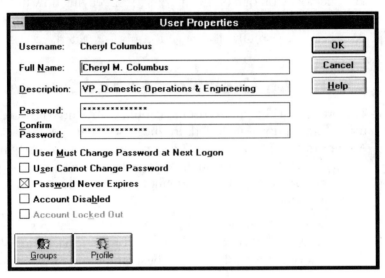

The User Manager's User Properties dialog box.

Within the User Properties dialog box you can see the username, full name, and description of the person who has the selected account assigned to them.

1. Double-click in the Password: entry and clear any previous entries that are represented as asterisks (*).

2. Type in the new password you want used in conjunction with the selected account.

3. Double-click on the Confirm Password: entry and clear any asterisks (*) that are present in the option dialog box.

4. To confirm the password, type in the exact upper and lowercase spelling you entered in the Password: option box.

5. Click once on any of the boxes that appear below the *Confirm Password:* option entry. The figure below shows an example of the *User Properties* dialog box with the options for having the password never expires, and the user not having the option of changing the password.

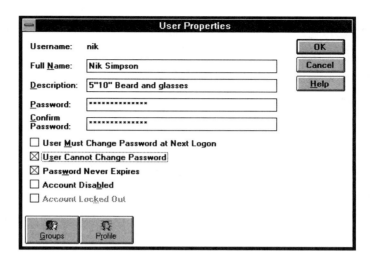

The User Properties dialog box with Password Options set.

6. With all the options set, and the password entered and confirmed, click once on OK. The password changes just entered will take effect next time the account is initiated from the Windows NT logon dialog box.

Working in the Windows NT Environment

Think of the Windows NT Desktop as just that—a Desktop—that contains the tools and applications you can use for getting work done. Presented in this section is a brief tour of the Windows NT Desktop. Throughout the various sections, you'll find out how you can use either the keyboard, mouse, or both to get around on the Desktop in the Windows NT environment. The figure below shows a typical Windows NT Desktop with its main components called out.

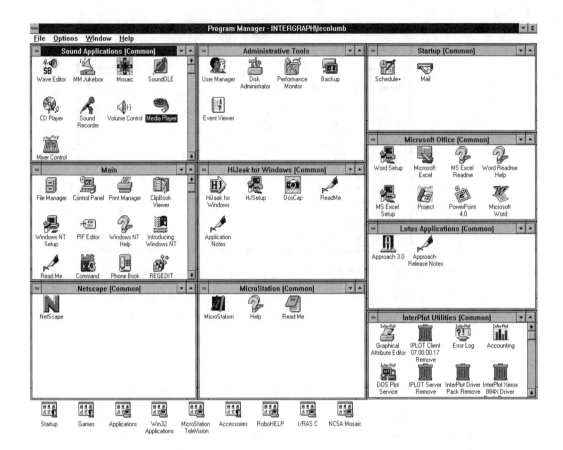

An illustrated Windows NT desktop.

The Parts of the Windows NT Desktop

So, You've Used Windows Before

If you are already familiar with how to use Windows 3.1 or Windows for Workgroups, then the NT desktop will be very familiar. This is natural because all three products share a common look and feel. Let's look at the differences between NT and its predecessors.

❑ **CTRL-ALT-DEL:** On Windows or Windows for Workgroups this will clear the display to a blue screen and offer you the chance to reboot or return to Windows. On Windows NT you are given the chance to reboot the machine, log off, lock the display and keyboard, or bring up a list of currently running processes.

☐ **Exit from Program Manager:** On Windows 3.1 this shuts down Windows and returns to a DOS prompt. On Windows NT it does not exist; instead you can either logoff or shut the system down from Program Manager.

Apart from these differences the interface is identical to Windows 3.1, so everything you've learned is still useful. If you are not familiar with Windows 3.1, then the Windows NT desktop will be a new experience for you. Part of learning any new operating system is getting an idea of how the Desktop is organized. In the case of Windows NT, you can quickly learn how the Desktop is organized by reading through the tips and insights in this section. The figure below shows an example of the Windows NT Program Manager with several Program groups open.

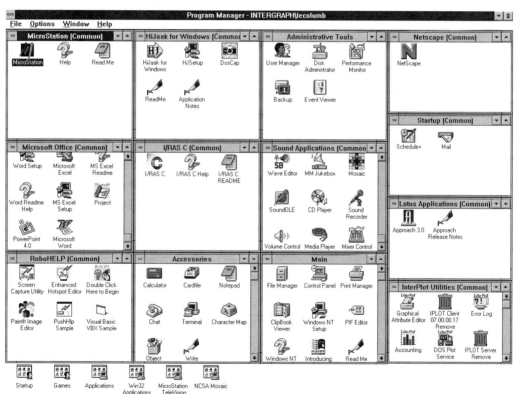

The Program Manager window.

Using the Keyboard

You can use either a mouse or a keyboard to use all the features of Windows NT. There's a series of keyboard shortcuts you can use for getting around in Windows NT, giving you the flexibility to get into and out of applications and to bypass menus with a simple keystroke sequence. Here's a reference of how to use keystroke sequences for accomplishing tasks from the Windows NT Desktop.

Starting an Application in Program Manager

Follow these steps for getting an application up and running by using keystroke sequences.

1. Press the CTRL+TAB keys together to select the Program group you want to open on the Desktop.
2. Press the ENTER key to open the Program group that contains the application(s) you want to use. The file group that is highlighted when ENTER is pressed will open onto your screen.
3. Press the TAB key until the icon for the application you want to use is highlighted.
4. With the application's icon highlighted, press the ENTER key. The application loads and begins running.

Opening a File in an Application

You can quickly learn these steps for loading a file while you are within an application program. Use these steps as a shortcut for opening files.

1. Press the ALT and F keys simultaneously to have the menu bar selected from within the application.
2. Select Open from the File Menu. An example of what this looks like is shown for Intergraph's MicroStation Version 5.0.
3. Press RETURN when the Open command is highlighted. The Open File dialog box appears and is shown below.

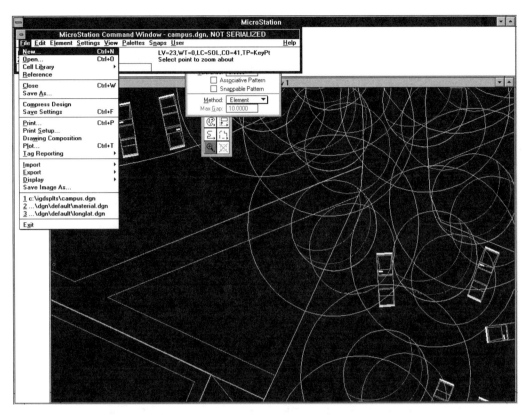

An example of using keystroke sequences to open a file.

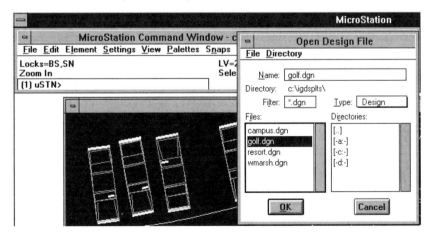

Open File dialog box in MicroStation.

4. Press the arrow keys to highlight the file you want to open.

5. With the filename you want to view or edit highlighted, press RETURN. The file is then loaded into the active application.

Case Study: How One Company Uses Windows NT Today

Windows NT includes many aspects of network computing systems that make it attractive as an operating system for companies with investments in UNIX and Intel-based workstations. One company that has successfully integrated Windows NT into the product development process is RJR Nabisco. Installing a Windows NT client system within the CAD Department, designers have had a chance to see how Windows NT complements their existing investments in Intergraph, Sun, and many third-party Intel-based PCs.

The criteria RJR Nabisco had in incorporating Windows NT into their CAD operations were interoperability, learning curve of the new operating system, and the support for existing investments in MS-DOS software. Windows NT was brought in and installed on several Intel-based 80486-based client systems. Intergraph's MicroStation Version 5.0 is being used in conjunction with Windows NT for completing initial design tasks that are then shared with other CAD designers using Intergraph workstations, Sun workstations, and Intel-based PCs.

The process flow uses the NT workstations as design verification and review stations. Once the drawings and designs have been checked, a plot is sent from the Windows NT workstation to the Intergraph server for plotting. Intergraph's InterPlot software is used for ensuring interoperability between the Windows NT and UNIX-based plotting resources. Once the plot is complete, it is reviewed with the product engineering managers.

Once the designs have been approved for production, the design files are sent via TCP/IP network from the Windows NT workstation to both the Sun and Intergraph systems for archiving and further use. One of the biggest reasons RJR Nabisco decided to be one of the early adopters of Windows NT was the ability to quickly configure network support, and the availability of CAD programs they were already using on both Sun and Intergraph workstations. The payoff to RJR Nabisco has been reduced product development cycles by streamlining the product development process.

Starting, Using, and Quitting Applications

Windows NT provides a consistent series of dialog boxes and menus for getting things done, regardless of the specific application. This makes it easier for you to learn the basics of a Windows NT application. Once you've learned one, you have a good idea of how the rest of them work. This is specially true with how you start, use, and stop applications. Throughout this section, you'll learn how to get up and running with Windows NT–compatible applications.

Starting an Application

You'll notice when you log onto Windows NT that there are several Program groups that make up the Windows NT Program Manager. The figure below shows the Windows NT Program Manager with several Program groups opened and tiled so that windows don't overlap.

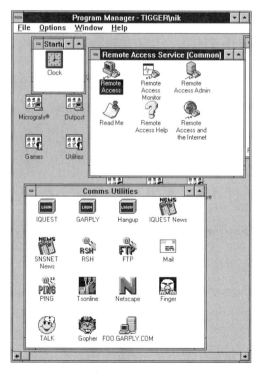

Windows NT desktop with tiled program groups.

Each of the icons that appear in the Applications group represent a specific application program. To launch an application, double-click on its icon.

Jump Starting Your Applications

Many engineers and designers use a design program and a word processing program at the same time. When you log on to Windows NT, you can have applications you use most often start immediately. Look at the figure below. Notice the group called Startup. This Program group is created when you complete the Windows NT Setup program. Any applications placed in the Startup group will be started when you login to the system.

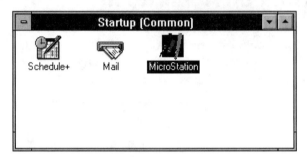

The Startup group with MicroStation version 5.0 shown.

To have an application start up every time you log on to Windows NT, follow these steps:

1. Click once to highlight the application's icon you want to move to the Startup group.
2. Copy that application or use the CTRL key as you drag the application's icon to the Startup window.

➠ **NOTE:** *You can have more than one application in the Startup group. The sequence applications will be loaded is from left to right, one row after another.*

If the application's icon is not in any program group, you can create a new icon in Program group using the File New option in the Program manager window.

Switching Between Applications

You can quickly move between all applications that are running on your Windows NT workstation using either the Fast Switching or Task List features. *Fast Switching* is when you press the ALT+TAB keys at the same time to move from one application to the next. The *Task List*, on the other hand, is a small dialog box that appears when you press the CTRL+ESC keys at the same time or by double-clicking on the desktop background. Either of these techniques is a good way to move from one application to another. The Fast Switching option is also context-sensitive. Once the icon appears for the application you want to access, let the ALT+TAB keys go, and the application becomes active.

To enable Fast Switching, follow the steps shown here:

1. Double-click on the Main group. The contents of the Main group are shown below.

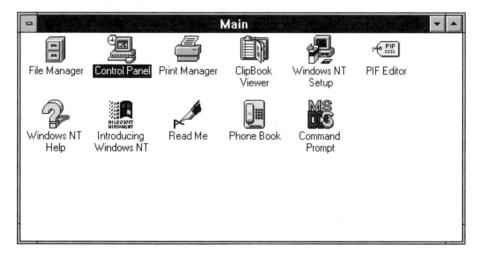

The contents of the Main Group.

2. Double-click on the Control Panel icon.

3. Double-click on the Desktop icon. The Desktop dialog box is shown below.

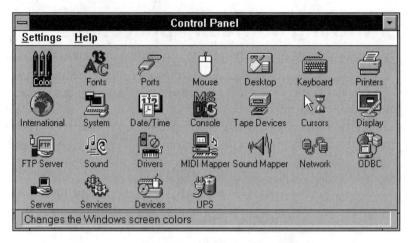

The Control Panel.

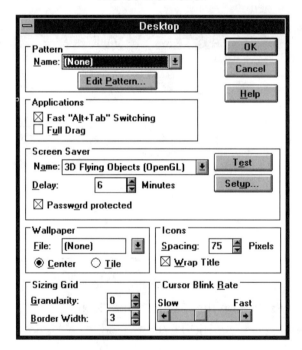

The Desktop dialog box.

4. Click once on the box located in the Applications area of the Desktop dialog box. This enables Fast Switching.

5. Click once on OK. The Desktop dialog box closes, showing the Control Panel's contents.

6. Press ALT+TAB. An icon for the next application that is currently running is shown in the middle of your screen.

Quitting an Application

For quitting an application, you can select EXIT from the File Menu. All Windows NT–based applications and even the 16-bit Windows 3.1 applications support this feature. You can also exit an application by pressing the CTRL+ESC keys to view the Task List. This dialog box shows the active or currently running applications. Follow these steps for shutting down an application from the Task List:

1. Press the CTRL+ESC keys at the same time to show the Task List dialog box. The figure below shows an example of the Task List.

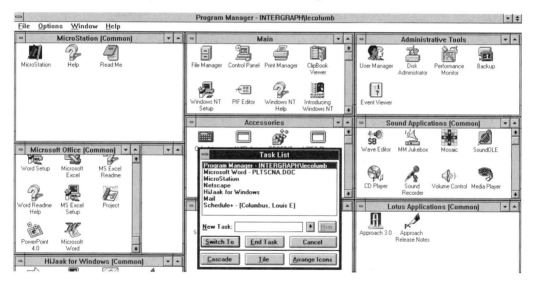

The Task List dialog box.

2. Click once on the application you want to stop so that it is highlighted.

3. Click once on END TASK. The application you selected is now stopped.

4. Click once on CANCEL. The List Task dialog box leaves your screen.

✖ **WARNING:** *This method of killing an application should only be used as a last resort for an application that has stopped responding.*

Shutting Down Windows NT

To quit or exit your Windows NT session, use the following steps:

1. Press the CTRL+ALT+DEL keys at the same time, or you can select Logoff from Program Manager's File Menu.
2. The Windows NT Security dialog box appears, and is shown below.

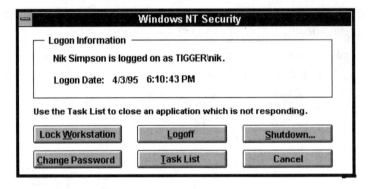

Windows NT Security dialog box.

3. Click once on the Logoff... button.
4. The Windows NT operating system saves the temporary data it was used to your system's hard disk, then stops.
5. After your workstation restarts, the Flexboot is again shown.

Logging Off Windows NT and Stopping Your Workstation

You can logoff Windows NT and turn off your workstation using the steps shown here:

1. Press CTRL+ALT+DEL keys at the same time to show the Windows NT Security dialog box.
2. Click once on the Shutdown... button in the Windows NT Security dialog box.

3. Windows NT backs up any temporarily used data, then presents a small dialog box informing you it's OK to turn off your computer.

➥ **NOTE:** *Like UNIX, Windows NT caches many writes to disk to allow it to optimize disk input and output. Never just turn off your Windows NT system. Shut it down first or you may lose data or corrupt a file system.*

How Was Your First Day?

Day in the Life: Becoming an NT Meister

In German, *Meister* means "one who has mastered a craft." Are you ready to accept the challenge of becoming an NT Meister? You can by reading through the following Day in the Life and ensuing chapters of this book. Let's look in on the progress being made on the new catalog StarFleet Flyers is getting together for WalShop's big meeting at the Louisville plant:

Once again, into the breach...

Frank walks in and gets right behind your desk, peering over your shoulder. You're in the middle of blasting design files through IPLOT to your screen. For a split second you see his image in the reflection of your screen.

"Hi, how's this project going?" Frank says, nearly startling you out of your chair. You've got to get a *real* office.

"It's coming along. I've just got a final run-through of the catalog to do and it's ready to go," you say, realizing that within 2 weeks this entire project needs to be done and you're skipping lunches to get it out. You stop working and turn around to talk with Frank face-to-face. It drives you nuts when people talk to their screens like you are in the computer instead of there in person!

"I need your help in getting MicroStation files pulled from the Microsoft Mail messages I've been getting from Engineering Department. See, these design files? How can I save them? I click on them and poof! Up comes MicroStation and I have to save the files and quit out." You step aside explaining your problem.

Frank straddles your chair and looks into your workstation's screen like Dr. McCoy would stare into Spock's ears during the early episodes of Star Trek.

Frank presses the ALT and TAB keys until Microsoft Mail is in the foreground of your screen.

"Here, just select Save Attachment," Frank says as he selects that command from Mail's File Menu. The file is then saved to your workstation's hard disk without activating MicroStation.

"I can't seem to get regular IPLOT to work. I can plot to the screen but not to any plotter we used to talk to when we had the UNIX plot server here." As you're saying this Frank moves through the open applications pressing ALT and TAB.

"Well I see one problem right now. You have quite a few applications open, and it could be slowing down your workstation." Frank press the CTRL and ESC keys to show the Task List of all open applications. There's a scroll bar along the right side, a sure sign that many applications are open.

You're beginning to think that you need to get back to work now if you hope to see a shred of your weekend. "Frank, thanks...." You hope your voice trailing off lets him know you need to get back to work.

"Wait, I see why you can't plot. You're going to a server that doesn't exist anymore. Your plots are heading straight into oblivion. Here, just connect to the UNIX plot server using the Connect To Printer command."

Frank clicks through the dialog boxes of Print Manager, connecting the workstation to the new PlotServe 2800 located on your same floor. "Now you don't have to go upstairs for your plots; they'll come out over there." Frank nods his head over to the UNIX plot server across the hall.

"Are we still saving iparms and metafiles?"

"Yes, I have a shell script that gathers and saves them to tape." Frank begins walking out of your office. "You saved your original design files, right? You haven't blown away any pen tables?"

"No, I haven't." Frank turns and leaves your office.

You press the ALT and TAB keys at the same time to scroll through the applications that are currently open. You then press the CTRL and ESC keys at the same time to see the active applications. Frank was kind enough to get out of the multiple copies of the Notepad you had running. You also had MicroStation up more than once. Frank fixed that and now your workstation is humming along.

Hmm, maybe I can take off for lunch today, you think.

Summary

Getting a solid foundation of how to log onto Windows NT and how the User Manager works are explained in this chapter. Setting up new user accounts in Windows NT is explained with step-by-step instructions, along with pointers on how to define passwords for new accounts. Windows NT has been designed to ensure that both the keyboard and the mouse can be used for completing tasks.

Chapter 3

Up and Running with Windows NT Workstation

Introduction

Windows NT isn't so much an operating system as it is a collection of software power tools. In order to use Windows NT efficiently you need to understand a number of these tools and utilities delivered with the system. This chapter covers a number of these tools. Subsequent chapters cover the balance. The most important tools to master are:

❐ Program Manager

❐ File Manager

❐ Control Panel

❐ Print Manager

❐ User Manager

Each of these applications provide you with a consistent set of tools for managing your Windows NT system and customizing it to your needs. The following figure shows each of these applications tiled on the Windows NT desktop.

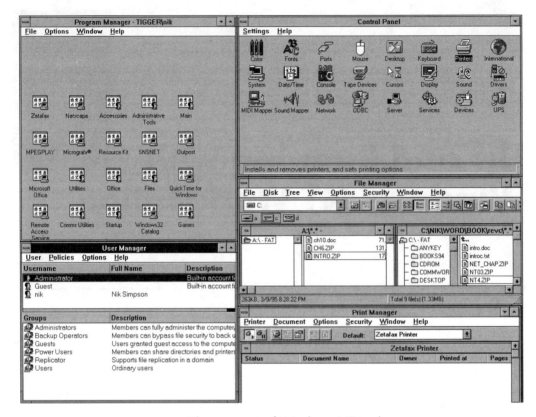

The core set of Windows NT tools.

Using Program Manager To Manage Tasks

Central to the organization of the Windows NT desktop is the Program Manager. The Program Manager acts as the coordinator or traffic cop for your applications. Hierarchical in nature, the Program Manager actually manages a collection of program groups where the actual applications reside.

The Program Manager is the one window that is *always* on your desktop. It is the graphical counterpart to the UNIX shell and just like the Shell, Program Manager is the first program to run when you login and the last thing to die when you logout.

Obviously, this is an important piece of software. So, what does it do? Program Manager performs the following functions:

❏ Organize files and programs into logical groups.

❏ Set up applications to be launched whenever you login.

❏ Launch applications either directly or through an associated data file.

❏ Customize the launch of applications to use specific switches and directories.

❏ Log out or temporarily exit Windows NT.

❏ Totally shutdown or restart Windows NT.

What the Program Manager Isn't

Both Windows NT and Windows 3.1 share a common user interface. Program Manager is used to start applications. File Manager is used for the common operations of naming, copying, and moving files. You cannot manipulate files in Program Manager.

Program Groups

When you look at the Program Manager for the first time, you see a series of icons usually found on the bottom edge of the Program Manager windows. These are Program Group icons. A Program Group is a window that contains icons for files and programs found on your hard disk. Each icon in a Program Group represents a program or data file. You can launch an application either by double-clicking on the application icon or by double-clicking on a file associated with that application.

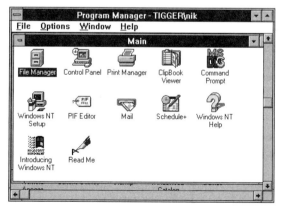

Program Group example.

Within Program Manager, a Program Group is represented as a window and can be moved, resized, and manipulated just like any other window. When collapsed or *minimized*, a Program Group itself is just another icon in the Program Manager window. The figure below shows the contents of the Main group.

When you install Windows NT it creates two sets of Program groups:

❏ Windows NT Groups standard on all systems.

❏ Windows NT Groups created from Windows 3.1 *.grp* files. If you are installing Windows NT over an existing Windows 3.1 or Windows for Workgroups installation, Windows NT will create a set of Program Groups identical to what you had when booting Windows 3.1. This will include applications.

The standard groups create are:

❏ **Startup (Common):** This group contains applications that should be started no matter who logs into the system.

❏ **Startup (User):** This group contains applications that will be started only when you login.

❏ **Accessories:** Simple applications such as the calculator and Media Player are found in this group.

❏ **Main:** Commonly used Windows NT applications such as File Manager and the Control Panel.

❏ **Administrative Tools:** Applications required to administer an Windows NT system, includes Disk Manager and User Manager.

❏ **Games:** Standard games supplied with Windows NT, includes Solitaire and Winmine.

Windows NT allows you to create new groups and modify existing ones. This facility allows you to organize your system in a way that suits you.

The Program Manager Menus

The Program Manager includes a complete series of pull-down menus used for completing tasks within Windows NT. Each of the menus in the Program

Manager provide vital functions to you. Program Manager includes a set of menus to assist you in configuring and understanding its functions, these are:

❑ **File:** Contains menu items for creating and manipulating program groups, as well as logoff and shutdown options.

❑ **Options:** Contains options that govern how Program Manager will behave when you launch applications from it or change its configuration.

❑ **Window:** Allows you to automatically layout the Program Manager window as well as quickly access any program group.

❑ **Help:** Access the Windows NT help system.

Exploring Program Manager's File Menu

Being able to quickly add Program Groups and Items within those groups is accomplished using the options in the File menu. The figure below shows the File menu for the Program Manager.

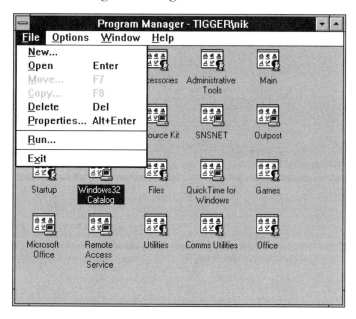

The Program Manager's File menu.

Using the File menu within the Program Manager you can create a new Program Item that becomes part of an existing Program Group, or even create a customized Program Group.

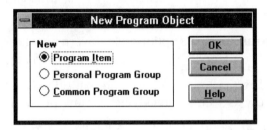

The Program Manager's New Item dialog box.

Using the options in the New... dialog box, you can easily add new program items to an existing Program Group or create an entirely new Program Group. The new program item is added to the active Program Group, which is either highlighted as an icon or as an open window.

Creating a New Program Group

A Program Group is used for storing related items on the Windows NT desktop. Think of creating a Program Group just like you would use a manila file folder to organize similar documents, images, or applications. The following are the steps involved in creating a new program group for your Windows NT Program Manager.

1. Select New... from the Program Manager's File menu. The New Program Object dialog box appears on screen and is used for creating both new program items and groups.

Note that you have several choices at this point:

❑ **Program Item:** A program or data file in a Program Group.

❑ **Personal Program Group:** A program group that only appears for you in Program Manager.

❑ **Common Program Group:** A program group available to anybody logged onto your computer.

We are creating a Personal Program group, so follow these steps:

2. Click once on Program Group within the New Program Object dialog box. The Program Group Properties dialog box appears and is shown in the figure below. If you decide to create a Personal Program Group, it will only be seen when you log on. If you create a Common program Group, then it will be seen by anybody using the computer.

The Program Item Properties dialog box.

3. Click once in the Description: entry and type in the name of the program group you want to create. This can be any name you want to use. For purposes of this example, type in the phrase *Project Designs* in the Description: entry. The Group File: entry in this dialog box is optional. Click once on OK.

Windows NT has two types of Program Groups, a personal group that is available only to the creator, and a common group that is seen in the Program Manager of anybody logged into the system.

Creating a New Program Item

Many programs automatically create a new program item when they are installed. Not all installation procedures are so helpful and you may have to create a Program Item yourself.

The simplest method is to open the Program Group in which the new item is to go and then drag the required file from a File Manager window to the Program Group. You can also create program items using the File→New menu in the Program Manager. The sequence for creating a new program item is quite simple:

1. Select New from the Program Manager's File menu. The New Program Object dialog box appears.

2. Note, that you have several choices at this point: Program Item, Personal Program Group, or Common Program Group.

We are creating a Program Item, so:

3. Click once on THE New Program Item radio button and click once on OK. The Program Item Properties dialog box next appears on your screen and is used for assigning a description, command line, working directory, and shortcut key.

4. Click once on the Description: entry. Type in the name of the Program Item you're creating. This can be any text including spaces and punctuation. Pick something that will help you remember what the item is for.

5. If you know the exact location and name of the file you are going to use, then just type it into the Command Line field, otherwise, click once on Browse.... The Browse dialog box appears as shown below.

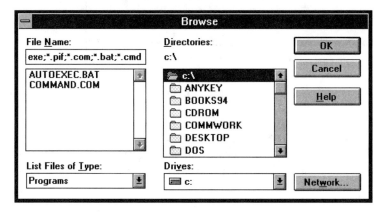

The Browse dialog box.

6. Using the options in the Browse dialog box, scroll through the executable files until you find the one you want to have represented as an icon on the desktop.

7. Click once on OK.

8. The new program item appears in the currently active program group. The figure below shows an example of the Windows NT desktop with the new program item.

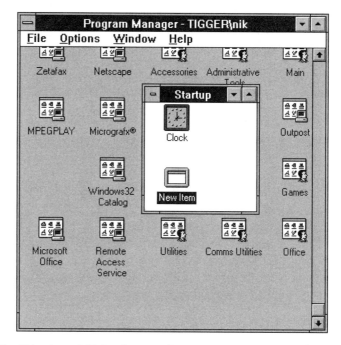

The Windows NT Desktop with a new program item shown.

Program items can also be data files. The simplest way to add a data file to a program group is just to drag it from the File Manager window. The file will show up with the icon of the parent application. For example, a *.doc* file would show up with the icon of Word for Windows. If the file is not associated with an application, then it will have a blank icon. The subject of creating file to application associations is covered in the section on File Manager.

The File Menu's Other Commands

You can also use the commands within the File menu to move, copy, and delete icons from the Program Manager's Desktop. You can see from the figure below where each command is located on the File menu.

➠ **NOTE:** *It is very important to understand that Program Items are links to files on the disk; when you delete a Program Item, you delete the link, not the file on the disk.*

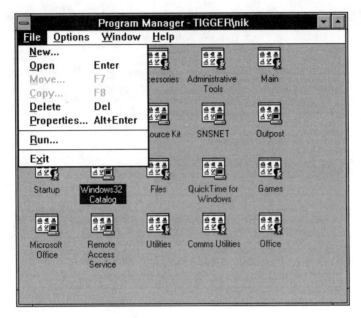

*Program Manager's File menu provides quick access
to many useful commands.*

Program Item Properties

Each item in a program group has a number of properties that affect the way it behaves when run. The properties that you can change are as follows:

❏ **Description:** The name of the program item. By default this is the name of the file represented by the item.

❏ **Command Line:** The location of the program or file, as well as any command line parameters to be used when the program is launched.

❏ **Working Directory:** Where temporary files will be created if required.

❏ **Shortcut Key:** Allows you to define a key sequence that automatically launches the file.

❏ **Run Minimized:** If checked, the application will collapse to an icon when run.

❏ **Run in Separate Memory Space:** This is new in Windows NT 3.5. Previously DOS and 16-bit Windows applications shared a common virtual machine. If one application crashed, then any DOS or 16-bit Windows applications went with it. In Windows NT 3.5, you can make Windows NT create a virtual machine for each application. This give you much greater stability as well as performance, especially on machines with more than one CPU.

❑ **Change Icon:** Allows you to select an icon to be associated with the Program Item.

Generally you'll not need to change the properties of a program item created by Windows NT. The most important property to anybody with an existing Windows 3.1 system is the "Run In Separate Memory Space" check box.

Using the Options Menu in Program Manager

You can quickly organize the Program Manager Desktop within Windows NT by using the commands available in the Options menu. The figure below shows the command available in the Options menu.

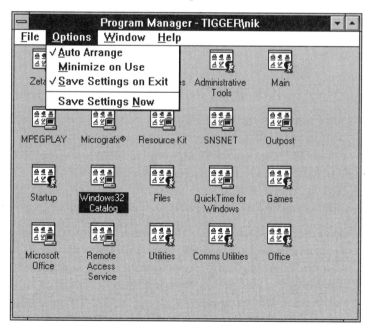

Program Manager's Options menu.

What can you accomplish with the commands in this menu? Let's take a quick tour by command to see.

❏ **Auto Arrange:** Selecting this option will automatically arrange the icons that represent applets within a selected group. This can be particularly useful if you have Program Groups that have a large number of icons or program items within them. To use this command you simply select it from the Options menu.

❏ **Minimize on Use:** Deflates the Program Manager to an icon in the lower left portion of the Windows NT Desktop. Taking a file group, application, or program item and minimizing it into an icon is called *minimizing* the item. The figure below shows an example of the Program Manager minimized to an icon. Selecting the Minimize On Use option within the Options menu shrinks the Program Manager into an icon when another application is launched.

Program
Manager

An example of the Program Manager minimized.

❏ **Save Settings on Exit:** Everyone has different preferences for how their Windows NT Desktop looks, the types of applications that are open, and the location of various groups and items within them. Once you have your Windows NT Desktop set just the way you want it to look, select this option. Using this option you can save the entire appearance of your Windows NT Program Manager window whenever you log off.

❏ **Save Settings Now:** Use this option to save the current settings of the Program Manager as permanent. Windows NT will honor your request to save the current desktop configuration just as it appears when you select this command from the Options menu. This is very similar to the Save Settings on Exit command, with the only difference being the latter saving the desktop selections only at exit from Windows NT. With this command the Windows NT Desktop is saved right now.

Arranging Program Manager Windows

The Program Manager-Windows menu includes command for organizing the various open Program Groups represented as windows on the Desktop. Here's a brief overview of the commands in the Window menu.

❏ **Tile:** Just as the name suggests, this command tiles the open Program Group windows so you can conveniently see the contents of each open program group. This is particularly useful if you want access to several applets and/or applications at once.

❏ **Cascade:** Arranges all open windows so that they overlap, allowing you to reach any window by selecting an exposed edge.

❏ **Arrange Icons:** Any Program Groups that have been minimized appear as icons. This menu option will arrange the icons along the bottom of the Program Manager window.

After you've arranged the desktop to your satisfaction you can select Options → Save Settings Now in Program Manager to defaults for Program Manager so that the current appearance is retained from session to session.

Shortcuts Around Program Manager

If you learned your first applications on UNIX, DOS, or a comparable operating system, you most likely became so familiar with the commands that you could actually type them before the screen was able to catch up with you. With Windows NT, you may feel that this isn't possible due to the graphical nature of the interface. Some graphical interfaces, notably the Apple Macintosh really have no command line interface. In Windows NT, the command line interface is basically a DOS shell; anything you are used to doing from the command line in DOS can be done in Windows NT.

Windows NT also supplies many keyboard shortcuts to help navigate areound the GUI when your mouse is impaired. Here are some of the more common shortcuts to use with Program Manager:

❏ **SHIFT+F4:** Arranges the currently open windows in a tiled format while Program Manager is active.

❏ **SHIFT+F5:** Cascades open windows within the Program Manager's Desktop.

❏ **CTRL+F4:** Closes the currently active window within the Program Manager.

❒ **ALT+F4:** Automatically logs the user off Windows NT. An interim dialog box is provided to confirm that you really want to log out of Windows NT.

❒ **ALT + TAB:** Switches between the active applications on the Windows NT desktop. Pressing these keys together scrolls through the active applications by presenting a small rectangular box in the middle of your workstation's screen.

❒ **ARROW KEYS:** Moves the active cursor to the location you want by using the up, down, left, and right arrow keys on your workstation's keyboard.

❒ **CTRL+F6:** Switches to the next active application.

❒ **CTRL+ESC:** Opens the Task List dialog box. This dialog box shows which applications are currently open. By default, the Program Manager is always listed as one of these applications. The figure below shows an example of the Task List dialog box.

The Task List dialog box, used to manage running applications on your workstation.

These keyboard shortcuts may be used in place of the mouse equivalents or in conjunction with them.

Using File Manager

The File Manager is located in the Main Program Group and is represented as a file cabinet. File Manager provides a graphical way of manipulating files on local and remote drives. File Manager is an alternative approach to the

UNIX commands ls, chmod, chown, chgrp, mount, cp, rm, mv, and find. By integrating all the functionality in a single application Windows NT provides a consistent and easily mastered system for organizing and managing files.

Using the File Manager you can create directories, move and copy files, connect to remote disk drives, find files with a particular name or pattern, launch applications, and many other day- to- day file administration tasks. Understanding the capabilities of File Manager is essential in learning to use Windows NT. Remember if you already use Windows 3.1 or Windows for Workgroups, much of this section will be very simple.

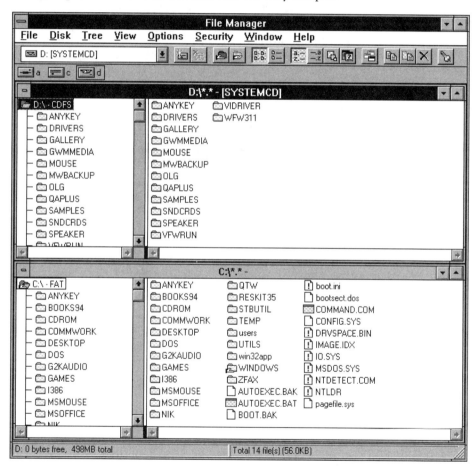

The File Manager in action.

At the end of this section you will know how to create, move, copy, delete, rename, and generally manipulate files on local disk storage or on the network.

Navigating Within File Manager

Let's suppose you're in the middle of trying to get out a series of rendered design files for your boss, who is leaving at 6 PM for the airport so he can present them to your company's board of directors tomorrow at 8 AM. You don't have much time. You know the files are scattered throughout subdirectories, and you need to pull them together fast. What can you do? Use the File Manager to get a complete view of your system's hard disk and then move all the files to the subdirectory where your plotting software will take them and plot them. Having all the subdirectories available at once gives you the opportunity to move through the various locations and get the rendered images all into a single location. The figure below shows an example of the File Manager's main window.

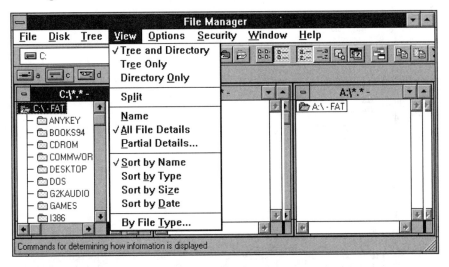

Navigating through the File Manager makes organizing files easy.

As you quickly grab the files you need, you notice the left side of the File Manager's window shows the complete series of directories on your hard disk. Along the top of the File Manager window in the preceding figure, there's a series of icons each with network lines going into and out of them. These are disk drives that you've connected to during earlier File Manager sessions. You can just as easily go over and use the networked disk drives by clicking once on them as well, but for now you're just getting the files on your hard disk organized.

Clicking once on the files you need, you move them all into the same subdirectory, then open up the application you use for plotting raster files. Your printer locks and then checks its pens, and suddenly there is hard copy being created. Spinning around you head for the Coke machine to take a break while the plots get done.

Notice also in the preceding figure there are subdirectories in the directory tree that show small <+> and <-> keys. These symbols designate expandable and collapsible subdirectories.

Opening Files and Directories from File Manager

You can use the File Manager's main window to open files, directories, or as was illustrated in the previous section, the File Manager has the ability to connect your desktop with other Windows NT workstations on your network or a related network. Files in the filesystem usually have a three character extension. The extension often has a special meaning for Windows NT. Every file has an action associated with it: double-clicking on a directory will open the directory, and double-clicking on an *.exe* or *.bat* file will run an application. Of course there are many more file types that correspond to application data files. Double-clicking on a data file associated with an application brings up the application with the selected data file loaded.

File Manager gives you the opportunity to start programs.

When you think of how to navigate through the subdirectories shown in File Manager it's best to think of a series of file folders on your desk. You can rearrange these folders by taking them and moving one to a level higher, one to a level lower, and another to an entirely separate location. File Manager has been designed to provide you with this same flexibility in organizing information.

Accessing Directories

Just as you would reach and open a file folder on your desk, it's basically the same approach in File Manager. Only you point at the subdirectory you want to open.

Normally you have one window open for each drive. Sometimes, though, you need two windows open on the same drive. Selecting the New Window command from the Window menu opens multiple windows in File Manager. Follow these steps to open and view a subdirectory in File Manager:

1. Double-click once on the disk drive that contains the subdirectory you want to open. Notice the disk drive icons along the top of the File Manager's window. The currently active disk drive is framed with a rectangular box.

2. The contents of the selected disk drive appear in a new window.

3. Click once on the subdirectory you want to view. For purposes of example, click once on the subdirectory where Windows NT is installed. The files in the Windows NT main directory are next shown in the right portion of the File Manager's window.

What if you want to compare one subdirectory's contents with another? Follow these steps:

1. Select New Window from the Window menu. A secondary window opens within the File Manager. The figure below shows the File Manager with a second window opened.

2. Select Tile from the View menu. The two open windows are then shown. The figure below shows the Tiled view within File Manager.

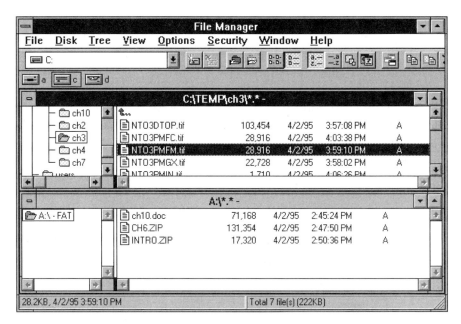

File Manager with two windows open at the same time.

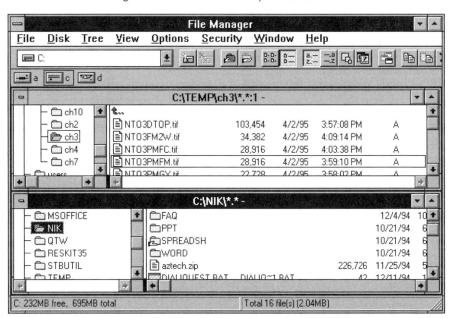

*You can tile multiple windows within File Manager
to have more than one subdirectory location shown at once.*

Changing and Closing Directory Windows

When using the File Manager, you can create several open views, each showing a different subdirectory structure, or even another disk drive's contents over the network. One of the strongest benefits of File Manager is the ability to connect with remote network-based disk resources. You can, for example, have separate windows open for each of the network-based disk drives you have available on your network. Here are the steps you can use for getting multiple windows open within File Manager, and how to change from one directory to another. The figure below shows an example of the File Manager with several windows showing the contents of networked disk drives.

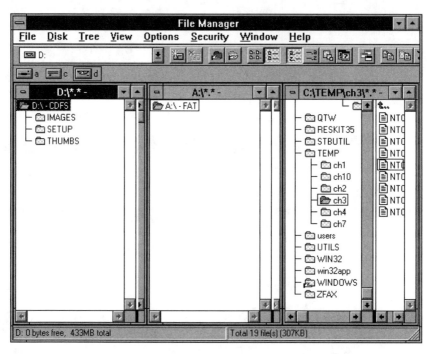

*Using the File Manager you can view the contents of
several disk drives at once.*

Here's how you can open and then display several subdirectories at once, and then change between each of them.

1. Click once on the first windows within File Manager you want to eventually tile.

2. Select New Window from the Window menu.

3. Click once on the new window to then select Tree Only from the View menu.

Sharing Data Using File Manager

One of the most important features of Windows NT is the ability to mount drives on other machines on your network as well share your own drives. Many operating systems have similar file-sharing capabilities to Windows NT. What sets Windows NT apart is the ease with which this is accomplished.

Before looking at how to mount a drive, let's look at how to make one of your drives or directories available to others. In File Manager select the directory you want to export to the network, then select Share As... from the Disk menu. The following menu is displayed:

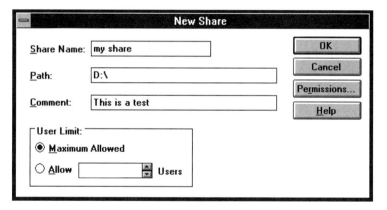

The New Share dialog box.

The dialog box has several fields to fill in:

❏ **Share Name:** The logical name for the resource you are sharing. This defaults to the directory name.

❏ **Path:** The Drive letter and directory path of the resource you are sharing. This defaults to the currently selected directory in File Manager.

❏ **Comment:** Users mounting network drives will see this comment. It should help them identify the contents of the shared directory.

❏ **User Limit:** Defines how many simultaneous connections are allowed. On Windows NT Workstation 3.5, there is a system limit of 10; on Windows NT Sever 3.5, there is no system limit. You might want to limit the number of connections for several reasons, including load on your machine or legal constraints on the number of simultaneous users for a particular shared resource.

For now we'll ignore the Permissions dialog box that can be accessed from the New Share menu. We'll talk more about it when we look at security and the NTFS filesystem in Chapter 10.

To mount a shared drive is equally simple. Select Connect Network Drive... from the Disk menu. The following dialog box is displayed:

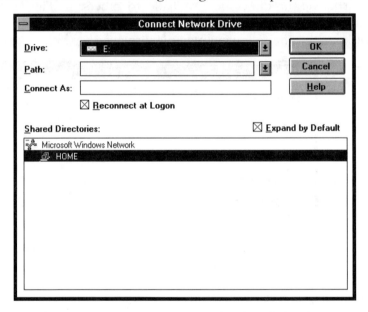

File Manager's Connect Network Drive dialog box.

The dialog box has several fields that you must fill in to connect to the network drive:

❏ **Drive:** This the drive letter on your system that will be used for the mounted drive. You can always accept the default. You can change the default if you want a particular letter associated with the mounted drive.

❐ **Path:** The path is a combination of a machine name and a Share Name. If the share were called designs and the machine called filesrv, then the path would be *filesrv**designs*.

❐ **Connect As:** If the share is protected, you may need to use a particular user name to connect to the drive. Talk to your system administrator if you don't have permission to connect to a shared drive that you need.

❐ **Shared Directories Window:** Presents a graphical view of all the shared drives available on your local network. This is useful if you don't know the share Path. If you select a machine in this window, all its shared drives will be displayed as shown in the previous figure. Selecting a shared drive in this window will cause the Path to fill in automatically for you.

This simple and consistent interface for mounting and sharing drives on the network makes access to shared resources very simple. In UNIX and other command line oriented operating systems you need to work with unwieldy command lines such as:

```
mount -fNFS,soft filesrv:/designs /usr/designs
```

For an experienced UNIX user this presents no great problem, but for a novice or someone not interested in learning the operating system, Windows NT's simple GUI approach is a much better solution.

Selecting Multiple Files and Directories

Within File Manager you can select multiple files for manipulations such as moving, copying, or deleting. To select a group of files, you need to understand the interaction of the mouse and the SHIFT and CTRL keys. If you simply select a file with the mouse, then selecting another file will deselect the first file. Using the SHIFT and CTRL keys you can change this behavior.

❐ **SHIFT:** If you hold down the SHIFT key when selecting the second file, all files between the first file and the second file will be highlighted.

❐ **CTRL:** If you hold down the CTRL key when selecting the second file, then it will be added to the selection list.

If you need to select several groups of files, then use the CTRL key to select each file individually. You cannot select files in multiple windows.

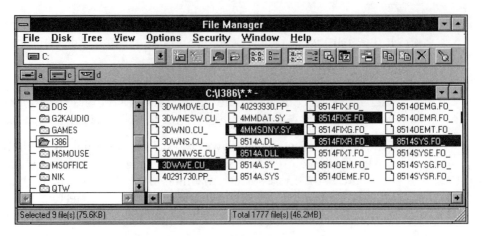

Using the File Manager with multiple files selected.

Once you've selected a group of files, you can perform simple manipulations such as copy, delete, or move. To delete the selected files, simply press delete on your keyboard. To move or copy files, just drag them to the destination directory or drive. File Manager has two modes when dragging files: move or copy. The default action will depend on the source and destination for the files:

❐ **Source and Destination on same drive:** Default operation is to move the files.

❐ **Source and Destination on different drives:** Default operation is to copy the files.

You can change this default action very simply: if you hold down the SHIFT key while dragging, then the system will always copy the files. If you hold down the CTRL key, then a move is performed.

Moving files from one location on the network to another is simple. First mount the destination drive. Then select the files to copy and drag them to the destination.

Selecting Files by Type

In the File menu of File Manager is an item called Select. This pops up the following dialog box.

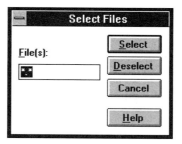

Using the File Manager Select Dialog box.

You can type in a *wildcard* search. For example, if you used **.bat,*exe,* all the files with those extensions in the current directory will be highlighted.

Searching for Files or Directories

You know that file has got to be on your hard disk somewhere, but where? Whatever happened to the design files for the Schmidt Project? On UNIX workstations, the find command gave you the opportunity to search through subdirectories and find the files you were looking for. File Manager gives you the same flexibility, and like the UNIX counterpart, the files meeting the specific search criteria are displayed as they are found. Let's take a look at how you can quickly find files on your local hard disk (most often known of as C:) and any network-based disk drive you have access to. Follow these steps to complete a search of a disk drive you a file.

1. Click once on the C: in the File Manager's window. The figure below shows an example of the File Manager with a window open on the C: drive. For convenience of the file search later, you'll want to have the root directory selected.

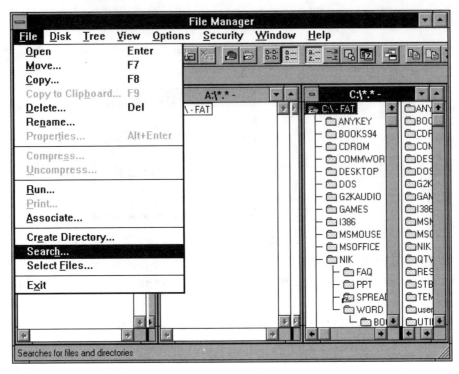

Where the search begins: Inside the File Manager.

2. Select Search... from the File menu. The Search dialog box appears and is shown below.

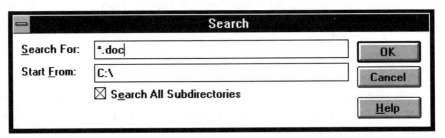

The Search dialog box.

3. Click once in the Search For: entry. Type in the name of the file you want to find. For purposes of example, type in the file extension of the type of design file you create. If you use MicroStation type in the text, *.dgn*. The * is a wildcard that tells File Manager to find all files that have the extension

.dgn. You can also search for specific files by giving the complete name of the file.

4. Click once on OK.

5. The file search begins, and a separate window opens, showing the search results. The figure below shows the results of a search session for all the files with a .dgn file extension.

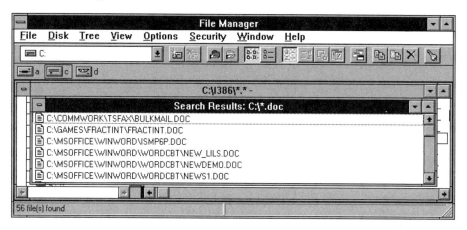

As a search is completed, a window is opened showing all files meeting the search criteria.

6. Click once on the file you want to open. Notice in the figure above there are icons, each representing a specific file. If there are little blue lines in the icon it means that the file is associated with an application.

7. Click once on one of the files that has the blue-lined icon. The file that originally generated the file or has the ability to read it launches, showing the selected file.

Changing the File Manager Layout

File Manager allows you to organize directory windows in several ways:

❐ **Cascade:** The windows are overlapped; select the window you want on top by clicking the mouse on any portion of the window you can see.

❐ **Tile Horizontally:** All windows are visible in stripes running the width of the File Manager window.

❏ **Tile Vertically:** All windows are visible in stripes running the length of the File Manager window.

Use these facilities to customize File Manager to your needs. The open directories and layout of windows is saved from one session to the next.

Specifying File Display Details

By default, the File Manager just shows file names. Sometimes you need to know more about a file than just its name. File Manager allows you to specify the amount of detail using the View menu. There are three options in the view menu that affect the detail displayed for each file:

❏ **Name:** When selected, this trims the detail to just the file name.

❏ **All File Details:** Shows size, creation, and last access time for each file.

❏ **Partial File Details:** Brings up a dialog box with *checkboxes*. Check each piece of detail that you want displayed.

Why would you want to show the contents of a specific subdirectory's files or the details for a specific file itself? Let's say you are comparing the revisions of files and want to get the latest one for a project. Using the commands presented here you will be able to get full information on files relevant to projects you're working on. Information on files is a displayed in the File Manager's various windows and appears in a tabular format. Central to this capability is the View menu in File Manager. The following figure shows the File Manager's View menu, which is used for showing the various attributes of files displayed in File Manager.

Let's get started with a hands-on example, showing how to use these commands for gaining better insights into how you manage files in File Manager. Use these steps for managing the files in File Manager.

1. Click once on the window in File Manager you want to have the various View options applied to.
2. Select All File Details from the View menu. The figure below shows the contents of a File Manager's window after this view is selected.

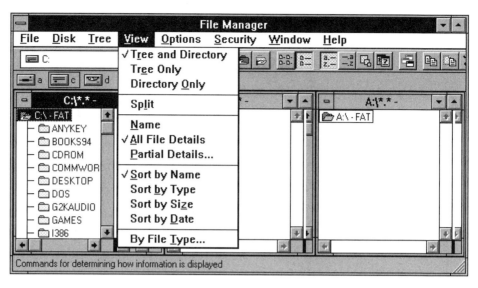

File Manager View control menu.

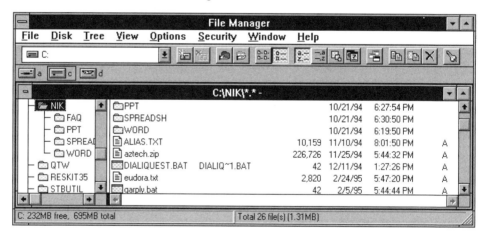

A window in File Manager with All File Details selected.

Showing All File Details provides a comprehensive listing of all details that pertain to a specific series of files. What if you want to see the files that have been updated since the last iteration of design reviews? You can also have the files shown that are sorted by the last modification date. Follow these steps to show files by the last or most recent modification date.

1. Click once on the window in File Manager that has the files you want to view the last update for.

2. Select Partial Display from the View menu. The Partial Display dialog box appears and is shown below.

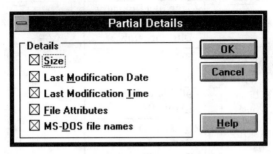

The Partial Details dialog box gives you the flexibility of viewing files by latest modification date.

3. Click once on the options Last Modification Date, Last Modification Time, and Size.

4. Click once on OK.

5. The Partial Details dialog box closes, showing the highlighted window in File Manager with the files displayed with the partial details shown.

6. To have these files sorted in descending order by modification date, select Sort by Date from the View menu. The files in the subdirectory window are then displayed in descending order by date of last modification.

Using the options in the File Manager you can quickly locate subsets of files you want to use in conjunction with a project, design program, or ongoing responsibility in your job. The View menu is very powerful in that you can quickly sort through a large number of files to find just the subset you're looking for.

Setting File Protections

If you are storing files on a FAT filesystem you have very limited control over what can be done to the file. Access rights are controlled from the File→Properties menu in File Manager. To set or modify the protection attributes follow this sequence:

1. Select the file or files you want to affect.

2. Select Properties... from the File menu. The Properties dialog box appears, as shown below.

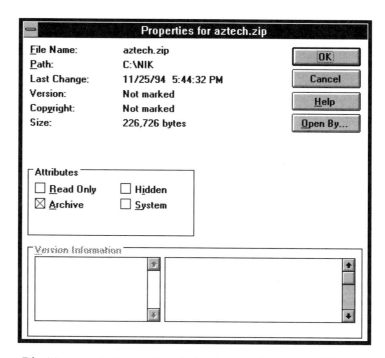

*File Manager's Properties dialog box makes it possible
to change attributes of selected files.*

3. Click once on each of the attributes you want to change for the file selected. Here's a brief explanation of each of the options in the Properties dialog box:

Read Only: Changes the file to Read-Only status, so no one can overwrite or change the original dates in any way. This is a useful attribute if you plan to have designs and drawings in a shared directory that others in your company can use for completing tasks. But remember, on a FAT filesystem anybody else can reset the Read-Only status.

Archive: The archive attribute is used to indicate to some backup programs that the file has been changed since the last backup was made.

Hidden: Gives you the option of displaying a hidden file or not. Several operating system files are hidden to minimize the chance of them being deleted.

System: Designates files that are essential to the operating system. These files are also hidden.

4. Click once on OK.

The attributes for the selected files are now changed, and the File Manager's window is updated to reflect your selections.

The more complete security system available on NTFS filesystems is covered Chapter 11, "Managing a Windows NT Workplace."

Working with Floppy Disks

In many environments, the floppy disk still represents a cheap and effective backup media as well as a way of taking work home. The File Manager can be used to format floppy disks that can then be treated exactly the same way as any other disk drive.

Formatting a Floppy Disk

Place the floppy to be formatted in the drive, then select Disk→Format in File Manager. The Format dialog box appears as shown below:

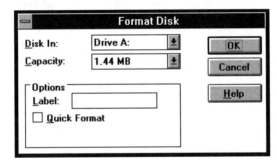

The Format Disk dialog box.

1. On most systems you only have one floppy drive. The Disk In: field will default to *a:*.If you have other floppy drives, you can select them by setting the drive letter to point to the drive. You cannot use this dialog box to format hard disks.

2. Most systems use a format that puts up to 1.44MB of data on a 3.5 inch floppy. If you need to use a lower density in order to transfer data to an older machine, you can select an alternate capacity by using the Capacity: field.

3. The label on a diskette is to help you identify the contents of the disk, you can leave it blank if you wish.
4. Quick format just writes a new filesystem to the disk. If you don't select this option, the disk is scanned for flaws before the filesystem is written.
5. Click once on OK. The diskette is now formatted per your instructions in the Format Disk dialog box.

If you format a floppy as bootable, it will not work on any system that does not have Windows NT loaded.

Copying Disks

If you've ever used MS-DOS, you know how easy it is to copy disks. You simply type *copy *.** to the destination drive you want to use. The Windows NT File Manager automates this process through the use of dialog boxes.

When you buy an application delivered on floppy disk, you should make backup copies of the floppies. The Disk→Copy Disk menu item in File Manager will let you make copies, prompting you each time you need to exchange the source and destination floppies.

1. Insert the floppy disk you want to copy into the floppy disk drive of your workstation.
2. Select Copy Disk the Disk menu.

The system will now prompt you through the whole process. Don't worry if you only have one drive, File Manager will tell you to change disks when appropriate.

Labeling Disks

If you're working on several projects at once, you probably have entire series of files and subdirectories that contain valuable files that you will want to save to a specific subdirectory and then onto tape for long-term archiving or onto diskette for use later on. You can do this easily enough by writing on the label that is easily attached to the side of the diskette. You could also label the diskette itself, so that every time you type the *dir* command in the Command Prompt to view a diskette's contents or use File Manager to view its contents, the same diskette definition is shown. Follow the steps shown here for labeling a diskette:

1. Place the diskette you want to label into the disk drive.

2. Select Disk Label from the Disk menu. The Disk Label dialog box appears.

3. Click once in the Label: entry and type the label you want written to the floppy diskette. This name can be up to 11 characters long.

4. Click once on OK.

Associating Files and Applications

Files in Windows NT have an action associated with them. For some files this action is built into Windows NT. An example of a default type is *.exe* files; whenever you double-click on one of these files it is launched as an application.

Data files created by an application can also have an action associated with them, for example a *.ppt* file will be associated with the Microsoft Powerpoint application. When a file is associated with an application, launching it will cause the application to execute and load the specified file.

You can modify or create *associations* using the File→Associate menu item in File Manager.

1. Select the file whose association you want to set or modify from a directory window in File Manager.

2. Select the Associate entry in the File menu. The Associate dialog box appears.

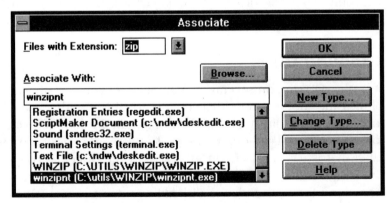

The Associate dialog box.

3. The Extension field will show the last three letters of the file name.

4. Use the Browse dialog box to select an application to associate with the file.

Remember, you cannot set an association for an individual file, only for files with a particular extension. Once you've created an association, File Manager can manipulate the file more intelligently. For example, if you select as file then select the File→Print menu item, File Manager will launch the associated application to print the file.

Summary

This chapter has explained the fundamentals of the two Windows NT applications that you'll need to get any work done. File Manager allows you to manipulate files with the same functionality found in half a dozen UNIX commands, but with a simple and consistent graphical user interface. Program Manager lets you create a more project-oriented view of the files on your disk. If you were already familiar with the Windows 3.1 counterparts for Program Manager and File Manager, you should have realized how similar the interface in Windows NT is.

Before continuing with the rest of this book, experiment with Program Manager and File Manager until you are comfortable with the way they work.

Using Control Panel to Customize Windows NT

Introduction

Getting started with any new operating system includes learning how to customize it for your specific needs. Whether you're an engineer who is using Windows NT Workstationfor completing designs and documentation, or a software developer writing a new application using Windows NT, you'll find this chapter helpful in understanding how best to master the Windows NT Control Panel.

The Control Panel is comprised of a series of smaller applications (sometimes called *applets*) that are used to configure virtually all aspects of your system, from changing how the desktop appears to loading new device drivers to support newly acquired hardware. This chapter looks at each of the important Control Panel applets and explains its use.

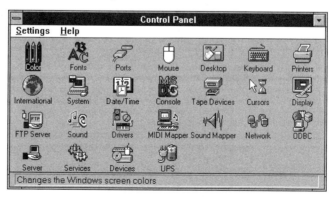

The Windows NT Control Panel.

You can launch the Control Panel from the Main Program group of the Program Manager.

Using the Desktop Control Panel

Everybody likes to inkjet a little individuality into their offices, layout of their offices, and even the color of their file folders. Windows NT provides plenty of opportunities to customize the desktop according to your own preferences. These tools that give you the flexibility to customize your Windows NT desktop deserve mention. Many of the ones not described here are self-explanatory. Let's take a quick tour of how you can customize the Windows NT desktop to match your preferences.

Changing the Background Pattern

Have you ever noticed on certain UNIX workstations there is a background pattern behind the windows and icons? This same desktop feature is included in Windows NT and is actually customizable directly from the Desktop icon in the Control Panel. Start the desktop control panel by double-clicking on the Desktop icon.

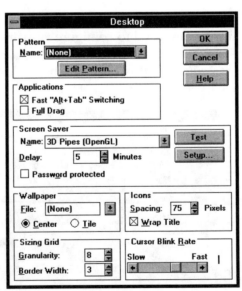

Use the Desktop dialog box to set the pattern on your workstation.

Windows NT allows you to choose either a simple background pattern replicated until it fills the screen or to load a more complex image that alone can fill the background. Remember, loading an image on the background will slow down screen refreshes as the background image has to be repainted.

Using just a pattern requires fewer resources; you can select one of the many patterns supplied or create one of your own with pattern editor. To select one of the predefined patterns, simply select the Name field in the dialog and select one of the choices. Using the pattern editor should be obvious.

Using an image instead of a pattern is equally simple. The only file type that is supported for background images is the Windows Bitmap or *.bmp* file. You use utilities like Paint Shop Pro to create in or convert images to this format. To select an image use the Wallpaper section of the Desktop Control panel. All the available files are displayed. Select one and then decide whether to have it centered (makes sense if the image fills the display) or have it tiled; when tiled, the image is replicated enough times to fill the background.

➼ *NOTE: Files used for Desktop Wallpaper must be stored in the Windows NT root directory. This is normally c:\windows or C:\winnt.*

Enabling a Screen Saver

If you've ever walked through a used computer store or even seen older monitors in your company, you no doubt have seen monitors with Lotus spreadsheets indelibly etched into the screen, even though it's turned off. To overcome the problem of burn-in and also to provide some security when you leave your system unattended, Windows NT lets you select a screen saver that will start after a set period of time. The screen saver has two functions:

❑ Generate a random or constantly changing pattern or image so that no one part of the screen becomes burnt in.

❑ Prevent unauthorized use by forcing a password login when dismissing the screen saver.

To enable the screen saver, open the Desktop icon in the Control Panel and select the one you want (you can preview the screen saver using the Test button. Then select a timeout value and check the password box if applicable. Some screen savers also have attributes that can be configured; these are accessed by selecting the Config button.

Selecting Fast Switching Between Applications

Being able to move quickly between applications that are running within Windows NT is called *Fast Switching*. This involves pressing the ALT and TAB keys at the same time to scroll through all open applications without having to minimize each window. How can you enable this feature? Simply select Fast ALT-TAB Switching in the Applications section of the Desktop applet.

Press the ALT and TAB keys at the same time. All the applications that are open are shown one after another via a small dialog box in the middle of your screen. These keystroke sequence shortcuts can save you time when you want to move through all the applications running on your workstation. You can also key in the values by highlighting the value you want to change.

The Applications section also contains the Full Drag option; this has nothing to do with alternate lifestyles. If Full Drag is enabled, windows will be dynamically updated as you stretch or move them. On a slow graphics card this is definitely not wanted; even on a fast card it can be distracting.

Customizing Date and Time

Control Panel contains an applet for setting the system date, time, and time zone. Any application that uses these values is affected. To set the time or otherwise change current setting, launch the Date/Time applet from the Control Panel.

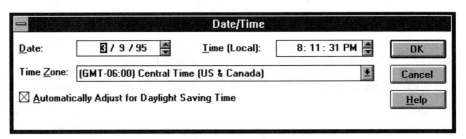

Use the Date/Time dialog box to set the current time and date used by your workstation.

1. Using the up and down arrow keys located to the right of the date and time entries, set the correct date and time.

2. Select the time zone the workstation will be used in from the Time Zone: entries. All possible time zone values are presented when you select the scrolling list at the right of the *Time Zone:* field.

3. Click once on OK.

The Date/Time dialog box closes, showing the Control Panel's contents. By changing the options in this dialog box you have changed what all applets and major applications use for time-stamping files.

Customizing International Settings

You can change the settings used within Windows NT for communicating the date/time format, the way numbers are represented, and what character set should be used for displaying text. Keep in mind that changes made in the International series of dialog boxes change the formatting conventions, not the actual character set and conventions of applications themselves. For example, changing the options in these dialog boxes will modify how numbers are presented, but to change the actual language of applications, you'll need to get a version of the software that has been translated into the language you want.

To customize the Windows NT desktop for a specific international area, follow these steps:

1. Double-click on the International icon located in the Control Panel. The International dialog box appears and is shown in the following figure.

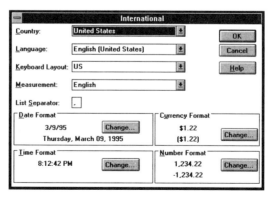

The International dialog box is used for changing country, language, date, time, currency, and number formats for specific locales.

Several aspects of the system can be customized to reflect your locations and local characteristics such as number formats and keyboard layouts.

❏ **Country:** Select the country in which you are located. If the country is not listed, then select one that is close (same time zone, etc.).

❏ **Language:** Select the language you want to use. This affects the way words can be sorted and several other things that are specific to different languages.

❏ **Keyboard:** Modify the keyboard layout and characters generated by certain keys to fit the standards of the country concerned.

❏ **Measurement:** Select between English (feet and inches) or Metric.

❏ **Display Formats:** Windows NT has the option of displaying several common objects such as date and currency in a variety of ways; select those that reflect your environment.

After selecting all your preferences, select OK to complete the process. Unlike MS-DOS, you don't have to reboot the workstation for the changes to take effect.

Working with Fonts

A constant problem in the evolution of computer graphics and plotting and printing technology has been making what you see on the screen look the same as what you get from the printer. This is most commonly a problem with fonts. The solution is to use the same fonts as the printer, or just have the printer print a bitmap and let the computer worry about the fonts.

With the advent of laser printers that are capable of producing an entire page in a single pass, fonts have grown in importance. The most common and easiest to use is the TrueType font. This font is independent of the resolution of your workstation's screen and printer. It carries its own rasterizer, which completes the interpolation process for making the font best match the output device being used, whether it is a screen or printer. Adobe has also developed an entire line of fonts called the Adobe Type 1 library. These fonts require both a corresponding character set on the printer as well as on the screen. For the majority of CAD applications, and especially for use on wide-format plotters, TrueType is the better and more reliable alternative. Later in this section you'll learn more about how TrueType fonts work.

Adding and Removing Fonts

There are thousands of public-domain (translated: free) fonts available on bulletin boards, through CompuServe's DTP Forum, the Internet, and even on local bulletin boards that serve the graphic artists in your area. You can add these fonts to those on your Windows NT system and make them available to all your applications.

1. Double-click on the Fonts icon within the Control Panel. The Fonts dialog box appears and is shown in below.

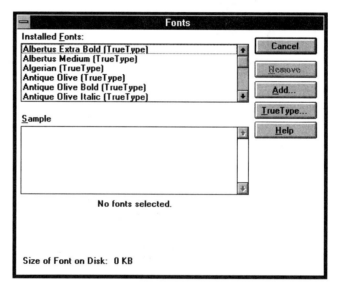

The Fonts dialog box.

2. Click once on Add.... The Add Fonts dialog box appears.

3. Use the Directory and Drives sections of the dialog box to tell Windows NT where your new fonts are. Windows NT will list all the available fonts.

4. Click once and hold down the SHIFT key as you select the fonts you want to install. Or you can hold the CTRL key down to select individual fonts.

5. When you've selected all the fonts you want to install, click once on OK. The selected fonts are then copied to your Windows NT workstation.

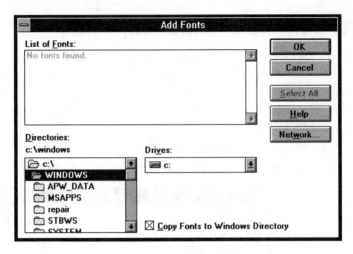

The Add Fonts dialog box.

6. When all the font files have been copied, the Fonts dialog box again appears. You can check to make sure the fonts you selected for copying are now active on your workstation by moving through the list and clicking once on each. The Sample: section of the dialog box shows an example of the font selected.

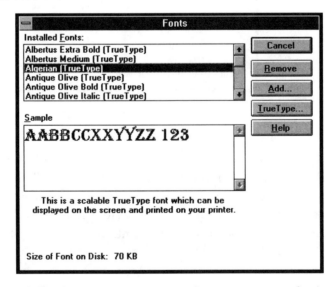

Using the Fonts dialog box, you can preview the appearance of selected fonts.

7. Click once on OK. The Fonts dialog box closes, showing the Control Panel on the Desktop.

TrueType Fonts

TrueType fonts have become a de facto standard because in combination with the PostScript printer language it provides a good match between text on the screen and what is printed on paper. The TrueType font technology is based on a scaleable character set that is easily modified within applications.

Within the Fonts dialog box you can ensure that all the fonts that are visible to you are TrueType by selecting the option, Show Only TrueType fonts. If you want to be sure that what you see is really what you get, then select the TrueType button in the Fonts control panel and then select this option.

Using the System Control Panel

The System Control panel gives you the ability to modify several aspects of the overall configuration of the system:

❐ Default operating system: If you have DOS and Windows NT loaded on the same platform, you can set which to boot by default.

❐ Timeout before system boots into default operating system: The default is 30 seconds.

❐ Virtual Memory: Sets the size and location of system paging files.

❐ Environment variables passed to an application.

❐ Action to take in the event of an error that Windows NT cannot recover safely from.

❐ CPU allocation between foreground and background processes.

✔ *TIP: The variables listed in the System Environment Variables dialog box are used by applications during run-time to ensure system resources are available. If you are unsure as to the function any of these variables perform, it is best to leave them alone.*

If you want to change the system to boot a different operating system, follow this sequence:

1. Double-click on the System icon located in the Control Panel. The System dialog box appears.
2. Select the scrolling list from Startup in the Operating System section and highlight the operating system you wish to boot by default.
3. Select OK to complete the operation.

Modifying Virtual Memory Settings

A modern 32-bit operating system like Windows NT can address up to 4GB (4000MB) of memory. Few if any systems actually support this amount of memory because of the cost (at $50/MB that's $200,000 just for memory). To overcome the limitations of real RAM, operating systems like Windows NT and UNIX allow you to specify space on disk to be treated like memory. Windows NT (like UNIX) handles this by subdividing real memory into "pages", then juggling pages of memory between the real memory and the space on the disk so that no more than 16MB is of real memory is required at any given moment. Consider a system with 16MB of real memory, if you launch an application that requires 5MB of memory to manipulate a 20MB data file then you need 25MB of memory. Windows NT will move "pages" of memory from the real memory onto the disk in order to make space for the executable image. It then dynamically shuffles the data file between real memory and the disk.

The sum of real memory and space on the disk (virtual memory) is the total space that can be allocated to all the programs you run. You can increase the amount of the virtual memory available using the System Control Panel with the following steps:

1. From the System Control Panel, select the Virtual Memory... button located on the right side of the System dialog box. The Virtual Memory dialog box appears.

    Usually you'll have a single paging file on drive C:. This dialog box will show you the minimum and maximum size of any pages file on your system. You can modify these settings and add new page files. The Drive [Volume] section shows all the paging space currently allocated.

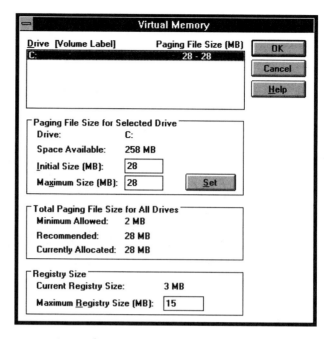

Virtual Memory Settings Dialog box.

2. To modify the size of a paging file, select the drive in the Drive [Volume] section. The Paging File Size for Selected Drive section will be filled in with the minimum and maximum sizes for the paging file. Enter the new values for the paging file in the Paging File Size for Selected Drive section and then select Set.

The process for adding page space on a previously unused drive is identical, simply select the drive and key in the minimum and maximum sizes.

When setting up virtual memory there are several things to remember:

❏ Performance for a paging file is improved if the minimum and maximum sizes are the same; this allows Windows NT to preallocate the space on the drive.

❏ If you have two drives, put half the paging space on each drive as this will improve performance.

❏ You cannot use more memory than the total of the real memory and the page file space allocated on the drives.

❒ Page files have the Hidden attribute set so that the chance of accidentally deleting them is minimized.

With its excellent handling of paged memory, Windows NT is able to offer performance and flexibility previously only found on UNIX workstations.

Crash Recovery Options

Even a system as robust as Windows NT will occasionally meet circumstances that cause it to crash. Typically these will be hardware errors because the operating system is very good at preventing software crashes. The Recovery.... button in the System control panel will display the following dialog box.

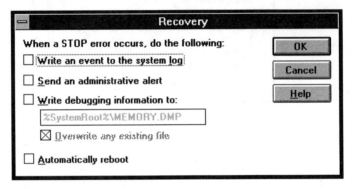

Recovery Options dialog box.

When an unrecoverable situation occurs, Windows NT generates a STOP event if at all possible. The Recovery dialog box allows you to customize behavior when this event occurs. You have the following options.

❒ **Write an event to the system log:** Windows NT keeps a record of all significant events. You can force it to enter an event in the log when a system crash occurs. This can be very useful for systems left running unattended for long periods.

❒ **Send an administrative alert:** Will send a broadcast message on the network so that the system administrator will know that the system is down even if he or she is located a long way from the system.

❐ **Write debugging information to:** Dumps a memory image to the file specified in the dialog box. This can be very useful if a crash is persistent, requiring investigation by your supplier. An experienced analyst can determine exactly what was happening when the crash occurred using this information.

❐ **Automatically reboot:** If you don't select this option, a crashed system will show a Blue Debug screen until you manually reboot it. With this set the system will reboot automatically if possible.

✔ *TIP: Unless you have a persistent problem that needs to be debugged, you should disable the Write debugging information and enable the Automatically Reboot option.*

Tasking

Windows NT Workstation allows many processes to share a single processor. Time is allocated by the operating system in small amounts to each process. The switching between processes is so fast and seamless that they look as though they are running simultaneously.

The tasking dialog box is reached by selecting the Tasking... button in the System control panel. This dialog box, shown in the following figure, allows you to modify the way Windows NT allocates time to different processes.

❐ **Best Foreground Application Response Time:** On a personal machine this is what you would always set. It ensures that the process you are using is allocated as much time as it can use.

❐ **Foreground Application More Responsive than Background:** This option still allocates more time to the foreground process than to background processes, but not as extreme as the first setting. This would be the setting for a machine that is primarily a personal machine but also offers file or print sharing services to other nodes.

❐ **Foreground and Background Applications Equally Responsive:** This would be the recommended setting for a system that is primarily used as a server.

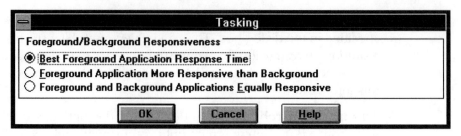

Tasking Options dialog box.

System and User Environment Variables

Sometimes an application will expect an environment variable to be set so that it can find some resource; many applications expect a TEMP variable to point to a directory where they should write temporary files. Windows NT allows you create types of environment variables:

❑ **System Environment Variable:** A System variable is seen by anybody who logs onto the system no matter what account they use.

❑ **User Environment Variable:** This type of variable is only seen when logged into your account.

You can only create System variables when you are logged in as the administrator account for your machine.

Creating a variable is very simple, at the bottom of the System control panel are two fields labeled Variable: and Values:, respectively. In the Variable: field enter the name of the variable. Enter the value assigned to the variable in the Value: field, and select Set.

Deleting a variable is equally simple, select the variable to delete and then select the Delete button.

Customizing the Mouse Operation

Computers, like most things in life, tend to be designed for right-handed people, even down to the selection of which mouse button gets used most frequently; just try to use a right-handed mouse when you are left handed.

Windows NT allows you to modify:

❏ **Mouse Tracking Speed:** Affects how a movement of the mouse is mapped to a movement of the screen cursor. The faster you set this, the less you have to move the mouse.

❏ **Double Click Speed:** Windows NT recognizes two mouse taps close together as what is called a *double-click*. Being able to double click is fundamental to working with Windows NT. You can adjust the intervals between clicks until you can consistently make the Test box change color by a double-click.

❏ **Swap Mouse Buttons:** For right-handed people, the most comfortable button for most actions is the left button. For the left-handed, the opposite is true. Use this option to swap the functions of the buttons.

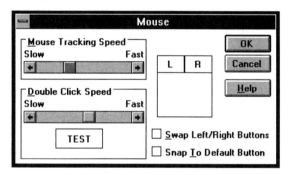

Mouse Control Panel applet.

All the options in this dialog box can be tested without actually dismissing the dialog box. If you don't like what you've done, then select Cancel.

Starting and Stopping System Services

System services are programs that Windows NT starts either at boot time or as a response to some condition. You can start and stop services manually as well as change some configuration information using the Services Control Panel applet.

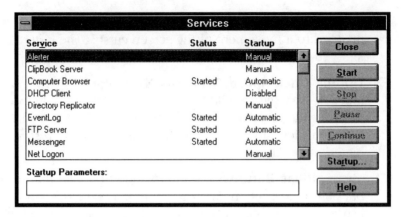

Services Control Panel applet.

The golden rule with services displayed here is "If you don't know what it is for, don't mess with it."

Services started here include all networking, the event logger, object linking and embedding, and many other components of Windows NT. You should leave manipulating these options to your system administrator.

Monitoring Connections to Your System

With the built-in networking abilities of Windows NT, any system can be a client and a server at the same time. You can provide several services to other Windows NT, Windows for Workgroups, and LAN Manager clients:

❏ **File Sharing:** Let other users mount your drives and directories over a network

❏ **Printer Sharing:** Let other users send print jobs to a printer attached to your system.

❏ **Mail Service:** Act as a mail clearing house for Microsoft Mail.

❏ **Network Clipboard:** Make data you've pasted into your Clipboard available to other users on the network.

Being able to monitor the number of connections is important for two reasons:

1. Windows NT Workstation 3.5 limits the number of incoming connections to resources. You cannot have more than 10 connections active at one time.

2. If you use a FAT filesytem, then the security you can put on shared data is limited, so it's useful to be able to check who is connected to your system.

You can monitor connections using the Server applet from the control panel as shown below:

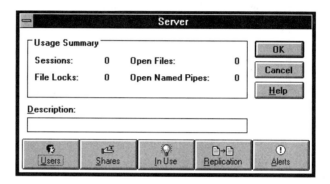

Server Control Panel applet.

Using the displays available from this applet you can monitor:

❑ **Users:** Any type remote access to your system counts as a User session. The User Session panel will show all these connections, giving you the nodename of the computer, the login name of the person using the resource, and the resource type.

❑ **Shares:** Lists all the directories and other shared resources as well as who is using them.

❑ **In Use:** Lists all the currently active sessions; an example might be a file open or a print job sent to a printer attached to your computer.

❑ **Alerts:** Allows you to send messages to machines that have made network connections to you. One use might be to warn people using shared files on your system that you will shut down the system.

You can also force a disconnect of shared sessions using these dialog boxes, for example:

1. Select Users. A dialog box showing all accounts connected to your workstation are shown.

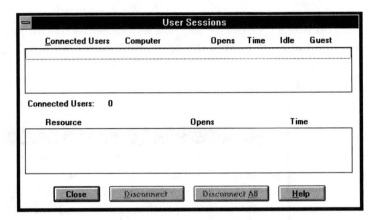

Users Sessions dialog box.

2. Select a session to disconnect.

3. Select the Disconnect button to drop the connection to the specified user. The Disconnect All button will close all active sessions.

Obviously dropping user connections like this is not something to do for fun. There are applications for it though. If you have a resource that somebody urgently needs to get to, but you have 10 sessions already active, then the only choice may be to disconnect a session.

For more information on managing connections, see Chapter 7.

Setting Display Attributes

Windows NT 3.5 offers the ability to change color and display resolution in the Display applet in the Control Panel. Modern graphics adapters have three characteristics that you change to suit your use of the system:

❑ **Colors:** Every pixel on your display is represented by a number in the screen buffer. The number maps to a particular color. The range of values represents the number of different colors that can be displayed. For example, if the computer uses 16 bits to represent the value of each pixel, then you can display 65,536 different colors.

❒ **Display Resolution:** Depending on the capabilities of your graphics adapter you alter the number of pixels displayed. Typically you'll have resolutions varying from 640x480 to 1024x1280. These represent the number of rows in the display and the number of pixels in each row.

❒ **Refresh Rate:** The number of times the computer will redraw the display. A constant problem in many environments is "Display Flicker," which is when the display appears to shake or pulse. You can experiment with different refresh rates to reduce this problem; the higher the refresh rate, the more stable the image becomes.

Remember, the larger the color palette and screen resolution, the slower the display will be. To change the settings on your system, select the Display applet from the Control Panel:

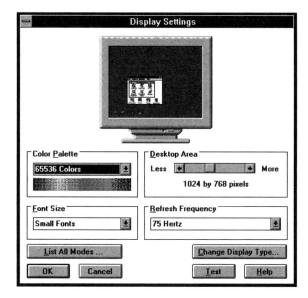

Display applet.

The applet lets you set up the display to suit your tasks and personal tastes:

❒ **Color Palette:** Selecting the scrolling menu in this section of the applet will show you all the supported palette sizes for your graphics adapter. The maximum size of the palette is governed by resolution of the display and the amount of RAM on the graphics adapter.

❐ **Desktop Area:** The screen resolution settings available to you will depend on the palette size. You will not be able to select a invalid combination of Desktop Area and Color Palette as the two options are intelligently linked.

❐ **Font Size:** If you choose a large desktop area such as 1024x768, you may find that text size in menus and other displays is too small. You can cause Windows NT to use a larger font by selecting Large Fonts in this section of the applet.

❐ **Refresh Frequency:** Selecting this will display a list of available refresh rates. Before selecting a particular rate you should check that your monitor can support the required rate. This information will be in the user manual for the monitor. Remember the higher the rate, the better the display will look.

❐ **Change Display Type:** If you change the graphics adapter in your system you'll need to load a driver suitable for the new adapter. The Change Display Type dialog box allows you to load new drivers or update existing ones.

❐ **Test:** When you've finished modifying palette, resolution, and refresh settings, you can test that the display will work correctly by selecting the Test button.

When you've confirmed that the settings are OK, you must reboot the system to see the new display. If you find that the settings you've chosen will not work despite successfully testing them, you can force Windows NT to boot into a Standard SVGA mode and use the Display applet to reset your display attributes.

Other Applets in the Control Panel

The functions controlled by several applets in the Control Panel are sufficiently complex to deserve their own chapter. The functions performed by the Networks applet and the Print Manager are described in the Chapter 7, "Networking," and Chapter 5, "Printing." If the function of an applet is not immediately apparent, check with your system administrator before making any changes.

Summary

In this chapter you've seen how easy it is to customize Windows NT via the Control Panel. This chapter has not covered all the applets available in Control Panel. Those applets that relate to system or printer administration are covered in later chapters; others are simple and require no explanation.

Sometimes, when you install a new application it will add an applet to the Control Panel that will be used for managing the application.

Using Print Manager

Introduction

Unlike other applications that you may have used in conjunction with the UNIX, OS/2, or MS-DOS operating systems, the Windows NT operating system provides a centralized printing and plotting resource that is used by all applications. The Windows NT Print Manager provides the necessary compatibility links between various printers and plotters on the one hand and your application programs on the other.

Print Manager includes many useful tools that make network-based printing and plotting more efficient than has been possible in the past. Through the use of GUIs that provide the necessary commands and options, Print Manager makes it possible for you to connect to network printers and plotters, create printers on other Windows NT workstations, and even print documents on printers attached to other Microsoft Windows NT–based workstations and servers. The following figure shows an example of the Print Manager icon located in the Main group.

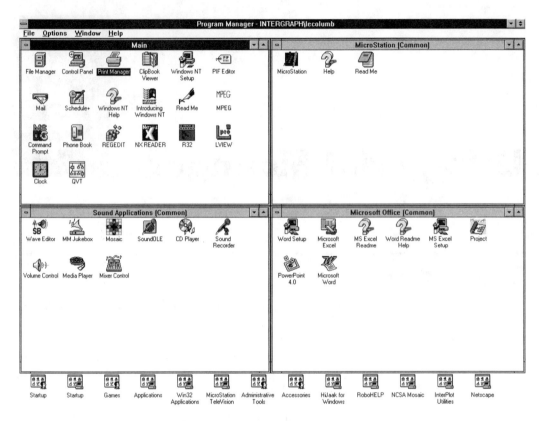

Print Manager's icon in the Main group.

Printing from an Application: How It Works

Windows NT Workstation is very similar to Microsoft Windows 3.1 in terms of making printing and plotting tools a readily available resource for any compatible application program. Both Windows NT and Windows 3.1 come with the Print Manager, which is a centralized series of devices drivers and printing tools. Although the Print Manager is available in both versions of Windows, their features and network capabilities differ significantly.

Throughout this chapter, you'll learn how you can use Windows NT's Print Manager features for completing printing tasks. The following figure shows an example of how the Print Manager receives tasks from the wide variety of application programs that run within Windows NT and then produces output using device drivers.

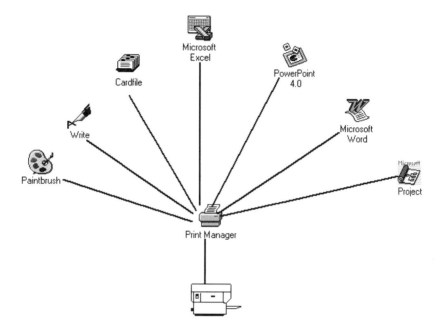

How Print Manager works.

Print Manager's Queuing Capabilities

If you're familiar with Microsoft Windows 3.1 Print Manager, you'll notice the big change in appearance of each printer's queue. Look at the following figure. This is the Windows 3.1 Print Managers' view of a typical printer.

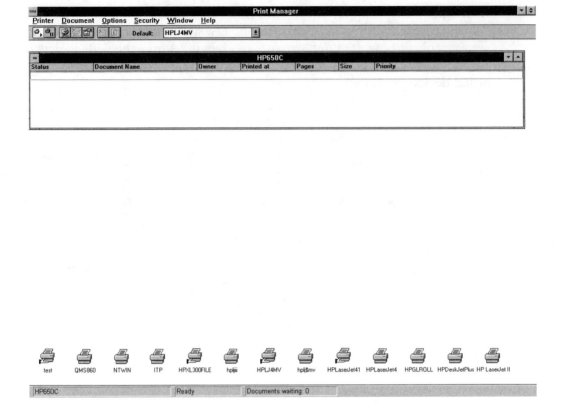

Windows 3.1 printer window in Print Manager.

Now look at the next figure. The Windows NT Print Manager is designed to make network-based printing and plotting more manageable. Notice how print jobs in each of the printer's window show the time submitted, status, and who the originator or owner is. Having this overview of activity for each printer makes it easier for you to see the level of activity for a given printer or plotter.

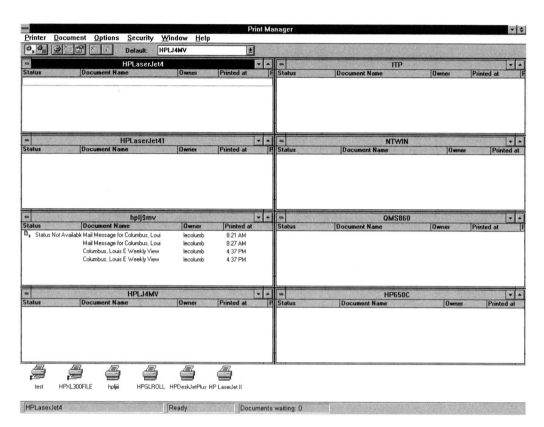

Windows NT Print Manager print windows.

Printing a File

Let's start our tour of Windows NT's Print Manager by looking at how you can print a file, document, spreadsheet, or any other type of report from within a Microsoft Windows NT–compatible application program. The steps shown here can be used with any Windows-compatible application program, whether the application program is 16- or 32-bit based.

1. Click once and hold the File Menu located in the upper left corner of your application's active window. The following figure shows an example of the File Menu selected while editing a Word for Windows document.

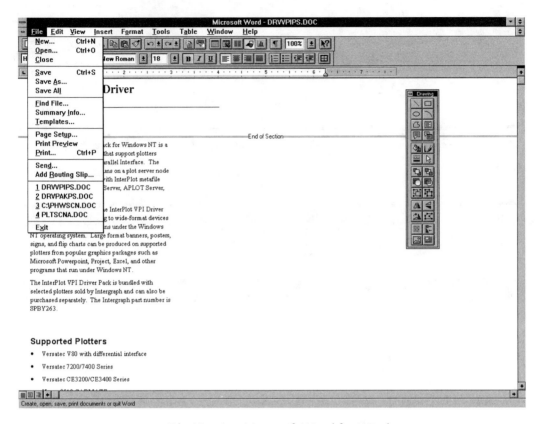

File Menu in Microsoft Word for Windows.

➥ **NOTE:** *Although Microsoft's Word for Windows is used as the basis of these examples, you can just as easily use the steps provided here with any other Microsoft Windows NT–compatible application program.*

2. Select Print... from the File Menu. The following figure shows an example of the Print dialog box.

Notice the printer name listed along the top portion of the Print dialog box. The printer name is shown, because this is the default printer as defined in the Print Manager's window. If this isn't the printer you want to print to, select Printer Setup... from the File menu and select the printer you want to use.

3. Click once on the Number of Copies: entry and type in the number of copies you want printed.

4. Click once on OK. Your document is then printed.

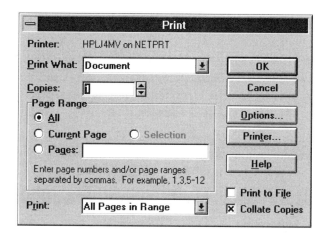

The Print dialog box.

↦ **NOTE:** *You could have also used any other server's printers, located at different points throughout the network. You'll find out how to use remote printers later in this chapter by using the Connect To Printer command.*

Understanding How Print Manager Works

You can see from the previous example of how a file is printed just how easily you can produce output from any Windows NT–compatible application. In addition to being a centralized resource you can use from any compatible application, Print Manager also includes tools for pausing, resuming, arranging the order of, and removing documents from a specific printer's queue. The following steps show you how to change the print order of a single document, or even a series of documents already submitted to a specific printer. It doesn't matter which application generates the print request. The Print Manager queues print jobs and then submits them in a first-in, first-out prioritizing scheme.

Changing the Print Order

Changing the print order of documents within Print Manager is accomplished by first highlighting the printing request, then moving it to the location in the queue you want it to print at. This is really like picking out a document and moving it closer to the printer. Having this capability can make your job go much faster. How many times have you had your boss call for your weekly activity report just after you submitted a design file for printing? Or sent a spreadsheet to your printer and have a customer call and ask for a copy of the letter you sent last week? Using the steps outlined here, you can quickly move documents to the top of the printing queue, giving you the ability to respond quickly to other's requests. Here are the steps that illustrate how easy it is to change a document's print order:

1. Click once on the print job you want to reposition in a specific printer's queue. The following figure shows an example of the HP DeskJet Plus queue with a print job several documents back highlighted.

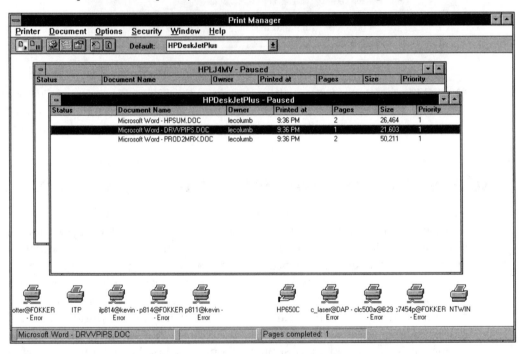

HP DeskJet Plus window with print job highlighted.

2. Click once and hold the mouse on the queued document.

3. Move the mouse up the list of queued documents, placing the selected document right below the currently printing one. The following figure shows an example of the revised printer queue.

➥ **NOTE:** *You can also use these steps to move a document back in any printer's queue.*

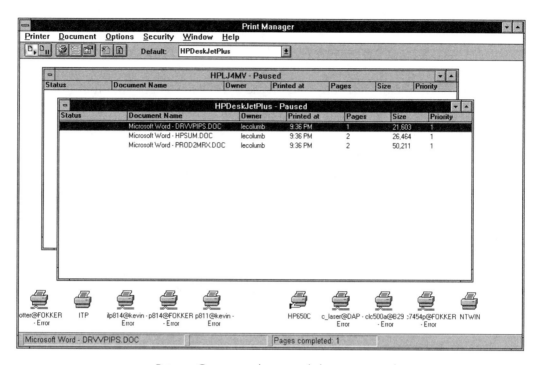

Printer Queue with revised document ordering.

Pausing and Resuming Printing

There are plenty of good reasons why you'd want to either stop or pause a document from printing. Within previous generation operating systems, this was a difficult task and required intimate knowledge of how the queuing systems and the printing software worked. The software developers at Microsoft have made these two tasks much easier for you than was possible in the past. In fact, you can pause all printing for a specific queue or for just a document. You can also resume printing for a specific queue or a single document. You'll learn how each of these works in the following sections.

Why Do People Pause Printers?

If you're going through a project, printing or plotting the necessary files you need, why would you want to stop or pause printing? This feature was first included in the Microsoft Windows 3.1 operating system when dot matrix and noisy daisywheel printers were being used in offices. A person working with a document or file being printed to a daisywheel printer would need to stop the printer to take a telephone call.

With the advent of laser printers, there's less of a need to turn a printer off while you speak with someone on the telephone. There are other reasons as well for pausing a printer. Here are a few:

❐ You'll want to pause a printer when it is nearing the end of a paper supply. Being able to pause a printer to add supplies leads to more complete printing tasks.

❐ If you're in the middle of printing or plotting something confidential and want to keep it that way, using the Pause button can preserve the privacy of your data.

❐ Being able to temporarily pause a printer that is getting jammed can help to alleviate any longer-term problems. In the case of using an electrostatic plotter, you could actually prolong the life of your plotter by alleviating a paper jam.

Pausing All Printing

To pause all printing to a specific printer, follow the steps shown here:

1. From within Print Manager, double-click on the icon of the printer you want to pause. The following figure shows an example of the Print Manager with the QMS 860 printer icon highlighted.

The QMS 860 printer window opens, showing any documents currently printing to this laser printer. The following figure shows a series of documents queued up within the QMS 860 printer's queue.

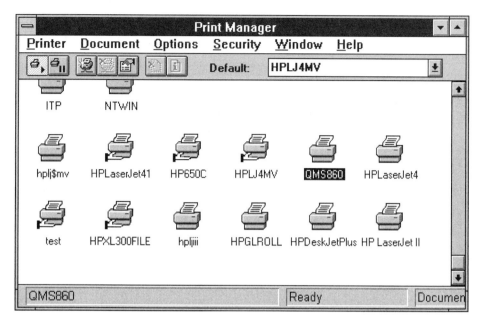

Print Manager with QMS 860 printer icon highlighted.

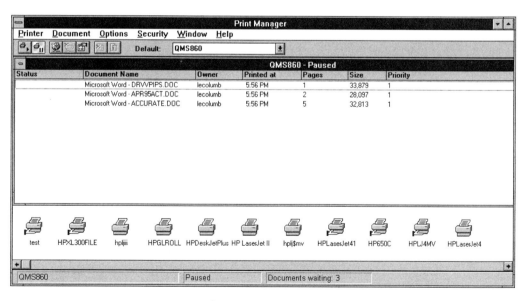

QMS 860's printer queue.

2. Select Pause from the Printer Menu. The following figure shows an example of the document in a paused state within Print Manager.

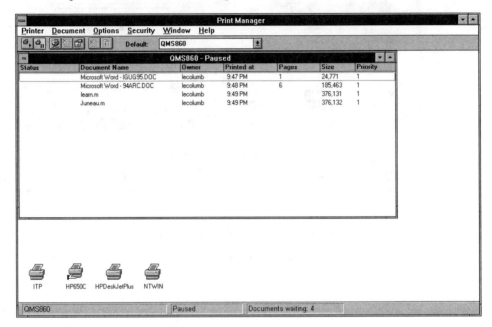

Paused document in Print Manager.

Pausing a Specific Document's Printing

Using the options in Print Manager you can pause any document being printed by any printer in Windows NT. This is particularly handy if you have to change the cartridge in a laser printer while your document is being sent to it, or when you need to put more paper into the inkjet, laser, or dot matrix printer you have.

Follow these steps to pause a specific document's printing:

1. Click once on the document you want to pause. The documents appear as entries in a printer's queue while they are printing. The next figure shows a document highlighted within a HP DeskJet 500 printer queue or window.

2. Select Pause from the Document Menu. The selected document is then paused from printing.

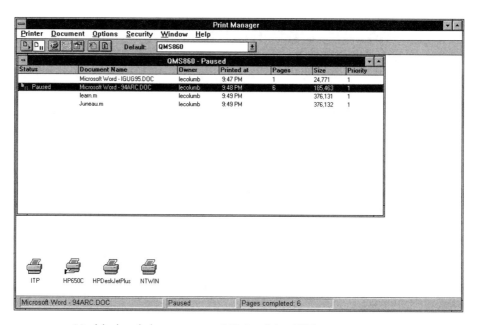

Highlighted document in HP DeskJet 500 printer queue.

Resuming All Printing

After having stopped all documents that are being printed by any printer, you can resume printing by using the steps shown here.

1. Click once on the printer window that had been paused.

2. Select Resume from the Printer Menu. The printer queue is then activated and begins to print again.

Resuming Printing a Specific Document

You can start and stop a document from printing just like you can pause and resume an entire printer. Once a document has been paused, you can begin printing it by using these steps:

1. Click once on the document you want to resume printing.

2. Select Resume from the Document menu. The selected document then begins printing again.

Removing Documents

After queuing up a big report for printing to the office printer, you decide you need to get over to another meeting, or you are going out for lunch and want to work on existing draft of your correspondence. You can remove documents that are queued within Print Manager's printer windows by using the steps provided here:

1.   Click once in the Print Manager printer's window in which you want to clear the documents. The following figure shows an HP DeskJet Plus window in Print Manager with a document highlighted.

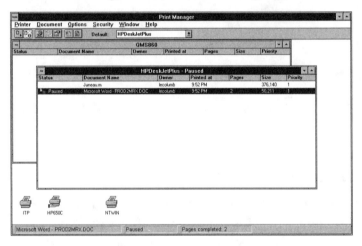

Highlighted document in HP DeskJet Plus window.

2.   Select Purge Printer from the Printer menu. The selected printer's documents are then purged.

Changing a Document's Priority

You can change the priority of documents once they are queued for printing within a Print Manager printer window. This can be particularly useful if you're in a hurry and need to get one report done quickly, ahead of other documents you have requested to be printed. Of course, it's always a good idea to check with others before you change the priority of your document relative to others in the print queue. Be considerate with the command of setting priorities.

To change a document's priority within a printer's queue, follow these steps:

1. Click once on the document you want to change the priority for.
2. Select Properties from the Printer menu. The Properties dialog box for the HP LaserJet Series 4 is shown on your screen.
3. Click once on the Details... button in the Properties dialog box. The Details dialog box appears.

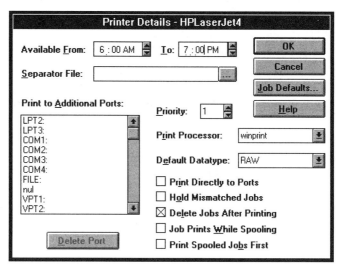

Printer Details dialog box.

4. Click once on the priority: option to move its value from 1 to the priority you want the document to be. The highest value is 99.
5. Click once on OK to close the Details dialog box, and then click on OK again to have the Properties dialog box close.

After having set the new priority on the selected document, it will be printed immediately after exiting the Properties dialog box. The Priority: entry in this dialog box is used for setting the relative level of importance for one printer and its requests relative to another. The highest priority is "1," with the lowest being "99." If you have integrated Windows NT into a Clipper UNIX (or CLIX) environment, then "31" is the default priority for the Network Queuing System (NQS). When a printing or plotting request is passed from a CLIX client to an NT server, the "31" priority level within NQS translates to the "1" priority level of the Windows NT Print Manager.

Closing the Print Manager

To close Print Manager, complete these steps:

1. Select Exit from the Printer Menu.

2. The Print Manager closes, showing the Main file group.

✔ *TIP: If you've printed using the Windows 3.1 Print Manager, you've had the experience of trying to close Print Manager and move on to their tasks. With Windows NT's Print Manager, you can close Print Manager, move through the Desktop to other tasks, and the print queues will continue processing and printing your documents. This is a big productivity improvement over Windows 3.1's Print Manager.*

Installing Your Printer

Installing a printer in Windows NT creates a printer window within Print Manager, where you can manage print requests as they are queued and then printed. An example of how a printer window looks in Print Manager when documents are queued up waiting to be printed is shown in the following figure.

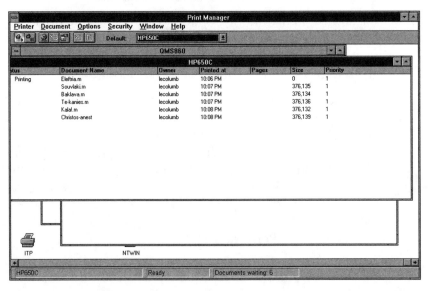

Documents queued in a printer window in Print Manager.

Once your printer is installed in Windows NT, all documents sent to it from any other workstation on the network appear in the printer window. If you've used Windows 3.1, you know that the Print Manager in that version of Windows assumes only a single user is going to be using the printer. In Windows NT, you can tell just from looking down the list of jobs queued for printing, as in the previous figure, that the way Print Manager works has fundamentally changed to compensate for sharing printers and plotters on a network.

✔ **TIP:** *You can create multiple printers in Print Manager, varying the properties of each for a single physical printer. This can come in pretty handy if you have a B-size laser printer that is capable of printing both letter and B-size pages. You can have one printer window created for doing letters, and a second for plotting B-size drawings and schematics. Each of these printer queues are equally accessible from within any Windows NT–compatible application.*

Creating a printer is possible using command selections from the Print Manager's window. Follow these steps for creating a printer:

1. Double-click on the Print Manager icon located in the Main group.

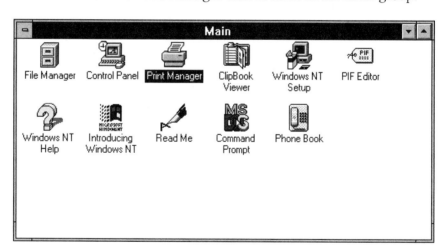

Print Manager highlighted in the Main Group.

2. Select Create Printer from the Printer menu. The Create Printer dialog box appears, as shown in the following figure.

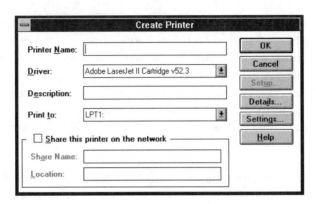

Create Printer dialog box.

Throughout the remainder of these steps, you'll learn how to get a printer installed and running. You can use these steps for defining two or more printers for the same physical printer.

⇢ *NOTE: For purposes of making the following steps concrete for you, substitute the name of the printer you own for the HP LaserJet Series III listed throughout these steps.*

1. Click once in the Printer Name: entry and then type the name you want the printer to be known as. This could be any name you want, but it's a good idea to use a name that describes the type of printer you're installing. Using the manufacturer and model is always good, as is having your name and the type of printer as well. For purposes of this example, type in the title HP LaserJet Series III.

2. Click once on the Driver: options area of the dialog box. There are hundreds of device drivers included as standard with Windows NT, and they are all selectable by scrolling down the list of device driver entries. Select the HP LaserJet Series III device driver from the list.

3. Click once on the Description: dialog box. Within this dialog box you can describe the printer you are installing. You can also use this Description: option area to describe the printer you are installing to others on the network. One CAD administrator has used this Description: entry to define the hours the printer will be available.

4. Click once on the Print To: options. A series of selections appears in the pulldown menu. The selections within this pulldown option listing include Centronics parallel port (LPT) ports, RS-232C ports (COM), FILE, and Network printing connections. Select LPT1 for connecting most laser printers to your Windows NT workstation.

5. Click once on the box labeled "Share this printer on the network." This makes the printer you are installing available to others on the Windows NT network. Upon clicking on this option, the name of the printer appears in the Share Name entry.

6. Click once on the Location: entry. While this entry is optional, you can use this to inform coworkers of the location of the networked printer.

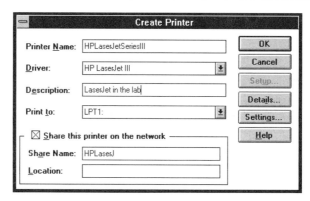

Completed Create Printer dialog box.

7. Click once on OK.

8. If the printer driver that applies to the printer you are installing isn't available, you'll be prompted for the diskette or CD-ROM that contains them. The interim dialog box prompts you for the path location of the device driver needed for completing the installation.

9. Once the device driver is copied and installed, the Properties dialog box appears for the printer you are installing. You'll learn how to work with Printer's Properties later in this chapter.

10. Click once on OK.

11. The printer is now installed and ready to be used in conjunction with Windows NT applications.

Printing to a File

Chances are you have used other operating systems and their printing utilities before learning Windows NT. Many of these operating systems have the capability of printing directly to a file. A limitation of previous operating systems is the process of getting the file into a format you can use in your job's process flow, or using the document in conjunction with a plot or print you are creating. Certain network-based plotting systems on the UNIX platform provide the capability of creating off-line files in specific formats.

❐ **Off-line file:** Within the Windows NT Print Manager, the printer queues can be configured to print either directly to a hardware port or to a file. When a printer queue is created that prints to a file, the resulting output is called an *off-line file,* because the printing task was diverted from an on-line hardware interface.

Windows NT's Print Manager can be configured to create an off-line file in any printer's format. So instead of having an off-line driver that just creates CCITT Group 4 files or HPGL/2 files, you can create off-line files compatible with any supported printer or plotter. This can be very useful if you are going to distribute your final document or plot electronically to other members of your workgroup or even to other divisions of your company. Having the document in a format that is readily recognized by a compatible printer makes it much easier for those receiving your documents. All they need to do is use the PRINT command in the Command Prompt window, or even the COPY command to send the file to a compatible printer.

Here are the steps you'll need to take to create a printer queue that can print directly to a file. For purposes of this example, the Hewlett-Packard XL300 printer will be used. For creating a print to file queue for any of your printers or plotters, substitute the name of your device for the Hewlett-Packard XL300.

1. Double-click on the Print Manager window if it isn't already open. The following figure shows an example of the Print Manager window with the existing printer and plotter queues tiled horizontally.

2. Select Create Printer from the Printer Menu.

3. Click once in the Printer Name: dialog box and type in the name you want the printer you are creating to be known as. For purposes of this example, enter in HPXL300File.

✔ *TIP: Network-based printing systems such as Intergraph's InterPlot need to have a printer queue name with no spaces in it so that the queue name will be recognized as a valid variable in the plotting system. Having no spaces in a printer queue name is a good idea if you plan to share the printer with users connecting from network operating systems other than Microsoft's LAN Manager or Microsoft Windows NT.*

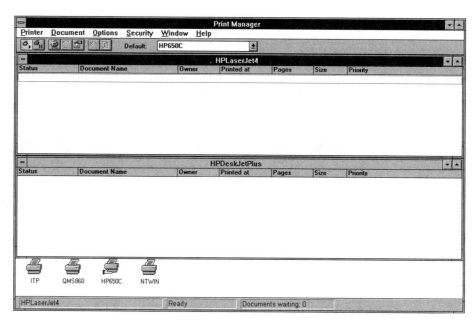

Print Manager window with printer queues tiled horizontally.

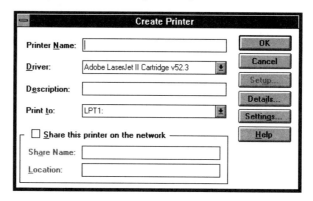

Create Printer dialog box is used for creating a print to file queue.

4. Click once on the Driver: entry. A pulldown listing of device drivers is shown on your screen.

5. Moving down the series of device drivers, select the one that best describes your printer. For purposes of this example, select the Hewlett-Packard XL300. Remember that printing to an off-line file is just like printing to a hardware port (like LPT1, 2, or 3), and the device driver being used in both instances is the same.

6. Click once in the Description: entry. This field is optional, yet can be useful in communicating the location and status of this printer to others who connect to it over the network. For purposes of this example, the location of the printer and the extension of the person responsible for it are provided. The following figure shows the Create Printer dialog box with the settings completed to this point.

Create Printer dialog box with device driver and description completed.

7. Click once on the Print To: option located just below the Description: entry. The Print To: entry lists all the ports and options you have to which to redirect output. Select FILE from the pulldown menu.

8. Click once on the box titled "Share this printer on the network." This enables others on the network to access the Hewlett-Packard XL300 using the Connect To Printer command also included in Print Manager's Printer Menu. Notice that when you select this option the name of the queue is placed in the Share Name: option automatically.

9. Click once in the Location: entry. You would typically use this portion of the dialog box to describe where the printer is that this queue represents. But because you're creating a print-to-file queue, put in a description that describes where the off-line files will be created. For example, if you have a guest account on your system, you can add text in this option that gives the Internet address and guest logon for your system. This would make it possible for others who have printed to a file to retrieve their files.

Alternatively, others on the network using the off-line printing capabilities of Print Manager could also access a common shared directory on your workstation through File Manager. You can use the Share Directory command from File Manager's File Menu to share a directory, series of subdirectories, or an entire disk.

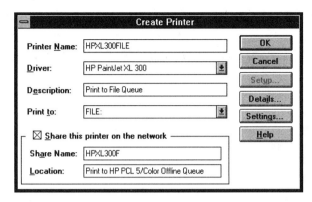

Create Printer dialog box completed for printing to a file.

10. Click once on OK.

11. The Device Attributes dialog box next appears and is specific to the printer or plotter you selected in the Driver: portion of the Create Printer dialog box. Click once on OK within this dialog box. The following figure shows the device attributes for the HP XL300's device driver in Windows NT.

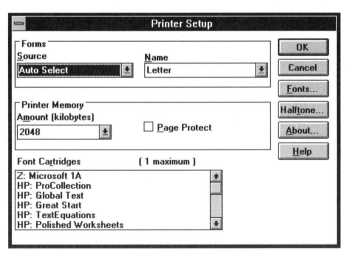

How device attributes are set for a specific printer.

12. The print-to-file queue is then created and appears as a separate window within Print Manager. The following figure shows the HPXL300FILE queue highlighted within Print Manager.

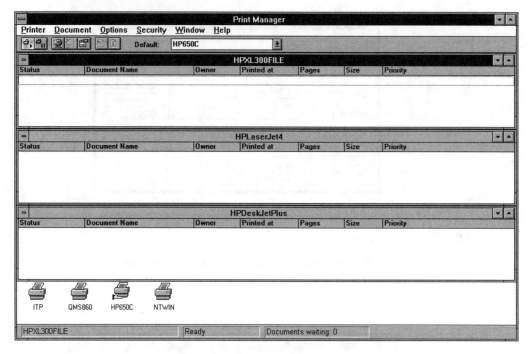

Completed print to file printer queue.

You can now select this queue from any Microsoft Windows NT–compatible application program and create a file using it. Once the file has been completed, you can either use the Command Prompt window to send the file directly to the printer, or you can send it over the network to others who also have an HP XL300, so they can print it when they need hard copies of your work.

➡ **NOTE:** *Windows NT will prompt you for an output filename whenever you print from an application to an off-line queue.*

Printing Over a Network

When you're working in a department that has networking capability, it's easy to get accustomed to printing to any available printer or plotter available over the network. Most larger plotters are typically installed on plot servers because they require significant stash partitions to complete larger, denser plots. With smaller printers, such as the HP LaserJets, Lexmark laser printers, and the Okidata printers, there are now Ethernet-ready interfaces available for making these smaller devices truly network-sharable. With Ethernet-ready interfaces, each printer has its own Internet address, where capabilities can be configured for sending documents, plots, designs, and drawings directly to the network-based printer. The use of Ethernet-ready printers and plotters is growing quickly. Hewlett-Packard has pioneered the availability of these Ethernet-compatible printers by creating the JetDirect card. This interface card is supported within Microsoft Windows NT. These Ethernet interfaces have become pervasive on plotters as well. A recent survey of Hewlett-Packard resellers has shown that one out of every three Hewlett-Packard DesignJet 650C plotters is sold with the Ethernet interface card installed.

Throughout this section, you'll learn how to connect to network printers, how to make your printers and plotters network-sharable, and how you can view network printer queues. You'll also learn how you can print directly to a network-based printer. If all this sounds pretty complicated, don't be daunted! The Print Manager has been redesigned over the Windows 3.1 version to make all these tasks driven by dialog boxes that you'll be able to move confidently through after completing the hands-on activities illustrated throughout the following sections.

Connecting to a Network Printer

You can connect to another workstation's printer or plotter and use it as if it was right next to your desk. The Connect To Printer command is used for getting connected with remote printers and plotters. Throughout these steps, you'll see how you can connect to, use, and even monitor how your document or plot is progressing. Follow these steps for getting connected to a network-sharable printer or plotter:

1. Double-click on the Print Manager. The Print Manager appears on your screen.
2. Select Connect To Printer... from the Printer Menu.

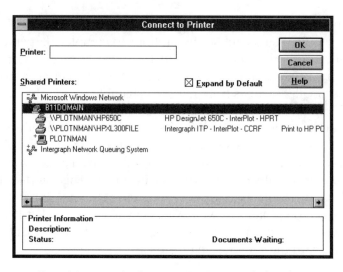

Print Manager's Connect To Printer dialog box.

Notice how the Microsoft Windows Network appears in the Shared Printers: portion of the dialog box. This portion of the dialog box is used for listing both servers and their attached printers and plotters.

3. Double-click on the Microsoft Windows Network line in the Shared Printers: entry. Workstations, servers, and other systems that are members of the network you are a member of appear in the Shared Printers: portion of the dialog box.

4. Click once on the workstation, server, or computer that has the printer or plotter installed that you want to use. After clicking on the individual system's name, all the printers and plotters installed on that system are shown. The following figure shows an example of the Connect To Printer dialog box with a series of printers and plotter queues for the workstation probe shown.

5. Click once on the printer you want to use. Be sure the printer's name is highlighted within the Shared Printers: portion of the dialog box.

6. Click once on OK.

7. If a printer driver for the printer you want to connect to is already installed or available on your system, the printer you are connecting to is then represented as a window in Print Manager.

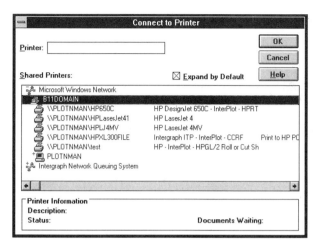

Connect To Printer dialog box with networked printers and plotters displayed.

If a driver is not already installed on your system, the Connect To Printer dialog box will prompt you with the Select Driver dialog box for the location on your system for the device driver needed.

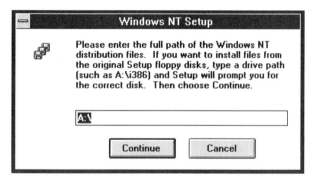

Select Driver dialog box used for installing local network printing support.

8. Type in the path location of the device driver that supports the network printer you are connecting to.

9. Click once on OK.

10. Print Manager installs local support for the network printer you are connecting to. A printer window appears, representing the remote printer you have successfully connected to. It's a good idea to think of this printer window as a "viewer" of what is happening on the remote printer or plotter. Once you submit a printing task to this queue, you will see it appear in the remote queue. The following figure shows the completed window in Print Manager. Notice along the top of the remote printer's window the remote system's name and share point (or shared printer) appear.

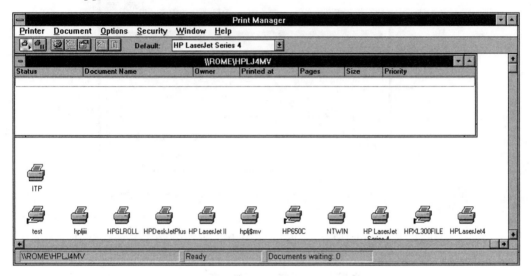

Remote printer windows in Print Manager.

Sharing Printers Over a Network

You've just learned how to connect to a remote printer or plotter using the Connect To Printer command. What's the difference between connecting to and sharing printers over a network? It's really a matter of getting printers and plotters that are attached to your workstation, server, or system available to others who are using the Connect To Printer command. Assuming that a printer has already been installed on your workstation that you want to share with others in your workgroup, company, domain, or other domains, follow the steps outlined here. You're going to need to change the properties associated with an existing printer queue. These steps show you how to do just that:

1. From within Print Manager, click once on the queue you want to share with others across the network.

2. Select Properties from the Printer menu. The Printer Properties dialog box for the printer you selected is now shown on your workstation's screen. The following figure shows an example of the Printer Properties dialog box for an IBM Lexmark laser printer.

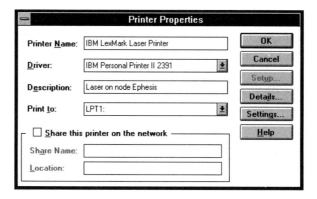

An example of the Printer Properties dialog box.

3. Click once on the option, Share this printer on the network. If not already selected, this option adds the printer's queue name to the Share Name: option immediately below this selection box.

4. Click once on the Location: entry located below the Share Name: option. While entering the location of the printer or plotter is optional, it is very helpful to others connecting to and using the printer. Users around the network will know where to get their printed documents and plots without calling you to determine where you are. The following figure shows an example of the Printer Properties dialog box modified to share the IBM Lexmark laser printer attached to the local workstation.

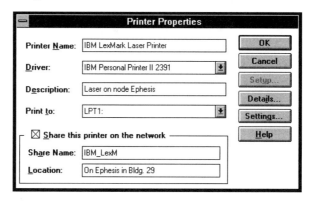

An example of a Modified Printer Properties dialog box
enabling network printer sharing.

5. Click once on OK. The Printer Properties dialog box closes and shows the Print Manager window again. Now others on the network can connect to your printer or plotter.

✔ **TIP:** *Many Microsoft Windows NT–based networks also include MS-DOS based clients, some of which use network-based plotting systems to increase overall productivity. Keep in mind that the Share Name: that is set in the Printer Properties dialog box needs to be 12 characters or less for an MS-DOS–based client system on the network to recognize the shared printer queue.*

Viewing Network Printer Queues

In order to view network printer queues you have two options. You can use the Connect To Printer dialog box to install support for the remote printer on your workstation and have a printer window show your printing tasks relative to others submitted to the same shared printer. The second option you have is to use the Server Viewer command located in the Printer Menu for viewing queues active on remote workstations, servers, and compatible systems. Use these steps to view printer queues on remote servers:

1. From within the Print Manager, select Server Viewer. The Server Viewer dialog box appears.

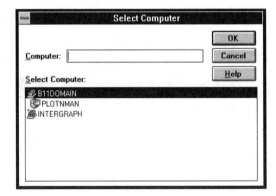

Select Computer dialog box.

2. Double-click on the server you want to view the queues of. The list of available servers appears in the Select Computer: portion of the Server Viewer dialog box.

3. Click once on OK.

4. Print Manager displays the printers attached to the server you've selected from the Select Computer: portion of the Server Viewer dialog box. The

figure below shows an example of the queues available on the server named probe.

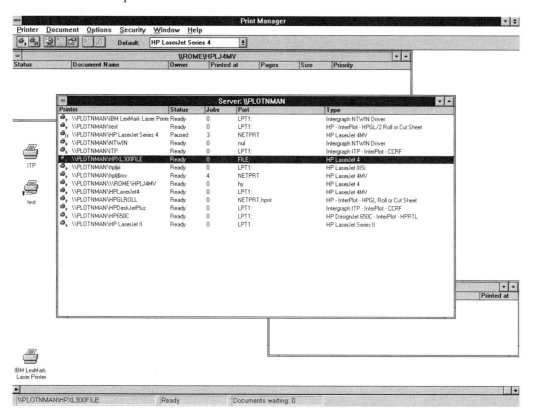

Available printer queues on server.

5. Double-click on the printer queue you want to view.

6. A window appears in the Print Manager, showing the active jobs in the printer queue you've chosen. The following figure shows an example of pending printing tasks in a remote queue attached to the server named probe.

7. After viewing the processing jobs in the selected printer queue, you can minimize the server viewer window by double-clicking in the upper left corner of the server viewer window.

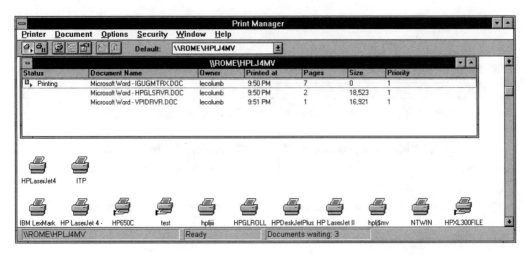

Server Viewer's printer window showing pending printing jobs.

Changing a Network Printer's Properties

The Server Viewer gives you a window into the pending and printing documents in a remote printer's queue. What if the remote printer is a QMS 860, for example, that has both letter and 11x17 inch document printing capability. You could, with administrator status or by being a member of the Power Users group for the active server, create a new queue for yourself that will print in 11x17 format. You could modify the existing attributes of the current QMS 860 queue, or create a new one. Because others may be in the process of sending letter-size documents to the printer as you work in Server Viewer, it's a good idea to create a B-size (11x17 inch) queue. How can you be sure the existing queue isn't already B-size without getting up from your desk and walking over to the host server? Use the Server Viewer command to first check and then modify a printer's properties. Using these steps to determine the properties for a given printer can save you the drudgery of tracking down where the server is and who has logon privileges.

Here are the steps for finding out what properties apply to the QMS 860 in this example. Keep in mind this can just as easily work for any other existing printer queue on the server you are viewing:

1. With the Server Viewer window active in Print Manager, double-click on the QMS 860 queue. The following figure shows an example of the Server Viewer window with the QMS 860 highlighted.

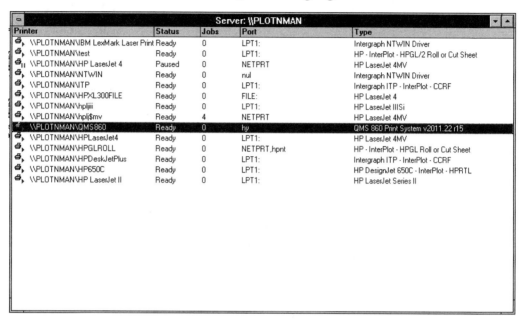

Printer	Status	Jobs	Port	Type
\\PLOTNMAN\IBM LexMark Laser Print	Ready	0	LPT1:	Intergraph NTWIN Driver
\\PLOTNMAN\test	Ready	0	LPT1:	HP - InterPlot - HPGL/2 Roll or Cut Sheet
\\PLOTNMAN\HP LaserJet 4	Paused	0	NETPRT	HP LaserJet 4MV
\\PLOTNMAN\NTWIN	Ready	0	nul	Intergraph NTWIN Driver
\\PLOTNMAN\ITP	Ready	0	LPT1:	Intergraph ITP - InterPlot - CCRF
\\PLOTNMAN\HPXL300FILE	Ready	0	FILE:	HP LaserJet 4
\\PLOTNMAN\hpljiii	Ready	0	LPT1:	HP LaserJet IIISi
\\PLOTNMAN\hplj$mv	Ready	4	NETPRT	HP LaserJet 4MV
\\PLOTNMAN\QMS860	Ready	0	hy	QMS 860 Print System v2011.22 r15
\\PLOTNMAN\HPLaserJet4	Ready	0	LPT1:	HP LaserJet 4MV
\\PLOTNMAN\HPGLROLL	Ready	0	NETPRT,hpnt	HP - InterPlot - HPGL Roll or Cut Sheet
\\PLOTNMAN\HPDeskJetPlus	Ready	0	LPT1:	Intergraph ITP - InterPlot - CCRF
\\PLOTNMAN\HP650C	Ready	0	LPT1:	HP DesignJet 650C - InterPlot - HPRTL
\\PLOTNMAN\HP LaserJet II	Ready	0	LPT1:	HP LaserJet Series II

Server: \\PLOTNMAN

Using the Server Viewer window in Print Manager.

2. Select Properties... from the Printer menu. Just as if the printer queue was local to your workstation, the Printer Properties dialog box appears on your screen, showing the specific properties set for the highlighted QMS 860 queue.

3. Click once on Setup from within the Printer Properties dialog box. The Printer Setup dialog box appears, showing the types of forms available, printer memory configuration, and font cartridges available for the QMS 860.

4. Click once on the Name: entry in the Forms: portion of the Setup dialog box. A pulldown menu shows the paper sizes available. Select B-size from the pulldown menu. The following figure shows the Printer Setup dialog box so far.

Printer Setup dialog box for QMS 860.

5. Click once on OK. The Printer Setup dialog box disappears, showing the Printer Properties dialog box.

6. Click once in the Printer Name: entry and type in the name you want the new printer to be known as. In this example, you could enter the name, QMS860/B. This signifies that the queue is for the QMS 860 and is configured to B-size printing.

✔ **TIP:** *You might be wondering if this will somehow disrupt the existing QMS 860 queue. It won't. Print Manager keys off the Printer Name: entry for creating new printers.*

7. Click once on OK. The new printer is now available on the remote printer.

What's next? You just created a new printer on a remote server, and you want to use it for printing designs and drawings. You can use the printer queue you just created by using the Connect To Printer command also located in the Printer Menu.

Printing Directly to Ethernet Interface Printers

Many printers and plotters now offer Ethernet interfaces as optional. Network-based printers and plotters make printing resources available to everyone. Network-based printers also have the ability to be transportable. In fact, one company puts their laser printers on carts, wheeling them to location to location on the production floor, tapping into the network as needed. A printer queue on one of the workstations that submits production drawings and schematics has the printer's Ethernet interface included in the Printer Setup dialog box. This way, before leaving every night, the designers responsible for getting drawings to the production floor select the appropriate queue for the networked printer, and then plot their schematics out of AutoCAD Release 12 for Windows. The Print Manager sends the print requests over the network, looking for the Ethernet address specified when the queue was created. Once the Ethernet interface is found, the documents are delivered and printed, ready for next morning's production.

How can you install printers or plotters that have an Ethernet interface within Print Manager? By following these steps:

➠ **NOTE:** *As with any of the other step-by-step instructions in this chapter, you can substitute the name of your printer in place of the one listed in this example.*

1. Select Create Printer from the Printer Menu.

2. Click once in the Printer Name: entry. Type in the name you want for the network-based printer you are creating. It's a good idea to use a printer name that is reasonably descriptive. You could, for example, give a Hewlett-Packard LaserJet IIIsi the name IHP3NET. This name lets others on the network know that this printer is a Hewlett-Packard.

3. Click once in the Driver: box. Select the HP LaserJet Series IIIsi driver from the pulldown menu.

4. Click once on the Description: entry located just below the Driver: entry. Type in a description of what kind of printer is being used and the location. It's a good idea to give the building and room number where the printer is located.

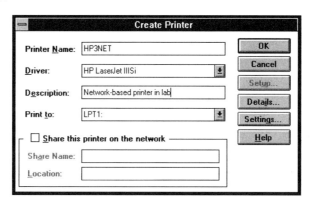

Create Printer dialog box so far.

5. Click once on the Print To: entry of the dialog box. Select the option Network Printer for using a Hewlett-Packard–compatible printer in Print Manager. The Print Destinations dialog box next appears.

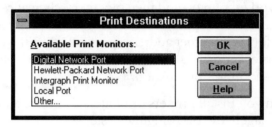

The Print Destinations dialog box is used for configuring Ethernet-based printers in Print Manager.

6. Within the Print Destinations dialog box, click once on the Hewlett-Packard Network Port, and then click once on OK. The Add A Hewlett-Packard Network Port dialog box appears. Enter the network printer's Ethernet added in the Card Address box.

7. Click once on OK. The printer is created and appears as a window in Print Manager. If the window doesn't appear it's because the device driver for the printer you're installing isn't installed on your system. An interim dialog box will prompt you for the path location of the device driver.

After you've installed a network-based printer, you can print to it just like one that has been installed on your workstation. You can also connect to it from other workstations, servers, or systems. If not already running, enable the Data Link Control protocol in the Network applet located within the Control Panel to make sure you and others can communicate with the network-based printer or plotter.

Solving Common Printer and Plotter Problems

Throughout this section you'll learn the answers to the most common printing and plotting problems from users of AutoCAD, MicroStation, and many of the other technically based applications compatible with Windows NT. These questions and answers have been collected from customer support departments at Autodesk, CalComp, Intergraph, and Xerox Engineering Systems.

Question: When I select Plot from within MicroStation Version 5, the plotter attached to my workstation doesn't plot. Why?

Answer: There are several reasons why this could be happening. The first area to look to solve this problem is within MicroStation Version 5 itself. When you select Plot in MicroStation Version 5, the first dialog box you get is shown in the following figure.

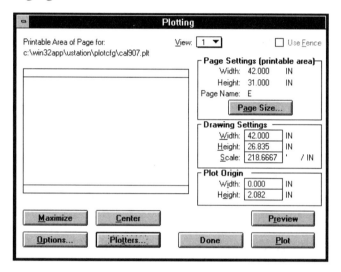

MicroStation's Version 5 Plot dialog box.

From this dialog box you can select which plotter you want to use. Clicking once on the Plotters... button opens a dialog box for selecting plot configuration files. These plot configuration files, or *.cfg* files, are ASCII-based and are easily opened and read using Notepad or Microsoft Write. The function of these plot configuration files is to take the plot request from within MicroStation and then translate specific vector elements into a data stream the individual plotter can understand. There are over 40 different plot configuration files shipped with MicroStation Version 5, with additional ones available on the Bentley Systems, Inc., and Intergraph bulletin boards.

After selecting the plot configuration file that best matches your specific printer or plotter, select OK from within the Plot Configuration files dialog box. The Plot Configuration dialog box closes, showing the Plot dialog box. Click once on Plot. A dialog box opens, asking you where you want to save the plot file, which is created at the subdirectory location *c:\win32app\ingr\ustation\plot*, and the file created is given the extension *.000* by default. You'll now need to copy the *.000* file to the port the plotter is connected to. For example, if your plotter is connected to the Centronics interface (LPT1), then from within Windows NT, open the Command Prompt, go to the subdirectory where the *.000* file is (*c:\win32app\ingr\ustation\plot*), and using the MS-DOS command, copy it to LPT1. The command is COPY *.000 LPT1:, which takes the entire series of *.000* files and copies them directly to the Centronics port (LPT1:).

What if you haven't had any success after completing these steps? Here's a list of items to check to ensure that MicroStation and your plotter are communicating.

1. Check to make sure the cables are solidly plugged into both the plotter and the workstation. If possible, swap out the cable you are using for another one to see if the one being used is defective.

2. Does your plotter have the ability to auto-sense which plotter interface is being sent data? If not, check to make sure the plotter is set up to accept data to the port you are copying it to.

3. How many emulations does your printer or plotter have? Be sure you have a clear idea of what data formats are available in your plotter, and that the plot configuration file you have selected during MicroStation plotting matches the data formats in your plotter. This is the most common reason people have problems plotting from MicroStation. The plot configuration file, or emulation, and the data format supported in the plotter need to be compatible with each other.

Question: I'm using AutoCAD Release 12 for Windows and don't have any plotters available in the Plot... command. How can I get plotters installed?

Answer: Using the utilities shipped with AutoCAD, you can install device drivers (software that makes it possible for AutoCAD and your plotter to work together) from the main desktop of Windows NT.

✔ *TIP: If you can plot from other Windows NT–compatible applications using printers and plotters installed in Print Manager, then use the Print... command from within AutoCAD for Windows. Both Release 12 and 13 support this capability.*

Question: I use Intergraph's I/RAS C continuous tone color imaging software and want to plot the hybrid (raster and vector) images I have created on-screen. When I use the MicroStation plotting routines, all I get is the vector lines, with no raster. Why?

Answer: I/RAS C requires IPLOT Client 7.0 for Windows NT on the workstation from which you want to plot. This is a plot submission interface that works in conjunction with MicroStation and MicroStation-based applications. The server side of IPLOT Client 7.0 is IPLOT Server, which is also required to handle the plot requests generated from IPLOT Client 7.0. Both IPLOT Client 7.0 and IPLOT Server are available on the Windows NT operating system. The I/RAS C design seat you are using can be configured as both a plotting client and server using these two pieces of software. This is the only solution to plotting hybrid images from I/RAS C at the present time.

Question: Our department has a XES/Versatec 8936-4R. When we switch from HPGL plot files to HPGL/2, the plotter only prints 30% or less of the HPGL/2 file. Why?

Answer: The XES/Versatec 8936-4R does not auto-sense each of the data formats being sent to it. Unlike some of the later-model HP LaserJet printers that do auto-sense the data formats being sent and then configure themselves on the fly to plot the data, the 8936-4R must be reset for each individual type of plot file being sent. Sending HPGL files in an entire block and then reconfiguring the plotter to HPGL/2 and sending that entire batch of plots alleviates this problem.

Question: When I plot from an Intergraph workstation using the CCRF-M drivers to the CalComp DrawingMaster Plus, plotting is very slow, and it seems as if the plotter is "filling up" with data until it plots.

Answer: The reason this happens is that CalComp ships the DrawingMaster Plus series of plotters with the CCRF-M (CalComp Compressed Raster Format - Monochrome) configured to be buffered to the internal hard disk. You can turn this off and get faster plotting from your Intergraph workstation by using the OPCOM parameters supplied with the DrawingMaster Plus. OPCOM is accessible after installing a serial-based terminal to the interface on the back of this plotter, and then rebooting the plotter. You'll notice on the screen that OPCOM begins counting and scrolling through the currently installed firmware in the plotter. Once plotter initialization is complete, access OPCOM and get to the CCRF parameters option. Turn Buffer to *No*. If you have any questions on how to access OPCOM, see the "User's Manual" that is included in the DrawingMaster Plus.

Question: I am trying to plot a PostScript file to the HP650C and nothing is happening. I am copying it to the LPT1 port. My HP LaserJet 4MV handles it without any problem, but the HP 650C doesn't do anything.

Answer: The HP 650C auto-senses HPGL, HPGL/2, and HP RTL. When a PostScript Upgrade is installed in this plotter, the controller needs to know it is there. Using the options in the HP 650C front panel, put the plotter into PostScript mode. Try resending the file to the plotter after doing this. By default, the HP 650C does not include PostScript emulation; an optional upgrade card is needed to make it compatible.

Question: My company is migrating to Windows NT on a few of the client systems and several servers. One of the plot servers now is Windows NT–based when it was once a UNIX-based Sun workstation running Xerox's ServeWare. I use ModelView and want to plot *.RGB* files through the Windows NT workstation. How can I do this?

Answer: Using Raster Server from Intergraph on the Windows NT platform, you can submit raster files, even *.RGB* files, from Intergraph UNIX workstations using either RASSUB (a utility Intergraph provides with every UNIX workstation) or by using the qpr command line. This command line is integrated into the Intergraph Network Queuing System.

Question: There are several HP LaserJet printers and an HP 650C that have the JetDirect interface card installed. How can I plot to these printers and plotters from Windows NT? Can I use Intergraph's IPLOT from within MicroStation to plot to these printers and plotters that have the JetDirect interface cards installed?

Answer: Yes, using either Windows NT 3.1 or Windows NT 3.5 you can plot directly to these printers and plotters that are active on the network. H.Q. provides a Print Monitor for either of these versions of Windows NT that makes it possible to print directly to the printers and plotters as if they were directly connected to the workstation itself. Each of the JetDirect interface cards have Ethernet chip sets included that transmit the Ethernet address over the network. Each of the Windows NT workstations with the Print Monitor installed can pick up and store the Ethernet addresses from these cards and present them within the context of the Windows NT Print Manager. Creating a printer in Windows NT requires selecting the port to be plotted to. When creating a printer queue that queues up and sends jobs to JetDirect-based printers and plotters, you'll first select the Create Printer command from the Printer Menu. Next, you'll select the device driver you will use with the specific printer or plotter. For the HP LaserJet IIIsi, you would select that specific printer driver, and then click once in the Print to: entry. Scrolling through the list of entries select the Network Interfaces... section. Click once on this entry and the series of Print Monitors is shown.

Selecting the HP Monitor leads to another dialog box that shows the Ethernet addresses for each printer or plotter on the network. Select the one that is installed in the LaserJet IIIsi and click once on OK to close the dialog box. You're now ready to begin printing and plotting to the LaserJet IIIsi. To recap, you'll need the following software and information to get a printer or plotter with an HP JetDirect interface card up and running on a Windows NT–based network.

Check to make sure HP Print Monitor software was shipped with your JetDirect card. Install this software on the Windows NT workstation you want to plot from using the steps provided.

1. Check to make sure the Windows NT workstation you want to plot from is active on the network. Check to make sure the network cabling is attached and that other network functions, such as using a shared file directory on someone else's workstation through File Manager, works.

2. To get the Ethernet interface address for the printer or plotter with the JetDirect card installed, print out the self-test page for that specific device. On that page you'll find the Ethernet address for the specific printer or plotter of interest. Many system administrators send out these Ethernet addresses using email to everyone who is interested in plotting to JetDirect-based peripherals.

✔ **TIP:** *Once a queue has been created to a JetDirect-based printer or plotter on the network, you can plot directly from within IPLOT Client 7.0 from within MicroStation directly to this device.*

Question: I want to hook up my CalComp 68436 to the network and use the 970 controller. I'm planning to plot from MicroStation and can't seem to get the 970 controller recognized. What can I do?

Answer: MicroStation by itself does not support network-based peripheral controllers like the CalComp 970. Originally developed to make it possible for CalComp plotters to be used on a variety of networks and network topologies, the functionality of the CalComp 970 is present in the HP JetDirect EX Print Server. The EX Print Server is a network interface that has a network connection on one end and both an RS-232C serial and Centronics Parallel interface on the other. The EX Print Server makes it possible for MicroStation users to plot to any RS-232C or Centronics-based printer. Using the following steps, you can plot from MicroStation to the CalComp 68436.

1. Decide if the CalComp 970 controller is the one you want to use. You could more easily configure the HP JetDirect EX Print Server, so that it would be possible to create a queue directly within Windows NT.

2. After setting up the queue in Windows NT's Print Manager, you can use the Print command in MicroStation Version 5 to get the image submitted from directly within the application to the plotter over the network.

3. You can use the queue created from within IPLOT as well. Invoking the IPLOT Client 7.0 interface from within MicroStation, you could select the queue that points directly to the CalComp 68436. If your company has standardized on Intergraph's Windows NT Plotting products, you must attach pen and feature tables during plotting. IPLOT Server, the server component of Intergraph's plotting software also needs to be present on the workstation you are plotting from, or the plot server you are plotting through.

Summary

The Microsoft Windows NT Print Manager has been designed to give you more flexibility in creating, using, and managing printers and printing tasks. Using a separate window for each printer that resembles a printer queue, you can view all submitted and printing documents for any printer available on the network of which you are a member. Using the Create Printer command you can install support for your printers and also create a printer queue that could be used for printing directly to a file.

The Print Manager has tools for managing the flow of documents through each printer's queue as well. You can pause and resume the printing of a document, or stop and start an entire printer's queue. Using the queue-like printer windows in Print Manager, you can also modify the sequence of documents to print. Also included in the Print Manager is the command, Create Printer. Using this command, you can create a printer's window in Print Manager. This command is versatile enough to be used for configuring printing to a file or directly to an Ethernet-ready printer or plotter.

You can also use the Print Manager's command, Connect To Printer, for using network-based printers. The Connect To Printer command provides a list of the Shared Printers that are available on the network of which you are a member. This can be particularly useful for printing documents on a printer that has little or no traffic. You can "shop" for a printer that isn't too busy if you are. This makes getting your documents printed much easier than if all members of the network needed to be funneled through a single printer. It is the intention of Windows NT's Print Manager to give you more flexibility in how printing tasks are completed.

Windows NT: CAD, CAE, GIS, and MS-DOS Applications

Introduction

Changing how efficiently tasks are accomplished is the implied objective for every operating system. How tasks are accomplished in applications running within an operating system is often the measure of how truly efficient a new operating system is. Throughout this chapter, application programs written specifically for the technical professional using Windows NT are profiled. You'll also learn about the major 16-bit applications that are commonly used within Windows NT as well, including AutoCAD Release 13 for Windows. Autodesk has committed to a Windows NT version as well, fulfilling the entire range of CAD application programs that will be 32-bit compatible. Profiles of each application are meant to give you an idea of the capabilities of each one.

The second half of this chapter defines the role of MS-DOS applications and their use in conjunction with the Windows NT operating system. Migrating from one operating system to another always requires consideration of which applications that you presently use will still be available to you on the new operating system. The Windows NT operating system has been designed with that critical migration issue in mind. Windows NT includes the ability to run many existing applications from DOS, Windows 3.1, and earlier character-based versions of OS/2. All these applications as well as native Windows NT applications can all run at the same time and share the resources of your computer. More importantly they are protected from each other in a way that their native operatings cannot match. For example, a DOS application may have a bug that under DOS will crash the system; under Windows NT the most it will do is crash itself. Since each of these subsystems exists within the multitasking framework of Windows NT, you can happily run several applications simultaneously, sharing information between them

Exploring how to use MS-DOS applications in the context of Windows NT is the goal of this chapter. Since Windows NT includes a subsystem that emulates the MS-DOS operating system, you can run applications in much the same manner as you would on any of the Intel-based PCs located throughout your organization.

A Day in the Life: Designing a New Bike

When StarFleet Cruisers Bicycle Company first began working with Microsoft Windows, all the coordinates, design data, and relevant statistics that described new bicycles were kept in Excel. As time progressed, the Design Department migrated from MicroStation Version 4 to MicroStation Version 5, switching from Clipper UNIX (CLIX) to Windows NT–based workstations. With this change, the original data used for designing bicycles was kept in Excel format and brought onto the Windows NT workstations. Using dynamic data exchange (DDE), the spreadsheets created within Excel were linked directly into a MicroStation design file, so that the resulting bicycle parts could be easily created from the existing database created earlier in Excel. Let's walk through the steps used at StarFleet for getting the bicycle parts designed using MicroStation as it is being driven by Microsoft Excel.

Using a series of templates designed within Excel to drive MicroStation design file construction, StarFleet Cruisers begins studying the market for a new bicycle. Using the market research reports available, StarFleet tries to get an idea of the bicycles that are selling today, and that have potential in the future. Having standardized on Windows NT, the Microsoft Office suite of products, and AutoCAD and MicroStation, the StarFleet Marketing and Engineering organizations easily accomplish the process of sharing market data and transforming it into product specifications.

The product managers for the StarFleet line of bicycles review the past sales history of bicycles sold around the world for the last three years. The following figure shows an example of the Excel spreadsheet that the product managers and engineering staff review when trying to decide the class of bicycle that will be produced.

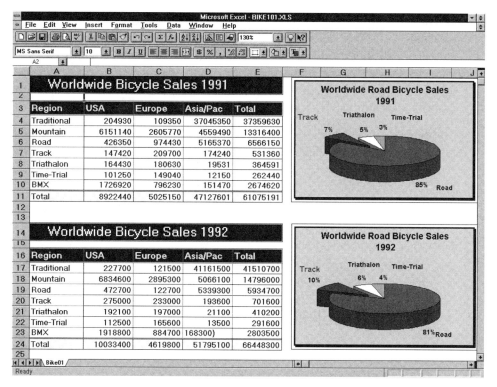

WorldWide Bicycle Sales Analysis from StarFleet.

With the data in the context of regions, StarFleet's product managers see that all market segments except the road bikes have grown from 1991 to 1992. How does this extrapolate into 1994 and beyond? Using the tools in Excel, the compound annual growth rates of each of these segments is included in the spreadsheet, and the result is that Time-Trial bikes continue to grow as a market segment, with little competition. The other bicycle segments continue to grow as well, but attract more than their share of competitors because the costs of producing a bike for the traditional and mountain segments are lower than those for creating a new bike for the time-trial segment. StarFleet sets its sites on this market segment and begins looking at the existing competitors, the market requirements of its users, and the overall trends impacting the entire bicycle industry. The results are used for creating the initial product design of the StarFleet's Time-Trial prototype.

With the creation of any new bicycle, there are frame coordinates to calculate, densities of tubing, head, and seat angles, and frame size differences. Using the Bicycle Frame Specification Sheet, which is an Excel template that calculates all these values, the designers at StarFleet can quickly get an idea of what the engineering specifications are for the bicycle being created. The following figure shows an example of the Bicycle Frame Specification Sheet used at StarFleet for creating the specifications for a new bike.

The figures for a new bike are entered into this Excel template in the upper left corner. These specifications are then used for driving the entire design of the bike. After the designers have used these specifications for defining the new time-trial bike, they use the spreadsheet underlying this template to drive MicroStation and actually create the initial models.

Using the calculations in the Excel spreadsheet, MicroStation constructs a wireframe model of the proposed frame. Using the frame as a reference point, the designers begin creating each of the component assemblies using a template that is linked within the Excel spreadsheet to MicroStation as well. The initial frame created from the Bicycle Frame Specification Sheet is shown in the figure on page 168.

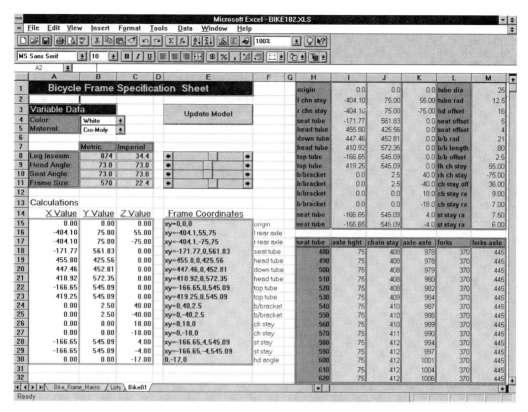

StarFleet's Bicycle Frame Specification Sheet.

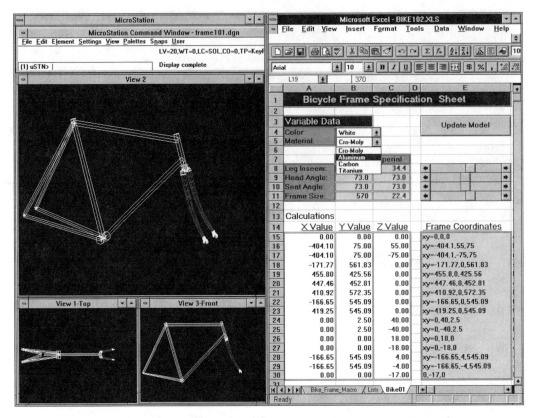

Initial MicroStation design file generated from Excel template.

The designers can review the initial frame design and modify its appearance using the options in the Excel spreadsheet shown to the right of the screen. If the head and seat angle need to be adjusted, the compensating values are easily entered into the Excel template, and the resulting changes are reflected in the MicroStation drawing file. As the design is being generated using the Excel spreadsheet as the data calculation tool, the designers can also zoom into a specific part of the bicycle's design. For example, if the angle of the main bars supporting the bicycle's frame is too severe and could possibly snap if there was enough stress placed on them, the designers can zoom in and look at the specific angle and joint of tubs in the frame. The following figure shows an example of how the designers can use MicroStation on one side of the screen of their Windows NT workstations and have the Excel worksheet running on the other. Changing the values in the Bicycle Frame Specification Sheet leads to the change being made in the actual frame.

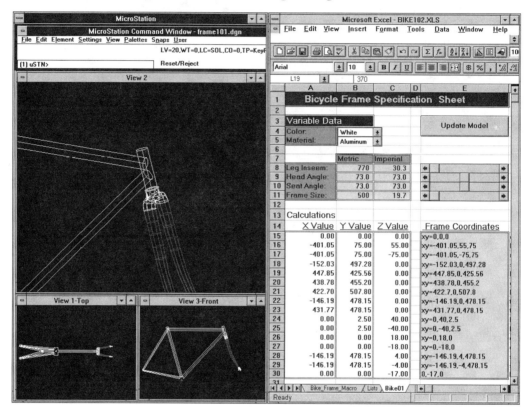

Zooming into a bicycle frame.

After going through an initial series of design review meetings between the product managers and the designers, the Product Development Team at StarFleet decides that it's time to begin the design of the actual wheels used on the bicycle. The following figure shows the initial designs of the wheels that have been designed for StarFleet's next generation of time-trial bicycles.

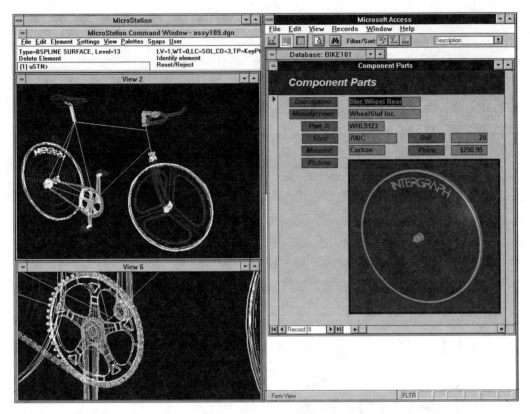

StarFleet's initial wheel design.

Notice how the Component Parts template is used for defining the specifics of the wheel assembly. For example, the description of the part is available, along with the part number, size, material, reference number, price, vendor, and even a rendered image of the actual part. As additional parts are added to the bill of materials for the bicycle, the additions are made into the Component Parts listing.

As the design process continues, it is decided that the chain being used on the prototype needs to have higher torque. With the increased torque, it is hoped that the typical racer will be able to get more speed from the bike. Using MicroStation to modify the circumference of the gears, additional torque is included in the bicycle's gear mechanism. The following figure shows an example of the gears being increased in size to allow for more torque per revolution.

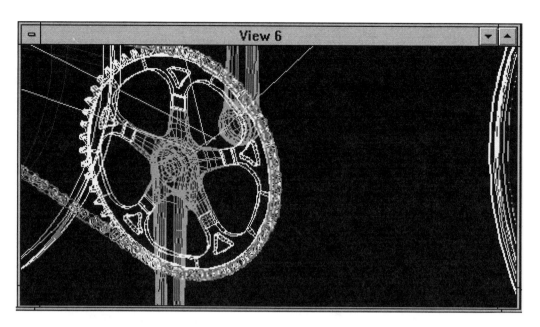

Increasing the torque ratio for the time-trial bicycle design.

With the design nearly complete and the schedule looking pretty solid for an initial production run, the engineering and marketing departments decide that it's time to announce the new time-trial bike to a few select distributors around the world that will be instrumental in getting new orders. An initial product flyer is created, with a rendered image created in MicroStation. Using the Rendering tools in MicroStation Version 5, the design team creates a smooth-shaded image, and then saves the image as a Windows bitmap (*.bmp*) file for use in marketing and sales announcements. One reason StarFleet uses the *.bmp* file format is that it can be imported easily into word processing applications like Word for Windows 6.0, and spreadsheets like Microsoft Excel for Windows. The following figure shows an example of the product announcement with the *.bmp* file inserted, showing the next bicycle design.

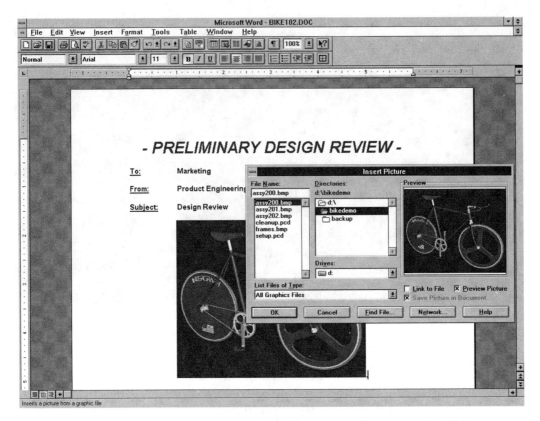

The new product announcement for the StarFleet Time-Trial Bike.

With the National Sales Meeting just around the corner, the Sales Department really wants to make a big deal about the Time-Trial bike, now called the Mach 7. In addition to having the design team wheel out the new Mach 7 and show it to the distributors, dealers, and sales people from around the world, the marketing vice president also wants to have an animated video showing how the Mach 7 handles extreme racing conditions. Further, he wants to show the bicycle moving at different speeds, showing how the increased torque capacity increases speed. He wants an animated demo.

The designers and the system administrator work together to animate a sequence showing the new features of the Mach 7. At the end of the new product presentation, an audiovisual file (*.AVI* file) is shown and appears against a backdrop of the Mach 7 frames awaiting custom orders from the bicycle racers around the world.

Throughout this demonstration, the ability of MicroStation to be driven by Excel spreadsheets, save rendered images in a variety of image formats, and even create a simulated video showing the new capabilities of the Mach 7 time-trial bike exemplify the capabilities that Windows NT provides for technical applications. Similar scenarios are also accomplished using technical applications that have Windows NT compatibility and are able to fully use the capabilities of Windows NT.

AutoCAD's Release 13 for Windows NT

Autodesk's latest version of AutoCAD reflects the requests from a large and varied customer base. With AutoCAD Release 13, Autodesk has offered its first 32-bit application specifically developed for the Windows NT operating system. The performance should increase with the introduction of a true 32-bit version of AutoCAD Release 13 for Windows NT. With Release 13, Autodesk now has a product that is actually slower than its predecessor, Release 12. The decrease in performance can be attributable to the larger file size in the native AutoCAD *.DWG* format, and the slower times for saving files. Autodesk's product strategy is to move away from Windows 3.1 and toward Windows NT and Windows 95.

With this latest release of AutoCAD, Autodesk had the opportunity to move DOS-based AutoCAD users solidly into the world of Microsoft Windows, where the majority of AutoCAD shipments have been for the previous five years.

There is an increase in the number of features included in Release 13.

❏ Designers can now include multiple lines of text (up to 100 lines can be added within a design file).

❏ There's also support for TrueType fonts in Release 13, making it possible to include comments within a *.DWG* file with your favorite font style. You could annotate a *.DWG* file using Times New Roman, Helvetica, or any of the other typefaces you typically use with other Windows-based applications.

With the introduction of AutoCAD Release 13 for Windows NT has come an entirely new user interface for the Windows version. The following figure shows the AutoCAD Release 13 for Window's new graphical user interface.

You'll notice that AutoCAD Release 13 for Windows user interface is more Windows-like compared with the DOS versions. There is support for object linking and embedding and the ability to have raster data displayed on-screen in conjunction with a *.DWG* file. There also are floating toolbars that can be detached and placed anywhere on the screen, making the options within these toolbars easy to access and use. These toolbars are activated using specific selections from each of the main palettes accessible from the main window of AutoCAD Release 13.

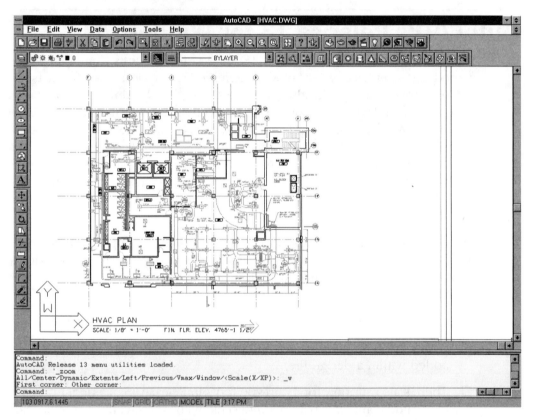

AutoCAD's Release 13 for Windows user interface.

MicroStation Version 5 for Windows NT

Both Intergraph and Bentley Systems, Inc., have continued to develop MicroStation-based application programs that meet the needs of technical professionals in the architectural, engineering, construction, mapping, and many other market segments that use CAD application programs. MicroStation includes features that make it easy to use on one hand, and robust enough to complete larger projects on the other hand.

Just as AutoCAD has been ported to a wide variety of hardware platforms, the same is true of MicroStation Version 5. It is available on the MS-DOS, Microsoft Windows, Windows NT, Apple Macintosh, Intergraph Clipper UNIX (CLIX), Sun SPARC, HP-UX, and IBM RS6000 platforms. This has made it possible for companies with a diverse hardware environment to standardize on MicroStation and seamlessly integrate applications into their workflow, since each workstation in a workgroup can share design files with the other.

What's New in MicroStation Version 5?

With each major MicroStation release has come additional functionality, increased performance and an increase in the usefulness of commands and features. There are a significant number of new features in MicroStation Version 5, many of which are briefly described here:

❒ **New and Improved GUI:** With MicroStation Version 5, tasks that previously took several steps have been consolidated into single commands to make completing designs and projects easier. The MicroStation Version 5 interface is also now constant across all platforms.

❒ **Raster File Viewing and Plotting:** Rendered images and design files can now be saved as raster files. Using the Binary Raster MDL application included with MicroStation Version 5 (called BRAS), raster images can be previewed as well. Rendered images can be saved as Windows *.BMP* (Bitmap), COT, Intergraph Type 27 Raster (called RGB), and RLE. In addition, rendered images can be saved in *JPEG, JFIF, TIFF, GIF,* Sun Raster, *.TGA* (or Targa), and Bump files. Using the BRAS Utility it is possible to convert *PICT,* PostScript, *TIFF* (both compressed and uncompressed), and WordPerfect *WPG* formats.

❒ **Fonts:** MicroStation Version 5 includes a font installer that makes it possible to use Adobe PostScript Type 1, AutoCAD, IGDS-formatted, and even TrueType fonts. Using the font installer you can create a font resource file that is used every time MicroStation is invoked.

❏ **Improved Patterning and Hatching:** MicroStation Version 5 now offers "intelligent" hatching and patterning, which makes it possible to create objects quickly with the intended patterning or hatching.

❏ **User Control Over Line Styles:** MicroStation Version 5 includes the option of specifically controlling the appearance of a given line style. You can modify the styles of lines by changing the dash and gap length definitions. Also included is the capability of having automatic symbol placement, offset lines, line widths, and the option of having lines displayed completely, or only in "fast" mode, which shows the files in an abbreviated format.

❏ **File Format Compatibility:** Being able to bring in AutoCAD *DWG, DXF* (Document Exchange Format), *IGES* (Initial Graphics Exchange Specification), and *CGM* (Computer Graphics Metafile) files directly into a MicroStation design session is possible using the File Import command. Instead of using filters to first interpret incoming data files and then converting them, MicroStation now takes these file formats directly from other applications or systems located throughout the network.

❏ **AutoCAD Upgrade Path:** MicroStation Version 5 includes the ability to import and export *DWG* files and also supports the AutoCAD *SHX* fonts, reference files, block attributes, and line styles. Using MicroStation, AutoCAD users can also construct 3D orthos and wedge surfaces and change line style settings to reflect their preferences in AutoCAD. There is also a complete series of help files provided in the MicroStation Online Help system, guiding AutoCAD users through the process of migrating to MicroStation.

Intergraph's MGE Product Family

Intergraph is comprised of a series of separate product centers that have the same goal of integrating their applications with MicroStation, and in a broader sense, with Windows NT. The Mapping Sciences Division of Intergraph is working on true 32-bit mapping applications.

The acronym MGE stands for Modular GIS Environment and includes many applications based on MicroStation and Windows NT. At the heart of MGE is a series of tools for completing vector and raster warping, editing, and image enhancement. In the context of the MGE products, warping is the process by which a vector file is overlaid to a raster one, with key vector points being applied to the raster file to anchor the vector one to specific points. The raster file can be any area or part, and the vector file is typically drawn in MicroStation to correspond to the topology, definition, or image of the raster image. The following figure shows an example of a vector and raster image being edited within I/RAS C.

Using I/RAS C to edit a hybrid image.

Intergraph's I/RAS C

One of the most commonly used applications in the MGE suite of products is I/RAS C. This application makes it possible to display continuous tone raster images, and then overlay vector design files to accentuate specific structures, streets, or any other item of interest. Commonly used within the business community and by utilities companies, I/RAS C runs on top of MicroStation. The following figure shows an example of an I/RAS C editing session.

In the case of a builder working with the city and county inspectors, having the ability to overlay property lines, show easements, and even define the utilities lines makes it possible to complete a project with less government intervention and on-site inspection. The accuracy tools available within MicroStation Version 5 ensure that placement of lines within the context of a given scale will be accurate. Accuracy within the context of I/RAS C is also possible because it supports "warping" or the joining of the vector file to the underlying raster file. This ensures that after the file has been worked on and saved, the same coordinates are also available for the next designer.

Using I/RAS C to plan a new home development.

Being able to change the color and composition of the background raster data is also possible using I/RAS C's image editing capabilities. Using the color gradation curves, color correction tools, and the ability to merge multiple raster images makes I/RAS C an excellent tool for completing geographic analysis. Adjusting the contrast of a raster image can alleviate shadows that are present in the image and make it possible to fully show the structures, land formations, and impact of the proposed development on the existing landscape.

ArcView 2

ArcView, from Environmental Systems Research Institute, Inc., is a GIS software that allows PC users to display, browse, query, and analyze geographic data, linking spreadsheets and graphics with maps, tables, and charts. ArcView has an easy-to-use GUI, but has advanced functionality and an object-oriented programming language, Avenue, which extend ArcView's reach beyond desktop mapping.

ArcView running in Windows NT can directly access data from UNIX workstations running ARC/INFO or other PCs or Macintoshes running database applications. ArcView has a Windows-based GUI. It includes standard protocols such as dynamic data exchange for Windows.

ArcView 2 includes the following features:

❐ Seamless access to data across networks.

❐ Strong support for standard output formats and devices.

❐ Strong integration with tabular databases.

❐ Interapplication communication; for example, ArcView and ARC/INFO can trade data or requests back and forth.

❐ An object-oriented architecture.

❐ A client/server architecture.

Some examples of users of ArcView within Windows NT include natural resource organizations that need to transfer field data gathered through global positioning systems to the home office networked on Windows NT; electrical utilities, whose marketing departments need to prepare presentations for future clients; and state and city governments that need to exchange data from dBase and UNIX applications into a common map application for presentation at public forums.

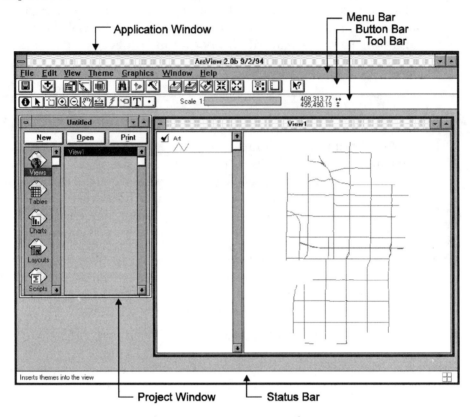

The primary ArcView interface.

Pro/ENGINEER Revision 14

Pro/ENGINEER is a mechanical and solids modeling package from Parametric Technology Corporation. It differs from other CAE programs in that it uses linked data to enable parametric design and support concurrent engineering. Using parametric design, one dimension of the design can be changed and the rest of the design is automatically adjusted.

Besides the core module, Pro/ENGINEER, there are many accessory modules, including Pro/DETAIL, Pro/ASSEMBLY, Pro/MESH, Pro/SHEETMETAL and Pro/MANUFACTURING. With Pro/ENGINEER, the design intent can be more clearly applied all the way through manufacturing. Production cycles can be shortened because revisions can be made more quickly.

Some features of Pro/ENGINEER include the following:

❑ Support for concurrent engineering.

❑ Flexibility in implementing design changes

❑ Associative data structure

❑ Features-based approach to modeling

❑ Rapid revision cycle

❑ Support for design through manufacturing

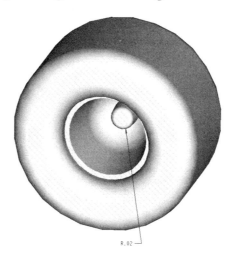

Part modeled in Pro/ENGINEER.

Running DOS Applications in Windows NT

The first question to ask about a DOS application is, "Will it run in NT?"

The best way to discover this is to try it. That said, there are some applications that definitely will not run:

1. **Applications that attempt to use hardware directly.** In DOS program-ming it is quite legitimate to put a a new value in a memory location or

CPU register simply addressing the location directly. This results in DOS applications that will not function in Windows NT. Any real operating system like Windows NT has to handle all the access to hardware otherwise it cannot control what goes on.

2. **DOS device drivers.** By definition these access hardware directly. To use a peripheral such as a sound card or disk controller in Windows NT you must have a device driver specifically written for Windows NT.

Fortunately, most applications that behave this way are games, which use the poorly defined DOS interfaces to hardware. Typical business applications are better behaved and are likely to run. Assuming a DOS application will run, you may still have some hurdles to overcome because of the eccentric and nonstandardized memory management extensions for DOS. Remember, DOS was designed originally for machines that would only use a maximum of 640KB of RAM. Techniques for accessing memory beyond 640KB vary. There are two widely used standards:

❏   eXtended Memory System (XMS)

❏   Expanded Memory System (EMS)

Often, when you first run a DOS application it will start briefly and fail; the error message will probably be gone before you even see it. To help get things working, you should start the application from a DOS prompt window started from the Main program group.

As you can see, this DOS application expects to find some EMS memory available for it to use. So the burning question is, how do we fool the application into thinking that it really is running on a DOS system with plenty of EMS memory. The answer is to create a startup file for the application that will initialize the DOS subsystem with everything the

application needs. The initialization file is created with a utility called the PIF Editor or Program Information File Editor. The PIF editor is found in your main program group and when started, it displays a dialog box. This dialog box has several fields:

❏   **Program Filename:** The name of the DOS executable to run.

❏   **Window Title:** The name to give the window it runs in.

❐ **Optional Parameters:** Any command line arguments you want passed to the application Startup Directory, which will become the current directory when the application starts.

After these fields you have the opportunity to define the memory available to your application. These fields are:

❐ **Memory Requirements:** This corresponds to the base 640KB on your computer. Some applications will refuse to run if they cannot find enough space in the base 640K of memory.

❐ **EMS Memory:** In our example, the application demanded at least 748KB of EMS memory. You can use this field to emulate the EMS memory system and provide the application with sufficient memory to run.

❐ **XMS Memory:** Some older applications demand XMS memory.

Once you've filled in the information, you save the file in the same directory as the application. The file has a extension of *.PIF*. This has a special meaning to Windows NT. When you run the application, you do it by executing the *PIF* file, not the application. Windows NT will initialize a DOS subsystem using the information provided then launch the real application.

Customizing *Config.sys* and *Autoexec.bat* for DOS Applications

If you are familiar with DOS, you'll know all about these files as they are fundamental to the system. In a DOS system you use these files to load DOS device drivers and set up shell variables used by your applications. Although Windows NT does not use these files itself, it gives you the option of loading psuedo versions of these files when you start a DOS application.

If for example you had a DOS application that required a variable *TEMPDIR* to be set when it runs, then you could add the line:

TEMPDIR=C:\temp

To the file *%SystemRoot%\system32\autoexec.bat*. This file is used to initialize the DOS environment whenever an application is run.

➥ **NOTE:** *Putting lines in config.sys or autoexec.bat to load DOS drivers into the DOS subsystem will have no effect as Windows NT will ignore them. In most cases, you will not be able to get DOS programs to use such facilities* *as your sound card because they want to access it without going through Windows NT.*

Running Windows 3.1 (Win16) Applications

In general this is much simpler. The Win16 programmers interface is relatively well defined, making its emulation comparatively simple. As a general rule, a Win16 application will run. The only ones that don't are those which:

1. Attempt to access hardware directly.

2. Require a Windows 3.1 Virtual Device Driver or VXD. This includes most Windows FAX programs and specialist applications that are tied to a specific piece of hardware such as a video capture card. Basically there is no set up required for Win16 applications. If the application works, then it will work by executing it in the same way you did under Windows.

How Windows NT Handles MS-DOS Applications

Windows NT is a modular-based operating system, comprised of a series of subsystems. Microsoft decided to include subsystems to run application programs originating from the MS-DOS, Windows 3.1, and 16-bit OS/2 operating systems. Think of each of these subsystems as columns, each independent, and providing the necessary compatibility with a wide variety of programs. The following figure shows an example of the Windows NT subsystem structure.

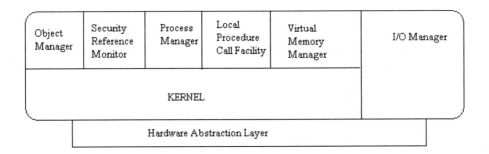

How the Windows NT/MS-DOS subsystem works.

Notice in the previous figure that each of the subsystems is discrete or standalone. This protects each of the subsystems, so that if for one reason or another an application running in the MS-DOS subsystem stops, the other subsystems can continue providing application program support. The Windows NT Executive located along the top portion of this figure coordinates how each of the respective subsystems are managed. The Executive makes sure that each of these processes runs in its own area of memory, not overriding another subsystem's working area. With each subsystem having its own area within memory, each subsystem can stand on its own, not affecting other subsystem's applications.

Loading and Running MS-DOS Applications

Think of the Command Prompt window as the monitor screen of your MS-DOS personal computer. You can complete many of the tasks that are possible when using a PC/AT. Here are the steps that profile how to install Lotus 123 within the Command Prompt window. You'll notice the steps are very similar to how this application program is installed on an MS-DOS personal computer;

1. Double-click on the Command Prompt window located in the Main group.

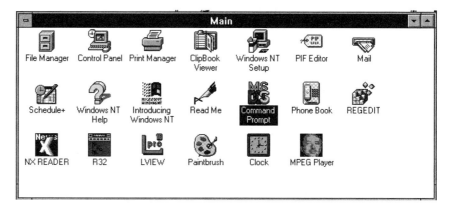

Command Prompt icon highlighted in Main group.

2. Place the MS-DOS diskette into the A: drive of your system. Type the MS-DOS command *DIR*. The contents of the floppy diskette you just inserted into the A: drive are shown.

3. Type INSTALL. Since this example shows how to install Lotus 123 within Command Prompt, the Installation Screen for this program next appears on screen.

Lotus 123 installation screen in the Command Prompt window.

4. Follow the instructions for installing the MS-DOS program you want to use in the Command Prompt window. These steps are identical to the ones you'd take if you were installing the program on an MS-DOS system.

5. Type 123 at the system prompt (or type in the command that launches the application program you have loaded). In the case of our example, the program Lotus 123 loads and runs on screen.

The Lotus 123 introductory screen appearing in the Command Prompt window.

Managing MS-DOS Applications on the Desktop

Running MS-DOS and Windows-based applications in Windows NT is actually like multiplying the number of sessions you have going on at a single time. Instead of just having Lotus 123 or WordStar running in one window to the exclusion of all other applications, you can have multiple Command Prompt windows open and available with the MS-DOS programs up and running. So the Windows NT Desktop gives you the flexibility of moving back and forth between several MS-DOS based applications just as if you were moving from one PC to another to complete separate tasks.

Managing these tasks requires knowledge of tools for navigating and changing from one MS-DOS application to another. Using the ClipBoard, for example, you can easily take data from an MS-DOS application and place it into a fully compatible Windows NT application like Pro/ENGINEER Version 14. So instead of being limited to MS-DOS and its single-tasking orientation, with Windows NT you have the opportunity to have several things going at once. This is particularly useful if you are using the Windows NT workstation you have as a plot or file server; several tasks can be accomplished at the same time under Windows NT.

Switching Between Applications

Since each of the Command Prompt windows is actually a "thread" or process occurring within Windows NT, you can treat each one as a separate application in itself. This means that just as you can press the ALT+TAB keys to move from one window of an application, or from the Program Manager, to other applications, you can do the same to move from one active Command Prompt window to another. Pressing the ALT+TAB keys places a small rectangular box in the middle of your screen, indicating the currently active application. Letting go of the two keys makes the application listed in the small gray rectangular box active. This could be the Command Prompt window or Microsoft Mail. The following figure shows an example of the small rectangular dialog box that appears every time the ALT+TAB keys are pressed.

The second approach to switching from one application to another is by using the Task List. Pressing CTRL+ESC at the same time shows the Task List of applications currently running, including the Command Prompt windows that have applications running inside them. Notice that the titles of the Command Prompt windows in the Task List show the MS-DOS applications being used within them.

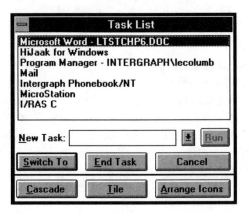

The Task List is a complete listing of all applications currently in use.

Printing from DOS Applications

Typically DOS applications print to a local port such as LPT1: for the parallel port and COM1: for the serial port. Assuming you have a local printer, these applications will continue to print just fine. However, if you used a DOS print redirector to make LPT1: send the print to a remote device, you'll need to use the Windows NT Print Manager to carry out the redirection. This is most easily accomplished from the command line.

For instance, the local port LPT1: might have been redirected via the Print Manager to a remote print que called "que1" on a node called "printserver."

The "PERSISTENT=YES" switch will cause this connection to always be established when the system boots.

Sharing Data Between Applications

Applications that are running within the Command Prompt window have access to the ClipBoard and ClipBook Viewer, just as any other Windows NT-based application.

Pressing the PrintScreen key captures the entire screen of your Windows NT workstation, while pressing the ALT+PrintScreen keys at the same time captures only the Command Prompt window.

If you are putting together a report that includes a series of graphs that can only be created within an MS-DOS application, you can first open the word processing document, or the design file, then press the ALT and TAB keys to view the Command Prompt window. With the Command Prompt window in view, pressing the ALT and PrintScreen keys at the same time captures the entire Command Prompt window. After pressing those two keys (ALT and PrintScreen), only the Command Prompt window is active on the Clipboard.

Since you don't want to paste the entire image into your report, drawing, or design file, open the Paintbrush application found in the Accessories group of Windows NT. Select Paste from the Edit menu. The entire Command Prompt window is then copied into the workspace of Paintbrush. The following figure shows an example of the Command Prompt window with a graphic highlighted within it. Using the Crop Tool in the upper left portion of the Paintbrush Tool Palette to isolate only the graphic created in the Command Prompt window, you can then paste it into your report.

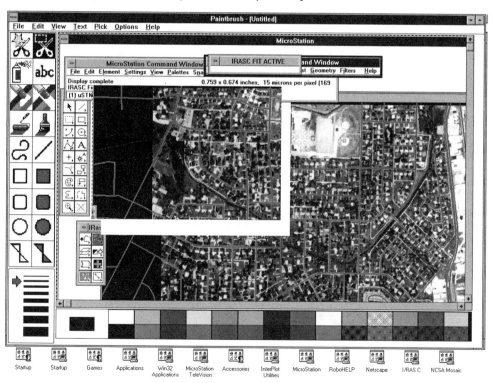

Using Paintbrush to cut and paste images.

Capturing a screen image from a window is not the only option. If the window contains text or figures from a spreadsheet, you can cut and paste from it, almost as you would from an application window. To cut text from an application running in a DOS window, carry out the following steps:

1. In the DOS Window select the Mark option in the menu.

2. You will now see a blinking cursor in the DOS Window. Using the mouse you can highlight any portion of text.

3. Now go back to the submenu used to select Mark and select copy.

4. The text is now in the Clipboard and can be pasted into any other window using the normal mechanisms.

Summary

Windows NT provides software developers with a solid platform from which the full capabilities of their programs can be used. Microsoft's efforts at recruiting software vendors that previously considered the UNIX operating system to be the only platform for their applications have been successful. Autodesk, Parametric Technologies Corporation, Environmental Systems Research Institute, and Intergraph have all made substantial commitments to the Windows NT platform.

In positioning Windows NT as a valid alternative to UNIX for technical applications, Microsoft has successfully persuaded developers of the performance and reliability features of their new operating system. Having the ability to interactively share data from one application to another, the option technical professionals have for Microsoft Office products to run at the same time as technical applications, and the strength of Microsoft's networking strategy, are all reasons why software companies continue to bring their applications to the Windows NT platform.

The benefits to technical professionals of this migration from UNIX to Windows NT for technical applications include increased connectivity options, more efficient use of resources since many Intel-based 80486-based systems now running Windows can be upgraded to Windows NT, and the option of sharing technical data with other Windows NT–compatible applications designed for office automation tasks.

Chapter 7

Windows NT Networking

Introduction

Windows NT Workstation was designed to include a range of networking capabilities from its inception. Included in the standard operating system are:

❏ **Server Message Block (SMB):** The native Windows NT networking protocol, SMB provides file and print sharing services between Windows NT nodes as well as Windows For Workgroups. This protocol is often referred to as NETBEUI.

❏ **TCP/IP:** Windows NT includes a complete implementation of the TCP/IP protocol and several applications to access TCP/IP based services on the network. The implementation provides support for standard WINSOCK applications.

❏ **IPX/SPX:** Allows Windows NT nodes to be clients to Novell Netware servers for file and print sharing services.

❏ **Remote Access Services (RAS):** Provides modem connectivity to Windows NT networks as well as TCP/IP-based networks such as the Internet. TCP/IP connectivity over modem lines uses either Serial Line Internet Protocol (SLIP) or Point-to-Point Protocol (PPP).

❏ **Support for Many Network Interface Cards:** Windows NT includes device drivers for many different cards, including most Ethernet and Token Ring interfaces. For a full list of supported cards see the latest copy of the Windows NT Hardware Compatibility List.

❏ **Support for a variety of popular modems.**

The inclusion of a complete networking implementation in Windows NT is particularly important in the modern office where the network is a fact of life.

Windows NT Networking Fundamentals

Large-scale networking of computers is a comparatively recent development. The standards that are used to create today's local area networks are not much more than 10 years old. Unfortunately, several different standards or protocols have been developed for connecting systems together, including TCP/IP, NETBEUI, and IPX/SPX to name a few. Different protocols are the networking equivalent of spoken languages—in order to have a meaningful conversation, both sides must understand the same language.

Despite its youth, networking is fundamental to most computing environments today. To be successful Windows NT has to connect to a variety of different network services:

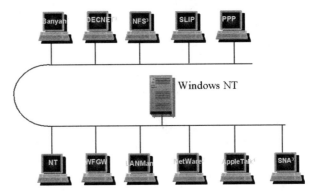

Heterogeneous network environment.

Layered Architecture

As networking has become more important, operating system designers have worked to hide its mechanics from applications and users. The goal is to make a whole network of computer resources behave as if they where attached to your own machine.

This level of integration requires that the applications use network resources in exactly the same fashion as local resources. Windows NT achieves this by providing a set of operating system services that hide the network from an application:

User Applications	
Networking Interfaces	
Local Area Network Interfaces	Remote Access Services
Token Ring, Ethernet etc.	MODEMs, ISDN, X.25 etc.

Operating System

Hardware

Layered architecture.

This sophisticated abstraction allows any application to work with network resources in the same way that it works with local resources. The model extends to resources on systems separated by thousands of miles whether connected via high-speed digital communications or low-speed serial devices such as modems.

Multiple Protocol Support

Windows NT speaks several protocols natively. This ability is required in the splintered world of network protocol standards. With built-in support for NETBEUI, TCP/IP, IPX/SPX, AppleTalk, SLIP, and PPP, Windows NT is well equipped to connect to most network resources.

Network Security

The number of systems connected to networks throughout the world continues to grow at an almost exponential rate. Access to the resources of woldwide networks is no longer the sole preserve of large companies and government organizations. Assumptions about professional and responsible behavior on the network are no longer valid and security is a concern to many.

The protocols used by Windows NT for networking with other Windows NT nodes and Windows for Workgroups are designed for maximum security. By contrast, the protocols used between UNIX nodes rely on nobody misusing the net. A good example of this is the transmission of passwords. Many common TCP/IP applications that transmit passwords do so in clear text. Windows NT sends passwords encrypted.

Because of the advanced security architecture of Windows NT, it is easier to secure from outside attack than UNIX. Many UNIX networking functions have portions that run as "root" and introduce potential security holes. The UNIX Sendmail mailer is a classic and often exploited example of this problem. With the powerful security provided by the access control list, Windows NT is able to offer much finer granularity in assigning security to networked resources.

Standard Networking Components

Windows NT is ready to connect to most networks without any additional software. The standard package includes:

❑ **Drivers** for most popular Ethernet and token ring network cards.

❑ **TCP/IP Protocol** and applications.

❑ **NETBEUI Protocol:** This enables such features as connecting to network drives and print sharing on Windows NT, Windows for Workgroups, and LAN manager nodes.

❑ **Remote Access Services:** These services allow the user to connect to networks using a modem. RAS supports several networking protocols over serial lines. This enables you to connect to many network resources with only a modem.

This combination of networking allows Windows NT to work well in corporate networks as well as platform for "surfing the Information Super Highway."

Installing Networking

Normally, the networking components of Windows NT are installed when you install Windows NT. If you add a network card or modem to the machine later, you'll need to install Networking. You can install the networking services or add new services using the Networks applet in the Control Panel.

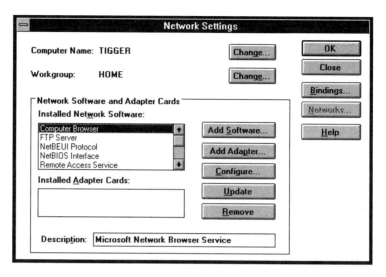

Windows NT Networks Control Panel.

If no networking is installed, you'll be prompted to install networking the first time you use the Networks control panel.

Because of the facilities provided by RAS, you can install networking services even if you have no network interface card.

NETBEUI Installation and Setup

NETBEUI is the natural language of Windows NT. An NT node with NETBEUI installed can share files and resources with Windows NT and Windows for Workgroups nodes. Once installed, NETBEUI requires no configuration.

In Windows NT environments using Windows NT Server, you'll have to join the local Windows NT domain. To join a domain, bring up the Networks control panel and select the second Change button. The text by this will either say "Domain" or "Workgroup," depending on your current configuration. The Change dialog box will appear as shown below:

Change Domain/Workgroup dialog box.

To join a Domain you'll need to get account name information from your system administrator.

TCP/IP Installation and Setup

Before installing TCP/IP you'll need to get several pieces of information from your LAN or system administrator:

❑ **TCP/IP Address:** Each node on a TCP/IP network requires a number that uniquely identifies it.

❑ **SUBNET Mask:** Many TCP/IP networks are split into "subnets" for administrative or network traffic routing purposes.

❑ **Domain Name Server Address(s):** Remembering the TCP/IP address of a particularly node is difficult. In UNIX networks a standard has evolved so that names can easily be mapped to numbers. The mapping of names to numbers is stored on a single machine that is queried whenever a name is used. This machine is the Domain Name Server or DNS Host.

❑ **WINS Server Address:** Windows Internet Naming Service is a system introduced in Windows NT 3.5. You'll find it on networks consisting of many Windows NT and Windows for Workgroups nodes where it simplifies name administration and resolution.

Once you've obtained all the TCP/IP information, you can go ahead and install the TCP/IP protocol. In the Networks control panel, select the Install Software button. Windows NT will display a dialog box with a list of all the available networking software:

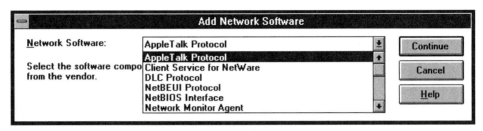

Add Network Software dialog box.

Select TCP/IP Protocol from the list of network software, then select Continue. This adds TCP/IP to the installed protocols. Before TCP/IP can be used it must be configured. From the Network control panel, select Configure. Windows NT will display the following dialog box.

TCP/IP configuration.

Enter the TCP/IP address and then select Advanced Options to configure other components of the TCP/IP setup. Windows NT will display the following dialog box.

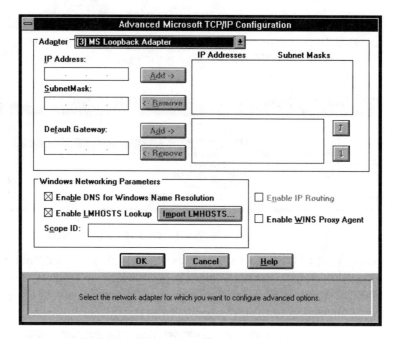

TCP/IP advanced configuration options.

TCP/IP addresses consist of four groups of digits. This net address is also mapped onto the machine name. Remembering names is always simpler than numbers, but Windows NT has to have some way of translating a name to an IP address. The TCP/IP implementation offers three choices for name resolution:

%SystemRoot%\system32\drivers\etc\lmhosts: This is the equivalent of the */etc/hosts file* on a UNIX system. The format is the same, for example:

129.135.252.227 nik

means that the nodename nik translates to the IP address "129.135. 252.227."

➡ **NOTE:** *The last line in the LMHOSTS file must have a carriage return following it or it will not be recognized*

Domain Name Service (DNS): Maintaining an LMHOSTS file is tedious. In the UNIX world this has been replaced by a standard referred to as DNS. In the DNS system a Domain Name Server maintains the database; others use the server to translate for them. Currently Windows NT only operates as a DNS client.

➥ **NOTE:** *The Windows NT 3.5 Resource Kit includes DNS server capability.*

Windows Internet Naming Service (WINS): WINS is the Microsoft equivalent of DNS. Currently only Microsoft clients can access a WINS server. In a mixed UNIX/Windows NT environment, DNS is much preferred.

You can get Windows NT to search various providers for DNS name resolution. They will be queried in the order you specify when adding them in the DNS setup dialog box.

IPX/SPX Installation and Setup

Windows NT can act as a gateway to LANs using the SPX/IPX protocol family. IPX/SPX is the protocol used by the Novell Netware File/Print sharing servers. Netware is the most widely used network protocol, so support for connection to its servers is critical.

You can install support for IPX/SPX during initial installation or at any time after the system is built. To install IPX/SPX you need to bring up the Networks Control Panel applet shown below.

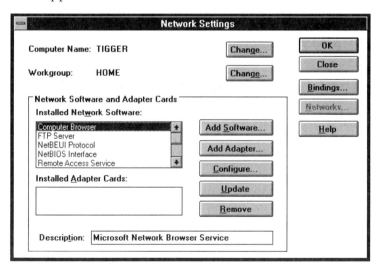

Network Control Panel.

Select the Add Software button. Windows NT will present a scrolling list of network software packages that can be installed.

Select NWLink IPX/SPX Compatible Transport. There is no user configuration, so once the software has loaded, select the OK button and reboot the system when asked.

AppleTalk Installation and Setup

Windows NT Server can provide file and printer sharing services for Apple Macintosh computers using the AppleTalk Protocol.

✔ **TIP:** *Because of the long filenames and other requirements of the Macintosh, only NTFS files systems can be shared. Appleshare protocols can only be started if Windows NT Server is installed on a NTFS filesystem.*

You can install support for Appleshare during initial installation or at any time after the system is built. To install Appleshare, you need to bring up the Networks Control Panel applet shown earlier.

1. Select the Add Software button. Windows NT will present a scrolling list of network software packages that can be installed.

2. Select the AppleTalk Protocol from the list of supported protocols.

3. Once the software has been installed, select the OK button and reboot the machine when prompted.

Client Service for Netware Installation and Setup

Windows NT can also be a client to a Netware 3.x server. To enable this facility, you need to install the Client Service for Netware module. This service implements the client of the protocol used by the Novell Netware File/Print sharing servers. Netware is the most widely used network protocol, so support for connection to its servers is critical.

You can install support for Client Service for Netware during initial installation or at any time after the system is built.

1. To install Client Service for Netware you need to bring up the Networks Control Panel applet.

2. Select the Add Software button. Windows NT will present a scrolling list of network software packages that can be installed.

3. Select the Client Service for Netware option. There is no user configuration, so once the software has loaded, select the OK button and reboot the system when asked.

➡ *NOTE: If you have a Windows NT Server node in the network, you can install the Netware Gateway service on that node and leave all the Windows NT clients alone.*

RAS Installation and Setup

You can install RAS on systems with or without a LAN connection. RAS provides the following capabilities:

❑ NETBEUI connectivity to remote LANs.

❑ TCP/IP connectivity using SLIP or PPP.

❑ IPX Connectivity to Netware servers.

The built-in SLIP/PPP connectivity makes Windows NT a very powerful system for connection to the Internet. Support for IPX over RAS gives you the ability to access Netware servers via a phone line.

During RAS installation, the system will attempt to find and identify a modem device. This takes a little time. If a modem is found, Windows NT will display the following dialog box.

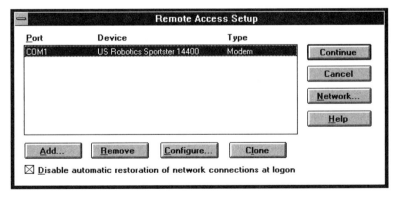

Remote Access Services Configuration dialog box.

If you don't need SLIP/PPP or IPX connectivity, you can accept all the defaults from the dialog box and continue. If SLIP/PPP or IPX is required, then select

Network and "check" the TCP/IP and/or IPX connectivity options in the following dialog box.

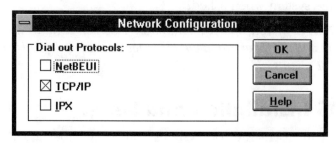

Remote Access Services Network Configuration dialog box.

RAS Serial Line Internet Protocol (SLIP)

Built in to the Remote Access Service package is a SLIP client. Using SLIP you can connect to TCP/IP networks, such as the Internet, using only a modem. Many Internet service providers can offer SLIP connectivity. Using SLIP and 14.4K modem you can access all the information available on the Internet. Before attempting to set up SLIP you'll need to obtain the following information:

1. TCP/IP address

2. DNS server addresses

3. Domain name

This information can be obtained from your Internet service provider or your system administrator if you are connecting at work. With this information you are ready to set up RAS to make SLIP connections. This is done using the following steps:

1. Start up the Control Panel and run the Networks applet.

2. If TCP/IP Protocol is not installed, then select the Add Software button and add the TCP/IP protocol.

3. With TCP/IP selected, select the Configure button.

4. Windows NT will display the TCP/IP Configuration dialog box. If you do not have a networking card installed, this will show with everything "grayed" out as in the following figure.

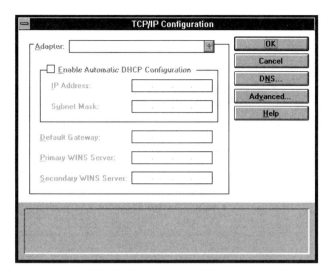

TCP/IP protocol configuration dialog box "grayed out."

5. Select DNS and fill in the DNS server information as well as a node name and domain name. The completed DNS Configuration dialog box will look like the following figure.

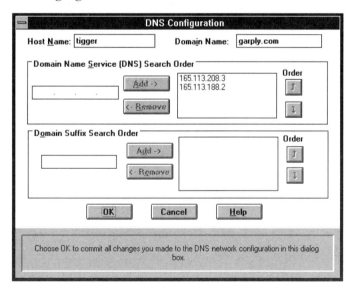

TCP/IP Protocol DNS configuration dialog box.

6. When you've added all the information, select the OK button to return to the previous dialog box.

7. Select OK from the TCP/IP Configuration dialog box.

8. From the Program Manager, open the Remote Access Service program group and select the Remote Access icon to launch the application.

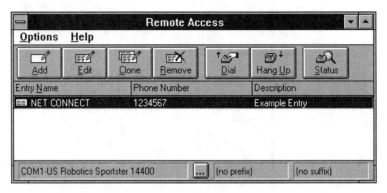

RAS session configuration.

9. Select the Add button. The remote access service will display the following dialog box.

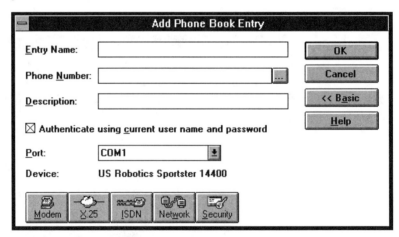

Add phone book entry.

10. Fill in the following text fields:

   ■ **Entry Name:** A name that will be used to identify this phone book entry for programs like RASDIAL and in the SWITCH.INF file.

   ■ **Phone Number:** The number to dial when making the connection.

   ■ **Description:** Optional text field to help identify the phone book entry.

11. Select the OK button when you've complete this stage.

12. Select the communications port that is attached to your modem.

13. Select the modem. The following dialog box is displayed.

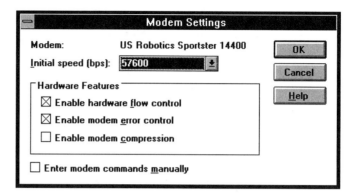

RAS modem configuration.

14. This dialog box is used to define the basic characteristics of the modem, such as speed and whether hardware compression is supported. Select the OK Button when you've complete this stage.

15. The ISDN and X.25 options are for sites using those facilities.

16. Select Network. The following dialog box is displayed:

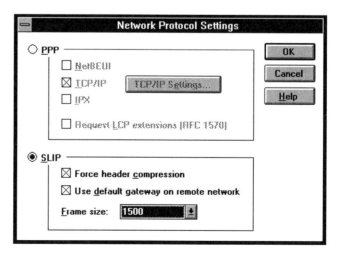

SLIP session parameters.

17. Select SLIP and its options will be highlighted. The options are:

- **Force Header Compression:** Many SLIP implementations allow software compression of the packet headers, often referred to as Van Jacobson SLIP or VJSLIP. Normally this is detected during the session initiation. If you know your remote site supports this, but it is not being recognized, you can force the connection to use this mode.

- **Use Default Gateway on Remote Network:** This allows you to route packets between a local Ethernet and the remote site.

- **Frame Size:** This is the maximum size of an IP packet transmitted during a RAS SLIP session. If the remote host supports a 1500 size, then it will be more efficient to use it.

18. Select the OK button when you've complete this stage.

19. Select Security, and the following dialog box is displayed.

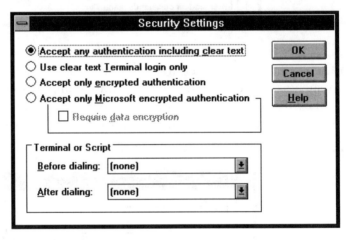

SLIP security settings.

20. The security dialog has several functions:

- How to handle authorization on remote host. The simplest one to use is "Accept any authentication including clear text." This works for most terminal servers as well as Windows NT and UNIX hosts.

- The terminal or script function allows you either run a script to complete connection or have the dialer pop up a terminal window for manual login. Scripts are created in the file *c:\windows\system32\ras\switch.inf.* In some cases you may need to have some actions taken before a connection is made. This can be done by defining a terminal as the script to run before a connection is made.

Once you've made all the necessary entries, you will have a phone book entry set up to make SLIP connections to the outside world.

RAS Point to Point Protocol

Setting up RAS point to point protocol (PPP) is almost identical to setting up SLIP. The only difference is in the Networks configuration dialog box.

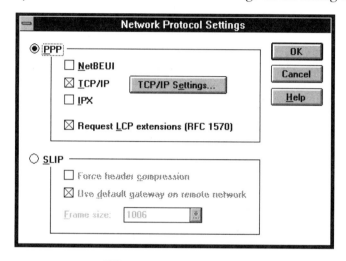

PPP session parameters.

Select the TCP/IP Settings button, and the PPP TCP/IP dialog box is displayed.

This dialog box allows you to configure the PPP protocol. You'll need some information from the PPP server to complete this dialog box, specifically:

❏ **Static or Dynamic IP Address:** Some servers will allocate you a IP address that doesn't change from one session to the next. The alternative is for the server to support the Dynamic Host Control Protocol (DHCP). DHCP allows the server to allocate an address from its address pool to each session.

❏ **DNS Server Addresses:** The Windows NT implementation of PPP allows the DNS information to be requested from the PPP host. If this does not work, you can force Windows NT to use DNS servers specified in this dialog box.

All other aspects of configuring PPP are identical to SLIP.

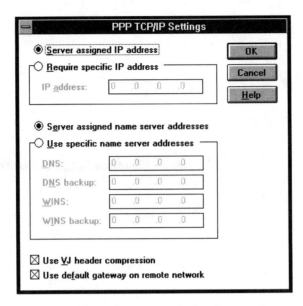

PPP configuration dialog box.

Sharing Files with Windows NT

Windows NT includes all the services required to share files on a network of machines that understand the NETBEUI network protocol. This includes the following.

❑   Windows NT running on any processor type

❑   Windows for Workgroups clients

❑   DOS with LAN Manager clients

❑   Several UNIX implementations including SCO UNIX and Solaris

❑   OS/2 LAN Manager clients

Using the file sharing services, you can create a network of machines that mount filesystems on remote machines. This allows you to store important files on servers where backups are conducted while continuing to work on the files on your local machine.

Mounting a Shared Filesystem

Filesystems can be mounted from the File Manger application or from the command line. In File Manager you can select the Disk→Connect Network Drive from the menu or select the Connect Network Drive icon as shown in the following figure.

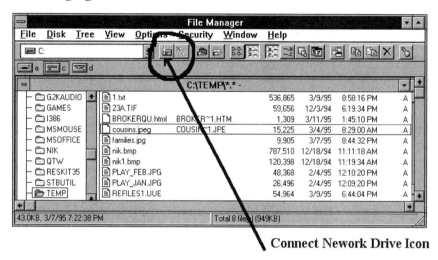

Connect Nework Drive Icon

Connect Network Drive icon.

The File Manager menu option and icon both display the Connect Network Drive dialog box.

This dialog box contains several fields and a display of all accessible shared network resources. The following list describes the fields.

❑ **Drive:** This is the drive letter that will be assigned to the next resource you mount. You can select a particular drive letter from the list button by this field.

❑ **Path:** The resource location is in the form of *//node/resource*. If you know what this field should contain for the resource you want to mount, you can type it in. Otherwise you can wait for the Shared Directories window to fill.

❑ **Connect As:** When a directory is shared, you can assign a username and password to it. If you are mounting such a protected resource, you will need to know the username and password.

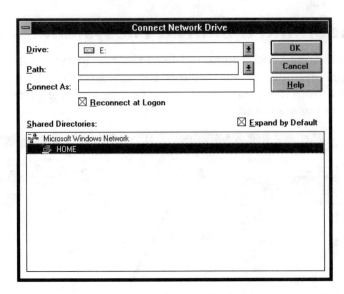

Connect Network Drive dialog box.

❏ **Shared Directories:** When you enter the Connect Network Drive dialog box, Windows NT will search the network for all mountable resources. The results of this search are placed in this window. On large networks this may take some time. To select a particular resource, use the mouse to highlight the appropriate entry in this window. The Path: field will fill automatically.

When you've selected the resource you want to mount, select OK. The resource will be mounted and its files will be accessible from File Manager in exactly the same way as local files.

Mounting a Shared Filesystem from the Command Line

Sometimes you may need to mount a filesystem from the command line. This is typically done in scripts. An example might be a backup script that mounts shared resources and does a backup of it files. The command line in Windows NT is accessed by running the DOS command line window. The icon in Program Manager is highlighted below.

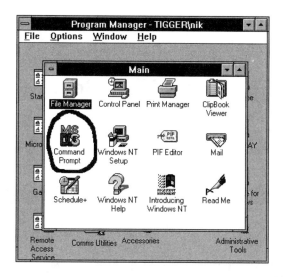

Program Manager command prompt icon.

This icon will launch a command window, allowing you issue DOS style commands. The command to mount a network resource is shown in the following command window.

```
Microsoft(R) Windows NT(TM)
(C) Copyright 1985-1995 Microsoft Corp.

c:\nik>net use /?
The syntax of this command is:

NET USE [devicename | *] [\\computername\sharename[\volume] [password | *]]
        [/USER:[domainname\]username]
        [[/DELETE] | [/PERSISTENT:{YES | NO}]]

NET USE [devicename | *] [password | *]] [/HOME]

NET USE [/PERSISTENT:{YES | NO}]


c:\nik>net use  g: \\archive\x29-project_
```

DOS Command Window with Net use command.

Note the syntax used to specify the net resource is the same as the one used in the Connect Network Drive dialog box Path: field.

Sharing a Local Filesystem

Windows NT also allows you to export local resources, allowing it to be both client and server in a network. To export a resource, first select the directory to be exported. Then you can either select the Disk→Share As option in the File Manager menu or select the Share As icon shown in the following figure.

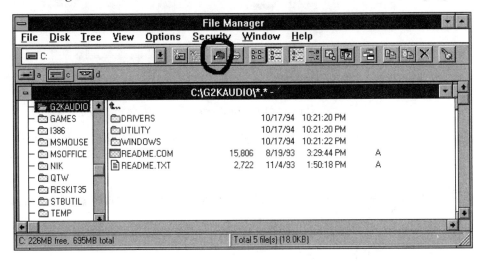

File Manager Share As icon.

Whichever method you choose, the following options are displayed.

❏ **Share Name:** This is the name that this resource will be known by.

❏ **Path:** The full pathname of the resource, including the drive letter and any directory path. This will be filled in from the directory currently selected in the File Manager.

❏ **Comment:** Any comments you want other users to see when they mount this resource.

❏ **User Limit:** The maximum number of remote connections that you will allow for this share.

When you export a resource, you can also set up protections so that only certain people can mount the resource. This is useful in office and project environments where you wish to limit access to sensitive or personal information. To set protections on a shared resource, select the Permissions... button. The following dialog box is displayed.

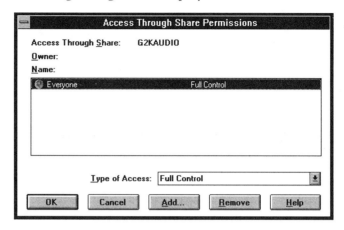

Share Permissions dialog box.

Permissions can be set for single users or for groups of users. By default the share is exported to everyone on the network. This dialog box has a complete context-sensitive help page that is accessed by selecting the help button. Briefly, the options and buttons here provide the following facilities:

❏ **Add:** This option displays the following dialog box, which lists all users and groups on the local network. Select the users or groups that you wish to have access to the share, and then select the type of access you will allow. When you've set up the permissions, select the OK button to return to the Permissions dialog box, which will have been updated.

❏ **Remove:** Select a user or group to remove from the list of users with access to the share and then select the Remove button.

❏ **Type of Access:** This option allows you to alter the type of access granted to a user or group. Types of access allowed are:

■ **No Access (None):** Allows no access to the share.

■ **Read:** Allows read-only access to files in the directory.

■ **Change:** Allows full read and write access to files and directories on the shared resource.

■ **Full Control (All):** Allows you to change ownership of the file and modify other file attributes such as read and write privileges.

This ability to assign individual and group permissions to files is often referred to as *Access Control Lists.*

Sharing a Local Filesystem from the Command Line

Windows NT also allows shares to be created from the command line. The next figure shows the syntax of the NET SHARE command as well as an example command line.

```
c:\nik>
c:\nik>
c:\nik>
c:\nik>
c:\nik>
c:\nik>
c:\nik>
c:\nik>
c:\nik>net share /?
The syntax of this command is:

NET SHARE sharename
          sharename=drive:path [/USERS:number | /UNLIMITED]
                            [/REMARK:"text"]
          sharename [/USERS:number | /UNLIMITED]
                  [/REMARK:"text"]
          {sharename | devicename | drive:path} /DELETE

c:\nik>net share tempdir=c:\temp /unlimited /remark:"Temp Directory"
tempdir was shared successfully.

c:\nik>
```

Syntax and example for NET SHARE command.

The command line versions of File Manager options are useful when writing scripts that cannot interact with GUI utilities like the File Manager.

Universal Naming Convention Paths

It is not actually necessary to mount a shared drive in order to access files on that drive. Assuming you have permission to access the files, you can refer directly to files using the following syntax:

```
\node\share\filepath
```

So for example to access file *fred.exe* on share *files* on node *server*, the universal naming convention path would be

```
\\server\files\fred.exe
```

This facility can be useful if you have a program on a remote system that you want to place in a Program Manager group on your system. You cannot easily use a "driver letter" path such as "e:/fred.exe" because the drive letter will change, depending on the order you mount shared directories. Instead you can use the universal naming convention path. The following figure shows the Program Item Properties dialog box from the Program Manager with a universal naming convention path:

Local program item using universal naming convention path to remote executable.

Summary

In this chapter you've seen many of the features of Windows NT networking, including the following:

❏ Simple setup through dialog boxes.

❏ Multiple protocol support.

❏ PPP and SLIP support from RAS.

❏ RAS scripting.

❏ How to connect to network resources.

❏ How to offer local resources to colleagues on the Internet.

❏ The Universal Naming Convention for accessing resources on the Internet.

No desktop PC operating system has ever offered such a variety of network options in such an easy-to-use package.

Windows NT, Multimedia, and CAD/CAE

Introduction

Using more than one type of medium for communicating an idea, selling a proposal, reviewing a design, or walking through a refinery as viewed on a workstation's screen is possible using the tools available in Windows NT. These tools have collectively been known of as *multimedia*, where sound, video clips, and animated images generated from modeling programs are used for illustrating complex ideas in a simple manner. Using the available tools, for example, a designer can "fly through" a completed building, processing plant, or campus that has been drawn and then rendered. Using the capabilities of electronic mail as a medium for sharing files, designers can share both the drawing files and comments on a proposed building using this approach.

Multimedia holds the promise of making the entire process of communicating and presenting concepts from a workstation clearer, because more than just the written word or the sketched drawing are presented to the person interested in the information. Throughout this chapter, the requirements that multimedia places on a workstation are described, along with a profile of how specific applications now have the capability of offering multimedia support without any additional software.

Upgrading Your Computer for Multimedia

Taking the steps to get your Windows NT workstation compatible with multimedia applications entails getting a sound card installed, purchasing speakers, and getting the utilities up and running for this type of application. Multimedia is a term that refers to all facets of having multiple sources of media used on a workstation. The most common type of multimedia is sound. For a complete list of sound cards that work with Windows NT, see the Windows NT Hardware Compatibility List. If in doubt, buy a Creative Labs Sound Blaster 16-bit card.

In looking at the options you have for upgrading your Windows NT workstation to handle multimedia tasks, let's examine the levels of application support available in technical applications. At the first level, and most pervasive, is support of sound and motion-based presentations. This level includes the ability to send and receive electronic mail with vocal messages embedded within the mail messages, the ability to listen to annotation designs and drawings with comments provided in sound clips, the option of retrieving and listening to sound clips pulled from World Wide Web sites and various sources around the Internet, and the ability to listen to music CDs on your workstation while completing other tasks.

At this first and most basic level (and most popular) Windows NT-based workstations are also capable of viewing files that show movement of objects, even animation. Because the minimum hardware requirement for a Windows NT workstation includes a VGA monitor and at least 12MB of RAM along with an Intel 80486 microprocessor, the various types of files that include on-screen video are easily shown. In fact, the Media Player in Windows NT includes the capability of playing musical CDs, viewing video files, and even listening to music and voice files that have been translated into digital form.

The world of the audiovisual operator is a far cry from when you saw English & American Literature movies in high school! Now, using multimedia you can write, produce, and display your own movies, all from the desktop.

At the second level of multimedia systems, there are more complex tools for editing and mixing sounds and visual effects. Although the Windows NT workstation may be the "brain" of this type of multimedia system, many of the peripherals have 32-bit processors themselves, and are typically used for creating special effects in commercials and movies of all kinds. These pieces of equipment provide for matte filming, a specific technique of having one portion of the screen stay constant as the animated portions of the presentation are projected electronically into the other areas of the screen. Equipment used to produce these effects and others costs thousands of dollars and is typically found in the production departments of Fortune 1000 companies. Staffs responsible for these systems are from the creative arts, film, and occasionally from the computer-generated art industries. This level of multimedia makes it possible to create short subjects, even complete movies using animation.

Multimedia and the Technical User

What are the implications of multimedia for you? As a member of the technical community, you have seen how fast computing technologies change. Multimedia is no different, as can be seen with every new application that provides for full motion animation, rendering, and the capability of creating MPEG files directly from a series of raster or vector images. What is certain that within the next five years multimedia will become a tool for more effectively communicating complex technical tasks in a simple manner.

Take for example the construction of a new building. The building is first defined in MicroStation Version 5, with renderings applied to ensure the walls appear as they should, and the light source shows the proposed building during a bright, spring day. Multimedia has made the building easier to sell to a potential client. The ability to embed verbal comments into a file makes it possible for the architect to give a "tour" of the building before it is even built. Customers interested in seeing why an architect added the entrance at the corner of the building can simply point and click on a comment box embedded in the file to hear the explanation.

Basic System Requirements

In considering a move into the world of multimedia, it's a good starting point to get a clear understanding of the characteristics your Windows NT workstation needs in order to be compatible with multimedia applications. Here is a listing of the various hardware and software requirements that a Windows NT workstation needs in order to play multimedia applications. As with any attribute or feature of a Windows NT workstation, more is better.

❑ **A dual-speed CD-ROM supported by Windows NT:** Having a dual-speed CD-ROM gives you the necessary speed to pull larger files from the CD itself, and the SCSI-based host adapter provides faster performance.

In the world of the technical professional, having a CD-ROM disk drive that can read larger, more complex files fast is a great advantage.

❏ **At least 32MB of RAM:** Although many Multimedia Upgrade Kits can run in 16MB of RAM, system performance will suffer as many applications contend for memory resources. Be sure to have at least 32MB of RAM on your workstation before using it for multimedia-based tasks. Memory is an area of computing where more is better, so if you can load up on even more than 32MB, the performance of multimedia tasks and applications will be that much faster.

❏ **An Intel-based 80486 workstation:** This is a minimum requirement for doing multimedia tasks, because many times you'll want to have either AutoCAD, Pro/ENGINEER, or any of the other processor-intensive applications up and running at the same time you are working with multimedia. Having at least an 80486-based workstation ensures that the foreground application, or the one that you use all the time, is not affected by the performance of the multimedia applications you are using.

❏ **Internet access:** Being able to pull images, entire video clips in MPEG format, sound files, and wave files from the Internet makes it possible to further customize a multimedia presentation. Either Mosaic from NCSA or NetScape from NetScape Communications are equally adept at navigating the Internet and giving you the necessary tools for getting multimedia files downloaded from the various World Wide Web home pages located throughout the Internet. Later in this chapter you'll see how you can use the Internet's vast resources to add the effects you want to your presentation. The following figure shows an example of the Silicon Graphics home page. Notice that there are sections on this home page where you can download various images if you choose. NCSA's Mosaic was used to reach the SGI Home Page.

❏ **Display:** At a minimum, having a VGA monitor is required to run Windows NT. With the added requirements of multimedia, consider getting a higher resolution monitor with a 17-inch screen, along with a screen buffer of at least 2MB. The difference in refresh rates is also important in multimedia, so choose a monitor that is specifically designed for graphics applications.

❏ **Accessories:** For producing multimedia presentations, it may be useful to have access to video capture hardware, a microphone for voice annotation, and a recordable CD-ROM drive.

Use the Internet to gain access to multimedia resources.

❐ **Output Devices:** Depending on the type of multimedia you are doing, you can select from the low-end 300 dots per inch (dpi) laser printers, through the ones that support 600 and 1200 dpi printing and plotting resolutions. These printers are monochrome and provide emulations or command sets that make it possible to place them directly on a Windows NT workstation. If you are generating color output, you have a wide range of choices, both from a price and performance perspective. At the low end of the color printer market, the HP XL300 is a good choice. It's based on inkjet technology and sells for under $4000 (U.S.). In the mid-range there are thermal transfer printers costing between $3000 and $5000. At the high end of the desktop color printer market there is the HP Color LaserJet at approximately $7000 or any of the dye sublimation thermal transfer printers at between $8000 and $20,000. Dye sublimation is a variation of the thermal transfer technology developed several years ago and creates photographic-quality output.

Multimedia: Hype or Reality?

Is multimedia a technology in search of a solution? Or is it like networking, where the market demands had to mature to meet the technology level of currently available products? Multimedia-based tools are being integrated on an application-specific basis, rather than multimedia itself becoming an application in itself. With the ability to "fly through" various designs or render a design file into a shaded image available in well-known applications, multimedia is slowly becoming integrated into design, drafting, and engineering applications. What was once a technology in search of market has become a set of tools now being integrated as point solutions in applications that have broader appeal that just the ability to record and play back sounds or motion pictures on screen.

Throughout this section you'll learn how multimedia works, the emerging standards, and levels of compatibility between existing multimedia-compatible applications. Keep in mind that multimedia is not an application in and of itself; rather, it is a series of tools for making it easier to communicate with others.

How Multimedia Works

At the center of multimedia are the efforts at universities and research centers to increase the quality of both still and animated image representation and to ensure the most accurate representation of sounds possible. Universities, companies, and research centers share their results through the use of home pages on the Internet. Later in this chapter you will learn of locations and http addresses on the Internet you can use to get the latest information on multimedia developments. With so much research being completed on multimedia, it's a good idea to get an idea of how multimedia systems operate, especially in the context of technical applications. Keep in mind that a multimedia system is just that—a system of interworking components that present a cohesive whole when combined.

A Windows NT workstation capable of being used for creating true multimedia applications will have the following characteristics. These product features can be relaxed if you plan to play musical CDs on your Windows NT workstation. If you are planning to create full animations or full video clips and save them into MPEG files so they can be recorded to CD or made available over the Internet, you will need the minimum system requirements in the following list. The following figure shows a diagram of a state-of-the-art multimedia system capable of creating and then saving MPEG files. The list of requirements earlier in this chapter describes the minimum requirements for a Windows NT workstation to be able to show multimedia files. The following requirements pertain to a Windows NT workstation being used for multimedia production.

A Windows NT multimedia production system.

System Requirements for Multimedia Production

❏ **Video Capture Card:** Inserted into a spare EISA or PCI slot, the capabilities of this type of card makes it possible to capture a single image from a video monitor and then change its appearance through the use of accompanying software. Also included in many of these video capture cards is the ability to record video images directly to an MPEG file on a disk. These video cards have the ability to read animated images on screen as well, and then save the recorded motion images into MPEG formats. Conversely, you can also use these video cards for taking motion images from the Windows NT workstation and recording them directly to a VCR running in NTSC or PAL formats. These video capture cards have interfaces for recording directly to CD-ROMs external to a Windows NT workstation as well.

❑ **Sound Card:** Many of the PC manufacturers are now selling upgrade kits for DOS and Windows-based systems so users can listen to CDs and play various games. For production of multimedia projects, it's a good idea to use a sound card that includes utilities for editing Windows-compatible audiovisual (*.AVI*) files. Sound cards vary in quality, with Turtle Beach Systems having one of the best rated sound cards available. This sound card requires a spare EISA slot in your Windows NT workstation.

❑ **Large-Screen Monitor:** This is the most essential component in a multimedia production system besides the hard disk. Reliability is key with this component, in addition to the resolutions supported. The NEC MultiSync 6FG and the MAG MX17F are two of the higher rated monitors designed specifically for multimedia application development.

❑ **System Memory and Speed:** A multimedia production system should have at least 32MB of system memory, with more available, the better.

❑ **Processor:** For best results you should use a Pentium, Alpha, or MIPS RISC processor-based system.

❑ **SCSI-Based Hard Disk and Adapter:** The best choice for drives on a system running Windows NT are those conforming to the Small Computer System Interface (SCSI) standard. SCSI is designed to provide performance in a multitasking environment offering several features not available on IDE or Enhanced IDE drives. Windows NT supports many different SCSI controllers. See the Hardware Compatibility List for a complete listing. Several companies have done excellent work in the development of SCSI protocol standards, and therefore have state-of-the-art products developed specifically for technical applications and multimedia production, two areas requiring large files and fast data transfers. Future Domain of Tustin, CA, and Adaptec of Mountain View, CA, are two companies that have adapters that meet the needs of the technical professional who is producing multimedia applications. Seagate and Maxtor both have excellent SCSI-based hard disks that are suitable for use in a multimedia production system. At a minimum, a Windows NT workstation used for multimedia production should include a 1GB hard disk drive.

❏ **Double-Speed CD-ROM:** This is an initial requirement since both the size of files being retrieved from CD and the frequency of file retrieval translate into at least a double-speed CD-ROM.

❏ **Write-Once Read Many (WORM) CD-ROM Disk Drive:** The Pinnacle Micro CD-1000 is an example of a WORM drive that multimedia developers use for writing their deliverable products to CD for distribution. This is an excellent product for doing limited production runs, where 100 CD copies are needed in a week. For larger production runs, it's a good idea to create a master CD and hire a service bureau to create the quantity you need.

❏ **High-Speed Modem:** This is a definite requirement to ensure Internet access for the developer. A 14.4K baud modem is a baseline requirement for logging onto the Internet and for transferring files from Mosaic home pages located around the world.

❏ **High-Resolution Printers:** For getting proofs of rendered images and printing documentation, two high-resolution printers are needed. A high-resolution color printer for printing out rendered images can be invaluable in presenting the results of a project to a customer, whether internal or external to the company or university. A high-resolution monochrome laser printer is useful for printing documentation showing how the multimedia product is used.

❏ **Internet Software and Access:** This is absolutely essential to the Windows NT multimedia production system. Having NCSA's Mosaic program (you'll learn how to get a copy of Mosaic later in this chapter) and a subscription to an Internet service provider make it possible to see what the current research in multimedia is yielding, in addition to downloading public domain images and MPEG files. If you decide to create a Mosaic home page for your multimedia products, the Internet access provider you choose can set up the home page for you by renting you disk space. This is a good idea since it means everytime someone accesses your home page, your system won't be tied up. If you have several Windows NT workstations available and want to create a home page on your own, then use the documents found in the Windows NT 3.5 Resource Kit.

❏ **Multimedia Authoring Tools:** Using Corel Draw and IconAuthor in conjunction with AutoCAD, MicroStation, and Pro/ENGINEER provide you with a powerful combination of tools for creating state-of-the-art multimedia presentations. In these technical applications, you can have a fly-through of a design completed. Once created, you can record the fly-through as an MPEG file and embed it within a multimedia project. The project could be anything—a game, instructional video on how to use a product, or a proposal to build a new airport.

Emerging CD-ROM Standards

With the intensive growth of multimedia fueled by dropping processor prices and the increased availability of files over the Internet, there are CD-ROM standards now in development and included in products that are being shipped. The dominant standards of CD-DA, CD-ROM, CD-ROM/XA, and CD-I are currently available in commercially available products. In addition, the Photo-CD from Kodak also exemplifies another type of CDE. Finally, there are single-session versus multi-session CD disk drives and disks. This section explains the differences between these technologies, helping you to understand how each plays a role in the world of multimedia for the technical professional.

CD-DA: In the beginning there was CD-DA (Compact Disc-Digital Audio) or standard music CDs. CD-DA was the predecessor to the CD-ROM when people realized that you could store large volumes of computer data on an optical disk. CD-ROM disks can save up to 650MB of data. CD-ROM quickly became an interchangeable storage media with hard disks. The only difference is that CD-ROMs cannot be written to multiple times.

CD-I: Next, the CD-I (Compact Disk-Interactive) format was developed. This format is used predominantly in the consumer electronics area of the market, where optical disks are used for entertainment. This format has been designed to deliver music, graphics, text, animation, and video all from the same optical disk. Unlike the CD-ROM drives, the CD-I disk drives do not require a complete workstation. They only require a player. The CD-I players available today plug directly into a TV and are typically used for playing back video clips of all types, including full-length movies. CD-I is actually backward compatible to musical CD-ROMs. A CD-I player can play musical CD-ROMs for example.

CD-ROM/XA: After CD-I proved that the entertainment audiences of the world accepted movies on compact disk, the CD-ROM/XA (eXtended Architecture) was developed. This approach to recording data moved the CD technology back to workstations. This CD-ROM/XA approach includes the capability of compressing audio, as found in the CD-I drives. Since CD-ROM/XA includes this capability, it became possible to record both compressed visual and audio, so that entire movies could be played back on a workstation. This technology began to revolutionize the approach multimedia developers used for creating products. The CD-ROM/XA technology actually brought back the features of CD-I that were originally developed for the consumer markets to the computing and technical professional marketplaces.

Photo-CD: After CDROM/XA was developed, Kodak pioneered the development of the Photo-CD. Kodak's approach is to include photographic quality images on a CD for distribution to a mass market. Philips, the electronics conglomerate worked in conjunction with Kodak to develop the format for storing images on CD that preserves the highest resolution possible.

Concurrent with the development of CD-ROM technology, there has been constant experimentation on write-once read-many (WORM) and write-many read-many (WMRM) optical disk technologies. These two technologies make it possible to create CD-ROMs for use with read-only disk drives. The Pinnacle Micro 1000 disk drive is one of the first disk drives to use WORM technology for creating either single-session or multisession CDs. A recordable CD that supports only the single session standard can only be written to once. Even if the first write operation only places one byte on the disk, it cannot be changed. A multisession CD writer can carry out several write operations to a suitable CD. This technology was originally developed for the Photo-CD standard where it was necessary to be able to add images to a disk as films were developed. Many CD players have the capability of reading single-session CDs, with more CD-ROM disk drives having the capability of reading multisession CDs. Why do people create multisession CDs? Because they want to create programs that overlay sounds and a great deal of other information.

Getting Multimedia Resources from the Internet

There's an entirely new approach to presenting information available to any computer user, especially those using Windows NT. Using the Internet as the medium by which messages are transmitted, thousands of companies are now making information about their products, services, even their employees known through home pages. A home page is really a graphical interface that makes it possible to organize key areas of a business and then provide a series of subsidiary screens, showing the various aspects of the company. In addition to businesses, thousands of universities, high schools, secondary schools, and elementary schools are now on line with their own home pages. The following figure shows an example of the Intergraph Home Page on the Internet. Notice how the various major categories of information are organized, making it easy for someone interested in learning about that specific area to simply point and click on the item of interest.

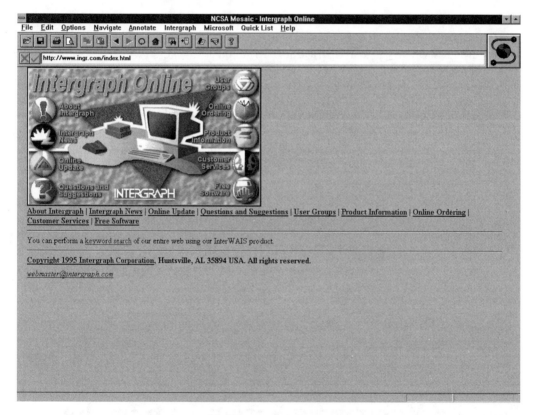

The Intergraph home page.

Each of these home pages has an http address that defines its location on the World Wide Web (WWW). This web is actually a network of mostly UNIX workstations that have the necessary software loaded to function as a server.

Recent market research studies suggest that over 75% of the Web servers in use today are running on UNIX-based workstations, with the remaining running on Intel-based platforms. Of those running on Intel-based systems, the majority are most likely running Windows NT. The majority of Internet users are technical professionals interested in both sharing and obtaining free information on subjects of interest.

Throughout the Internet, there are home pages dedicated to thousands of subjects. At present, there is no single software tool or search engine for navigating the Internet to find every single Web site that might have multimedia information. Instead, there are several search engines, each with a varying level of performance. For example, if you are searching for an MPEG file that represents an overview of an airport that has been drawn in vectors (much like the Intergraph video showing the Hong Kong airport), then you could use the Yahoo list on the Internet to find every site on the Internet that has a listing for *MPEG* files.

The *MPEG* file format compresses a series of video sequences using a common coding syntax as defined in the ISO/IEC 13818 Part 2 as defined by the International Organization for Standardization and the International Electro-technical Commission (IEC). In short, *MPEG* is the file format that makes it possible to create series of moving frames so they appear as a continuous motion. *MPEG* files are primarily used in education and the sciences, but are also being experimented with for animation and entertainment-based games and applications. The following figure shows an *MPEG* file being played on the Windows NT desktop.

Viewing MPEG movies in Windows NT.

The word *Internet* is sometimes used interchangeably with the phrase "Information Superhighway." In reality, the Internet is a network of computers spread throughout the world, with access to vast repositories of information. Until recently, navigating among these information resources was difficult and expensive. Today, there are several tools that make this much simpler. Foremost among these tools are "Web browsers," such as Mosaic or NetScape.

Imagine a building in downtown Manhattan a city block wide and over seventy stories tall. Now fill each floor with bookshelves and books, each one on a specific subject, complete with the most current writings and the most current graphics created to explain subjects. If we call this building Internet Central, then you get an idea of how much information is available free over the Internet using Mosaic or NetScape. For those interested in the world of multimedia, the Internet has actually contributed to the growth of this area by providing a medium of exchange (magnetic files containing both sound and imagery) that can be sent or requested from any location in the world.

Universities actively involved in the development of multimedia technology include the University of Arizona, University of California Santa Cruz, Boston University, Harvard, and the University of Chicago. One of the most interesting Web sites displaying the results of multimedia research is the University of Chicago's site, which shows current projects underway that show how multimedia can be more easily integrated into various application areas. There are many web sites located around the world containing valuable multimedia information. The two best I have seen for learning about multimedia and its various formats are the Naval Research Lab Network Navigator (*http://net-lab.itd.nrl.navy.mil/MM.html*), which includes pointers to a Gopher site that has plenty of text-based documents explaining the implications of network-based multimedia, and has several excellent reference documents on multimedia. Another site is Allison Zhang's Home Page, titled Multimedia File Formats on the Internet (*http://ac.dal.ca/-dong/contents.html*). The following figure shows Allison Zhang's home page.

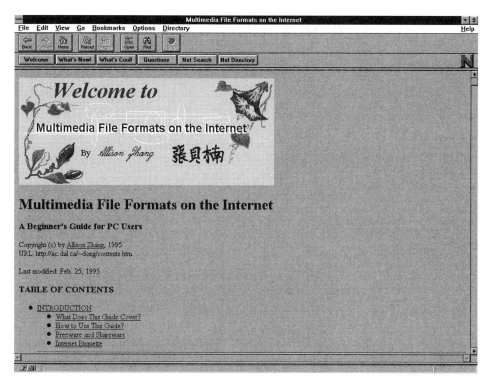

Allison Zhang's home page.

How Multimedia and CAD/CAE Work Together

With so many trends impacting the multimedia industry, how do CAD/CAE and these tools work together? CAD application developers are taking the tools that accentuate the strengths of their applications and placing them in their programs. With the introduction of visualization software, there now exists the opportunity to create animation directly from the technical desktop of a Windows NT workstation. What was once done using $100,000 systems specifically designed for creating animated logos such as the NBC corporate logo can now be done on a Windows NT workstation, costing less than a tenth of that amount. Throughout this section you'll learn about visualization software on Windows NT, applications of multimedia in CAD, and how to plan for multimedia in your business.

Visualization Software: The New Frontier

Taking complex data and representing it in simple terms is the goal of visualization software. There has long been powerful visualization programs on the UNIX platform, yet today there are companies just discovering the potential for visualization software on the Windows NT platform. The segments that visualization software serves include solids modeling and mechanical design. At the low-end of the solids modeling marketplace, there are the in-built capabilities of AutoCAD and MicroStation Version 5. In the mid-range of the market, there is ModelView from Intergraph Corporation. At the high-end of the market, there are programs for creating mechanical parts and assemblies, such as Parametric Technologies' Pro/ENGINEER. The following figure shows an example of an image being generated in Intergraph's EMS product.

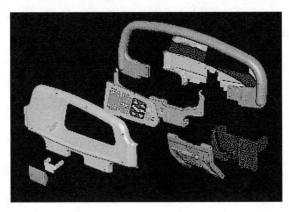

An image being generated in Intergraph's EMS for Windows NT.

Applications for Multimedia in CAD/CAE

How is multimedia being used in the CAD/CAE marketplace? How will it be used in the future? Here are a few of the areas where the tools and techniques of multimedia are finding use in architectural, engineering, construction, mapping, and mechanical application areas. The Windows NT operating system's 32-bit capability makes it an ideal platform for these applications. Keep in mind that this area of the Windows NT technical desktop is changing every few months and that more and more multimedia applications are being added to this list all the time.

❏ Computer companies are the ones pushing the envelope of creating multimedia applications to their maximum extent possible. Take for example national sales meetings where new workstations are being introduced. Sun Microsystems, Silicon Graphics, and Intergraph all use multimedia systems for creating life-like representations of animated sequences showing such diverse subjects as moonscapes, jet fighters, and space stations docking with new, slim line workstations. These presentations are written to video tape and distributed throughout the world coincident with a new product launch.

❏ Companies are increasingly putting their entire product catalogs on CD-ROM for distribution worldwide. In addition, the entire contents of a CD-ROM can be made available through the Internet to offices with dial-in capability. The following figure shows an example of the introductory screen for the Intergraph Interactive Catalog. Through the use of this catalog, both salespersons and customers can learn about the new product offerings, watch animated short subject films that illustrate how products are used, and view product summaries.

Intergraph's CD-ROM Interactive Catalog.

This catalog is revised every six months using a multimedia production system very similar to the one originally described earlier in this chapter.

❏   Proposals showing the impact of a new freeway on an existing landscape actively use multimedia to more precisely communicate the environmental impact of development. Recently, the Houston Chamber of Commerce used multimedia techniques to compare the impact of a proposed freeway on the existing urban environment. The results of the analysis showed that the appearance would actually be more pleasing with the roadway compared with how it looks currently. In addition, traffic flow would actually be enhanced with the new highway design.

❏   City governments are embracing multimedia as a tool for showing the impact of building modifications and design improvements. Working in conjunction with architectural firms, city governments have planned, proposed, and completed entire neighborhood restorations using multimedia to show the before and after effects of proposed buildings.

Planning for Multimedia in a CAD/CAE Business

There has been an increasing ability of CAD-based companies to win new business using multimedia to persuasively communicate a new product concept or proposed project. Using full motion video, for example, Fluor Corporation has been able to sell new development projects to government agencies from several foreign countries. Using the techniques of showing before and after images of a proposed renovation, architectural companies in San Francisco have had the opportunity to get contracts for renovating old office buildings into areas that can be put to new uses. Companies in the process of developing mechanical assemblies use multimedia to communicate how the actual part will function by itself and as a component of the larger system. Companies that actively use multimedia in their CAD operating share these common characteristics:

❑ **Multimedia Is a Business Development Tool:** Companies that have integrated CAD, mapping, or mechanical applications into their workflow see multimedia first as a tool for generating new business. Being able to propose a new bridge and stating that it will hold up to an earthquake can be proven through calculations, but it's much more persuasive to be able to show the proposed bridge being affected by a earthquake at 7.0 on the Richter scale. Showing how the various joints of the bridge flex and compensate from the stresses of an earthquake will lead that much more quickly to winning new business for the design firm.

❑ **Multimedia Is a Communication Tool:** Companies successfully using multimedia consistently use the various audio and visual components to make interesting, clear, and imaginative presentations of new product information for both internal and external audiences. For example, Sun Microsystems uses multimedia to communicate new product information to their sales force and customers, stressing the feature-to-benefit relationship and performance of a new workstation or peripheral. Sun also takes new product information at the technical level, making documentation that includes color images and multimedia capability.

❑ **Educational Uses:** The highest growth area of multimedia today is in the educational segment. Sun Microsystems uses a point-and-click approach for illustrating how a workstation can be serviced. In addition, the operating system parameters included in UNIX are also displayed within the context of a multimedia system.

Another approach used by CAD companies for educating their customers is demonstration diskettes and help files. Given the increasing complexity of CAD application programs, many companies are now using Robohelp II and IconAuthor to create on-line documentation that fully illustrates a specific command. Digital Equipment Corporation is one company that has embraced multimedia for documentation, shipping both the operating system and system documentation on the same CD. The following figure shows an example of how Silicon Graphics is using multimedia to communicate the aspects of their workstations customers need to know.

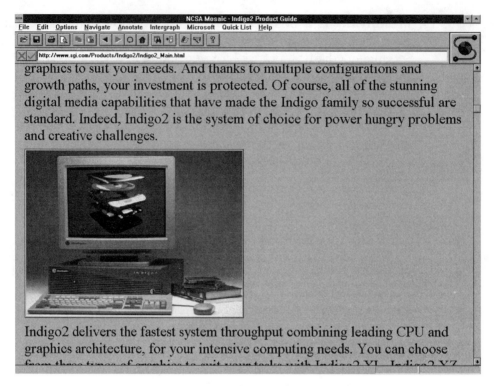

Using Multimedia to create on-line documentation.

☐ **Internal and External Communication:** CAD-based companies also are increasingly using the tools of multimedia for communicating the status of new projects to other members of the organization. Silicon Graphics and Intergraph both use this approach for communicating recent sales successes and innovative uses of existing products. In addition to sales and marketing information, technical information is extensively distributed on multimedia.

Take for example Microsoft's use of multimedia within their Win32 Developer's Kit and the Microsoft TechNet CD program, which makes the latest development information available to software developers creating new CAE and drafting applications. The extensive use of CD-ROM and multimedia technology is a model by which others creating multimedia-based tools for communication of concepts outside an organization should look at. In addition to the TechNet CD being available to Microsoft Developers, the same information is available directly over the Internet from Microsoft's home page (*http://www.microsoft.com*). The following figure shows the Microsoft TechNet CD available through the Internet using NCSA's Mosaic program.

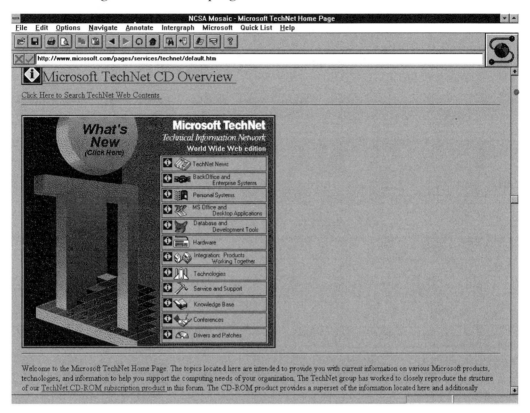

The Microsoft TechNet CD Program is available through the Internet at http://www.microsoft.com.

❏ **Willing To Make Investment:** Universities often receive grants for furthering the knowledge base of multimedia, with a significant portion of the budget going to new equipment. The ability of companies to make corresponding investments has limited the acceptance of multimedia production capability being integrated into engineering, marketing communications, or product development centers.

While this was certainly the case during the previous 20 years, recent developments on the Windows NT platform make it possible for companies to experiment with state-of-the-art multimedia production using the latest tools available. Intergraph's Video Engine 100 makes it possible for companies to create full-motion video using the dual-Pentium TD-5 workstation shipped as part of the entire configuration. Priced from $19,900 for the entry-level unit to $35,900 for the top model, the Video Engine 100 takes all the necessary components of a multimedia production system and places them into a single product. Included in the Video Engine 100 is the capability of creating *JPEG*-compressed motion files that can be converted into *.AVI* files for use on both Microsoft Windows and Windows NT workstation. The following figure shows the Video Engine 100 being used to create an animated video of a new bridge being constructed.

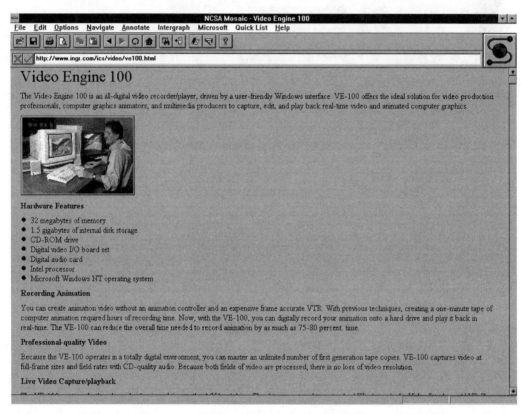

Using Intergraph's Video Engine 100 to create a new bridge.

The Video Engine 100 actually breaks the price point barrier previously in place for multimedia production systems. In addition to Intergraph, Silicon Graphics and Sun Microsystems are also planning to offer turnkey multimedia production systems.

Case Study
How JFS Consulting Is Using Multimedia in Proposals

Beginning as a service bureau that catered to the needs of Fortune 1000 customers interested in desktop publishing and CD-ROM production, JFS Consulting soon found a large potential market for multimedia production and consulting. Multinational companies interested in getting their message distributed quickly, accurately, and in the highest quality possible use the services of JFS Consulting to create multimedia CD presentations showing the features and benefits of their products. In addition, JFS Consulting has translation capability in-house, so a manufacturer that has the majority of their materials in German can have JFS Consulting translate the data into English, and then place it onto a CD for distribution. The need to show entire suites of products has lead several Fortune 1000 companies to use their services for multimedia presentations.

In an attempt to win additional business, JFS Consulting uses their own capabilities for creating multimedia presentations for such diverse clients as Fluor-Daniel, Bechtel, Toshiba America, and Compass Engineering Associates. Each of these client companies actively use CAD-based applications in their workflows, and rely on both the Windows NT and UNIX operating systems for sharing data and resources around the world. Structuring presentations using the capabilities of Windows NT makes each potential client more receptive to multimedia-based design proposals in general, and the techniques used to create them. For example, JFS Consulting typically leaves the multimedia presentation behind after a presentation to a potential client so that the interested parties can further query the concepts defined. An integral part of each proposal created is the use of object linking and embedding, where charts, spreadsheets, and database queries are embedded into the final presentation so the potential client can refer back to the data as the decision-making process continues. The following figure shows an example of the introductory screen to a JFS Consulting multimedia presentation.

An example of a JFS Consulting multimedia presentation.

Notice how each area of the introductory screen is used for communicating the various aspects of the potential client's business, along with a profile of JFS Consulting. In the above screen, you can see the potential customer is Compass Engineering Associates, a company that works in the geographical information systems market. Compass is interested in creating a multimedia presentation showing their latest series of products and their interoperability with ESRI's ArcView and the older Unigraphics Uniras application programs predominately found on mainframes. Using a series of icons throughout the screen, JFS Consulting has made it possible for the decision makers to quickly gain access to any part of the multimedia proposal.

Summary

Once considered an application in search of a market, multimedia is now seen as a series of tools that actually function as system components, complementing a wide variety of application areas. In the world of the technical professional, multimedia-based tools are advancing at a high rate of growth due to the increased processing power available at lower cost, pervasive use of the Internet for sharing both development data and finished products, and the increased willingness of software developers to integrate key multimedia tools into their applications. A case in point is Intergraph and Bentley System's inclusion of "fly-through" capabilities and file saving options for the *.AVI* and *.MPEG* file formats, in addition to *.JPEG* file import and export capabilities. Autodesk's inclusion of multimedia tools is also exemplified in AutoCAD Release 13 for Windows, where solid modeling is a supported feature, and the option of saving a file out in *.JPEG* format is supported.

What are the implications for the designer, draftsperson, or the architect? In a nutshell, the ability to communicate more persuasively by sharing the vision you have of a new product, building, or addition to an existing structure, all in full color. No longer will bridges be built using a series of coordinates showing stress levels at a specific point; rather, dynamic models showing the relative level of stress on a specific joint or juncture in the bridge design can be shown in color, with movement, ensuring that both the design team and the eventual customers understand how products will function before they are even built.

Chapter 9

Understanding Object Linking and Embedding

Introduction

If you've used a GUI before, you'll be familiar with cutting and pasting data from one application to another. For example, you might take an image from a MicroStation window and paste it into a document you are working on. The problem with this is, when you paste the image into the new application, all you get is the image. If the image is later updated as the design is modified, you'll need to update your document with the new image.

The solution to this problem is object linking and embedding (OLE). In OLE your document is a container holding links to information from different applications. It might have a MicroStation design file, some formatted text from Word for Windows, and some pricing information from a spreadsheet. If you call up the document in an OLE application such as Microsoft Word, it will handle all these links intelligently.

In practice this means that when you select the portion of the document that is a MicroStation design, then Microsoft Word will automatically switch to MicroStation to let you edit the figure, while staying in the document. The same intelligent handling would be applied to the embedded spreadsheet.

OLE is only really practical on a stable multitasking operating system like Windows NT. The reason is simple; when you load your document with its object links, the applications associated with the different embedded objects are started. Each application is responsible for displaying its portion of the compound document.

Now let's look at the impact OLE can have on the example of the shopping center being built. Instead of having each of the worksheets, schedules, and documents all done on separate computers using application programs that do not speak with one another, each part of the project is integrated and associated with the others, using applications supporting OLE. The spreadsheets for the project were done in Microsoft Excel for Windows, while the planning schedule was completed using Microsoft Project, and the final report was completed using Word for Windows 6.0.

Without OLE, you'd be running around trying to make sure that everybody was using the latest copies of the information being generated by each department. Using OLE, you can be sure that everybody is using up-to-date information.

Notice how the executive summary is captured in a single, integrated document while the accompanying files provide for the more detailed analysis. The following figure shows the Microsoft Mail message with the various files attached.

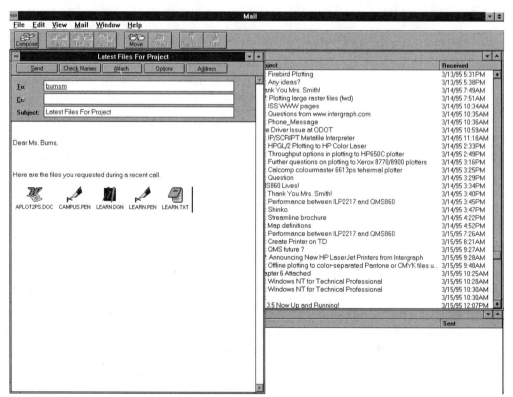

Distributing documents and files that are linked.

How Is OLE Different from Simple Cut and Paste

If you've used modern Office automation suites like Microsoft Office, you've probably already discovered how to cut information from one application and paste it into another.

When you paste information from Excel into Microsoft Word, it retains formatting information, but if you select it, it behaves like text entered in a Word table, not like an Excel spreadsheet.

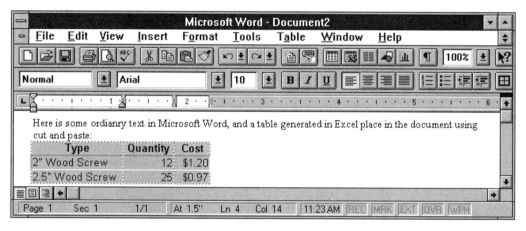

Embedded Excel information using cut and paste.

You can use the Paste as Object option when pasting the Excel data into word. This associates some intelligence with the new data. Now, when you select the Excel data, it will launch Excel as a separate window.

This is still not what you need, however. The data loaded into Excel will be the data from your Word document, not the master Excel spreadsheet.

The solution is use OLE to embed the spreadsheet in the Word file. To insert the information as an object, you use the Insert→Object menu in the application as shown in the following figure.

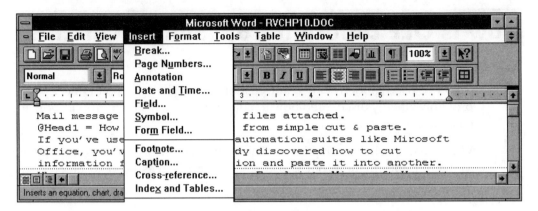

Microsoft Word's Insert Object menu.

Selecting this option will display the following dialog box:

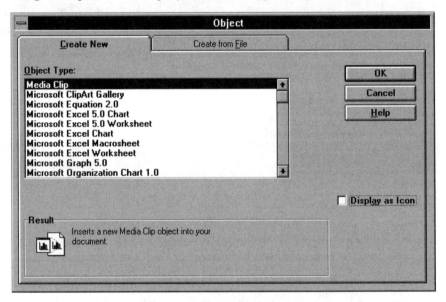

Microsoft Word's Insert Object dialog box.

The dialog box gives you a scrolling list of all applications that have been registered as supporting OLE. The registration of these applications takes place when they are installed on the system.

You can choose to insert an existing object from another file or just insert a empty object that you can add data to later. In this example, we'll insert an existing Excel object. To insert the object, in the Insert Object dialog box, select the Create From File option, and the dialog box changes to a familiar file select dialog box.

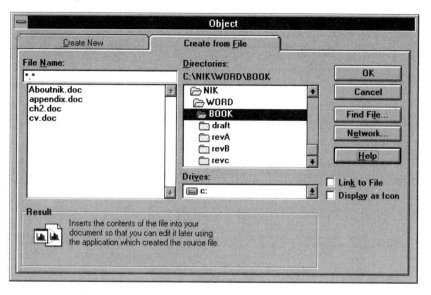

Microsoft Word's Create From File dialog box.

Use the disk and file selection windows in the dialog box to find the file you want to insert. Once you've selected the file, you have two more things to decide:

1. **How do you want the information displayed in Word?** You can choose to have it displayed as an icon or actually use the formatting abilities of the original application.

2. **Do you want to link or embed the object?** If you embed the object and later update the original file, the Word document will be become outdated. The other possibility is to make a link to the original file. When you link to the file, any changes in the original file will be reflected in your document.

In this example, we will use a link.

✔ *TIP: If you use links to filenames on your local disk and then mail the container file to someone else, they will not see the information correctly. There are two solutions to this. First you could mail the linked files as well, or second you could use the Universal Naming Convention (UNC) mecha-*

nism to name the file. To use UNC naming, select the Network option and select the file to link to.

For this example, we'll assume the file we want to link is on node ICS under the share "project" with a filename of *parts.xls.*" *Using the UNC convention we would refer to this file as* \\ics\project\parts.xls. Using the UNC name, you can mail out the container document. Whenever anybody looks at one of the objects, it will get the object via the network without any further assistance. This guarantees that anybody looking at the document always sees the latest and greatest information. The figure below shows the dialog box with all the appropriate fields filled in.

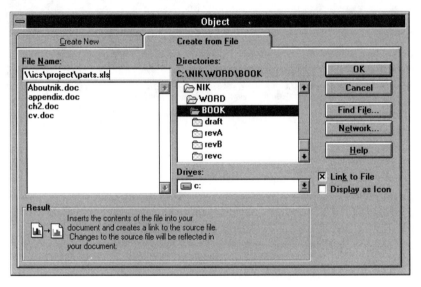

Microsoft Word's Create From File Dialog filled in.

Once you've inserted your object, you'll see a difference in how Word treats it. Instead of behaving like text in a Word table, it will have all the features and power of text in a Excel spreadsheet. Just selecting the table will cause all of Word's menus and icons to change to those of Excel. The following two figures show the file with Word menus, and then with the Excel object selected and Excel menus being displayed:

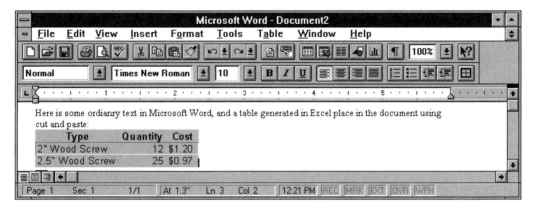

Microsoft Word with Word menus and icons.

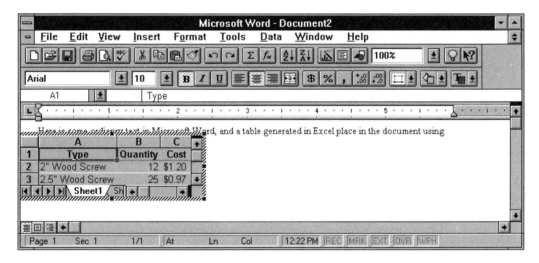

Microsoft Word with Excel menus and icons.

Using a combination of OLE and the UNC, you can keep all project data in one place and just make links to it in documents. When you send the documents to other members of the project, they will see it exactly as you want them to, and you are assured that the data they see is always up to date.

By contrast, if you use simple cut and paste, the document your colleagues see contains a snapshot of the project, which may already be out of date.

Another important feature of OLE is that it gives the ability to have the power of all you applications easily accessible from one document. If you need a drawing in a document, then simply embed a PowerPoint object in your document and then use the powerful drawing tools of PowerPoint. Without OLE you would need to follow these steps:

1. Start PowerPoint

2. Draw your picture

3. Copy it into the paste buffer

4. Exit PowerPoint

5. Return to Word

6. Paste your picture into the word document

Windows NT gives an unparalleled level of integration between all your OLE enabled applications.

OLE Client and Server Applications

The OLE capable applications are divided into three basic types:

1. **OLE Client:** MicroStation is an OLE client. You can use OLE to attach objects from other applications to MicroStation. You cannot attach a MicroStation object to another OLE document because MicroStation only supports the client side of OLE.

2. **OLE Server:** A OLE server-capable application can provide objects for embedding in OLE client applications. Microsoft Word can be a OLE server applications.

3. **OLE Client/Server:** A fully OLE-capable application can be either a client or a server. You can put OLE objects in its documents and you can attach its documents to other OLE-capable applications. Again, the Microsoft Office suite applications like Word and Excel are fully OLE capable.

OLE is rapidly emerging as a power tool for people working in a Microsoft Windows or Windows NT environment. Applications with full support for OLE are announced almost daily. You can expect the use of OLE to grow rapidly as people discover the power, flexibility, and integration it can bring to projects.

Day in the Life: Using Object Linking and Embedding in CAD

The following scenario illustrates how you could use the capabilities of OLE during a typical workday in a mechanical design department. As with many engineering firms, the flow of information, design specifications, schedules, and drawings are critical to deadlines being met and projects being completed.

Let's say your project consists of the following components:

❑   Designs done using MicroStation

❑   Costing estimates done using Excel

❑   Project proposal done using Word for Windows

❑   Product documentation done using Word for Windows

❑   Project schedule done using Microsoft Project

All the files for this project are stored on your central file server running Windows NT Server 3.5. In this example the central server is called "archive" and the shared directory where all the project files reside is called "project-X29."

Coming in on Monday morning, you first open Microsoft Mail on your Windows NT workstation and see that there is a message from Francine, the Product Development Manager for the new landing gear your company, Land Tight, is building for evaluation by several airplane manufacturers. The tell-tale red exclamation point is in the margin of the message, telling you the message was sent with the "Urgent" option turned on.

The message tells you that you have to produce a report for upper management, explaining why the project is over budget.

This sounds serious. You need to put together a response with all the relevant information very quickly, and the information better be up to date or your chances for that promotion could be somewhat limited.

OK, so what needs to be in the report. It had better include some information on what aspects of the project are over budget, what the latest costing estimates are, and what the revised project schedule is. Of course, you could just attach the project schedules and the cost spreadsheet to mail message and let them make up their own minds. But you realize that this is providing data to management, not information, and they will not be pleased if they have to wade through all the data to find out what is going on. We've all had that sinking feeling of losing our audience halfway through an hour-long presentation that should have been 10 minutes long. Remember, "Just the facts, ma'am."

A better idea would be to put together a quick status report on the project and include the relevant pieces of information from the cost and project schedules documents.

The trouble with a project like this is somebody, somewhere is almost certainly updating some of the information you want to show. Just pasting it into the document means that the information you include might be out of date before it is read by management. No, that will not do.

Then you have a brainstorm—why not use OLE to link the documents to your report? That way when management reviews it, they'll see the latest costs and project schedules. Better yet, if they want the same information a week later they can just look at the same document again, safe in the knowledge that it contains all the latest information. That should impress them!

Enough of this idle chat; you'd better get to work. You begin working on your trusty word processor, explaining what the problems are and why some things are going to cost more. You use the OLE features to link in the latest cost projections. Of course, you use the UNC filename for the cost projections; those darn things seem to change hourly.

Now to what they really want to know, when can they deliver one to a customer! Better grab that Project schedule file and include it, along with some explanation.

A couple of hours later...

Francine walks into your office, carrying her notebook and some other schedules.

"Hey, I just read your mail. Great job on the status report. How did you get cost information from an hour ago in a document you created two hours ago?"

You try to hide the smug smile. That promotion may still be within grasp.

How Does OLE Work?

When you create a report using OLE links to include the information from other applications, you are really creating a shell or container file with intelligent links to data stored in formats native to other applications. The next figure shows a simple container file with some explanatory text and links to other files:

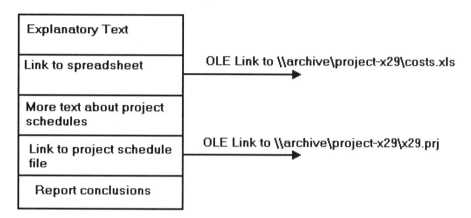

A container file with links to other information.

When you select one of the OLE links, instead of firing up the associated application, you OLE aware viewing program like Word just borrows the personality from the associated application and lets you carry on working in Word.

Since you've made the links using the UNC names, you mail this file to your manager and he'll see exactly what you want him to see; better yet it will be 100% up to date.

Another nice feature is that you can use all the nice formatting features of the OLE client to present the data in a really clear and concise way. No more hassles trying to get Word to crop and display a spreadsheet exactly the way you want it, you just set it all up in Excel, which is designed for the job.

The Future of Object Linking and Embedding

Ten years ago, OLE or technologies like it were being demonstrated on $200,000 workstations. With that sort of price tag, few people took much notice. Now you can buy a system for $3000, with all the power of the $200,000 machine. Suddenly everybody has the power to use objects in their day-to-day work.

You can expect several important developments in the world of OLE over the next few years. Here are some examples:

❑ Over the next few years even more object technology will find its way into the everyday life of the technical professional. Early in 1995, Intergraph, in conjunction with several other CAD companies including Autodesk, put the finishing touches on extensions for OLE specifically designed for the CAD marketplace.

❑ Release of Windows NT 3.51 makes OLE multithreaded, so that you get a real performance boost when you use dual processor Windows NT workstations such as Intergraph's TD-4 and MIPS-based workstations from NetPower.

❑ According to Microsoft, a new version of Windows NT, codename Cairo, will be released in late 1996 that will use OLE concepts throughout the operating system.

With ever more powerful systems finding their way to the desktop, you can be assured of one thing: Object technology is here to stay and it will change the way you work.

Case Study
How Juneau Design Center Uses Windows NT For Completing Design Tasks

Specializing in assisting contractors with the development of house plans, assisting individual customers with the development of custom home plans, and beginning to publish books and magazines of historical western home plans, Juneau Design Center has a workgroup of Windows NT workstations,

MS-DOS computers, and Macintosh computers all on a TCP/IP network. In addition, there are electrostatic plotters, high-resolution laser printers, color copiers, a fax server, and a color scanner. The Windows NT workstations also function as servers to the majority of this equipment.

The Windows for Workgroups client systems are tied directly to the Windows NT file server, and the other Windows NT clients are using AutoCAD for designing new homes. The MicroStation design seats are being used for the custom home plans, in addition to integrating vector files on top of color raster images. Called *hybrid plotting*, these design seats generate overview images of just how the building projects will be situated on land parcels. The Windows NT–based plot server uses the InterPlot VPI Driver Pack for Windows NT from Intergraph, along with IPLOT Server for plotting from I/RAS C to the Versatec 8936II-4R. The DOS-based seats directly access files on the Windows NT–based plot server as well, making it possible for the MicroStation designers to complete sample drawings to the LaserJet 4MV.

Let's next look at how documents and designs flow through this company. The designer initially completes the design file, working with either a contractor or the individual customer interested in a new home plan. Using a design seat on one of the available Windows NT workstations, the designer sketches the plan, working with the architects to plan exactly how the floor plans, elevations, and various components of the home are shown. The designer then completes the specific details on the entire plan and mails it to the project planning department with a series of Excel spreadsheets attached showing the bill of materials, costs of building the home, and the anticipated schedule. Each of these documents is linked directly into each file as they are processed, so that anyone reviewing the design file at any time can find out the current costs of completing the project, the location of the land parcel where the project will be completed, and the schedule to completion. At any point in the process these embedded files are accessible to architects, designers, and the customers when they stop by for a meeting to discuss their plans. During the presentation to a contractor, the total costs of the plan are accurate and as timely as possible, since there isn't any fumbling or searching for files.

"We have found this approach really puts our individual clients at ease.... They come in and review their home plans, and see exactly what the costs are given the changes made in a given design feature," Mike Richardson of Juneau Design Center says. "We use linking to make sure members of the design staff are in constant touch with the latest information on a project. And the customers like that too; they feel that someone is in control of their project."

In conjunction with object linking and embedding, Juneau Design Center also uses Microsoft Mail and email extensively. In fact, more and more contractors are now using email to schedule appointments, check into projects, and work with architects. Instead of having to stop in every few days, routine questions are easily answered between architects and designers through the use of Microsoft Mail. The following figure shows an example of a typical new home plan being created by Juneau Design Center, with the Excel worksheets attached, showing total costs and the schedule.

A completed design file from Juneau Design Center.

Summary

In this chapter we've covered:

❑ The fundamental concepts of OLE

❑ The difference between OLE and ordinary cut and paste

❑ How to make a dynamic document using the power of OLE

❑ How OLE will alter the behavior of your applications to be more intuitive

❑ A brief glimpse of where OLE technology is going

❑ A practical application of OLE

You should be able to see how OLE has the power to make you more productive by always making sure you have the latest information as well as making it easier to integrate information from disparate sources into one easily understood document.

Bridging the UNIX to Windows NT Gap

Introduction

Windows NT Workstation is targeted at many of the same market niches currently occupied by UNIX. Inevitably it must coexist with UNIX in these environments. Microsoft recognized this requirement by including support for the standard UNIX networking protocol of TCP/IP in the standard distribution of Windows NT.

Windows NT does not include some of the essential components for interoperating with UNIX; these tools are available from third parties. This chapter covers the setup and use of the tools included with Windows NT. Appendix A covers vendors of tools useful for making Windows NT interoperate with existing UNIX networks.

Interoperating with UNIX

Most networks use the TCP/IP protocol and a set of applications to tie UNIX workstations together. Windows NT includes the following TCP/IP client applications:

❐ **File Transfer Protocol (FTP):** A simple command line version of FTP allows you to make connections to FTP servers and transfer files to your system.

❐ **Telnet:** A simple terminal emulation program. Using Telnet you can create a terminal window to a UNIX host and login as though attached directly to the machine.

Windows NT has been criticized for a lack of UNIX connectivity because it is missing several commonly used services. Fortunately the Windows NT TCP/IP protocol conforms to the widely recognized WINSOCK interface specification. This means that Windows NT can use applications written for the following operating systems:

❐   Windows 3.1, sometime referred to as WIN16.

❐   Windows NT, sometimes referred to as WIN32.

With a choice of all the WINSOCK applications written, Windows NT has a good selection of UNIX networking applications from the public domain and commercial vendors. Currently packages exist for the following UNIX TCP/IP client services:

❐   **Newsreader for USENET news services:** Connect to and read news via the TCP/IP Network News Transport Protocol (NNTP).

❐   **WWW Browser:** Connect to resources on the World Wide Web using the TCP/IP Hypertext Transport Protocol (HTTP).

❐   **Gopher Client:** Connect to Gopher servers. Gopher is a network-based search engine, allowing you to look for specific pieces of information on the net.

❐   **Mail Client:** Connect to Simple Mail Transfer Protocol (SMTP) or Post Office Protocol (POP) servers to read and send mail.

❐   **Rlogin Client:** Make a connection to a UNIX shell on a remote UNIX host.

❐   **RSH/REXEC Client:** Run commands on a Remote UNIX host with the output being returned to the local host.

❐   **Wide Area Information Search Client:** A WAIS client is available that allows Windows NT clients to connect to WAIS Servers to search through large text and other databases maintained at sites, including the Library of Congress.

❐   **Talk Client:** Real-time conversations via the TCP/IP Talk or Ntalk protocols.

❐   **Finger Client:** Get information about a user on a remote node, including things like contact information, whether the user is logged in, etc.

❐ **NFS Client:** Connect to filesystems exported from a Network File System (NFS) server.

❐ **Network Time Client:** Allows the Windows NT system clock to be set from a time server on the Internet.

For a list of packages and FTP sites (where applicable) see Appendix A. Windows NT is not limited to being a client only on the Internet. The following server services are either provided as standard or available from independent software vendors or the public domain:

❐ **FTP Server:** Windows NT includes a FTP Server so that UNIX and other FTP clients can download files.

❐ **USENET News Server:** A public domain implementation of a USENET server is available to provide news access for NNTP clients (see Appendix A).

❐ **NFS Server:** Several commercial packages allow a Windows NT workstation or server to export a filesystem that a NFS client can read.

❐ **Netware Server:** Export filesystems that Novell Netware clients can access.

❐ **Telnet Server:** Allow Telnet connections. Clients logging in via Telnet get an MS-DOS shell, with access to all Windows NT command line abilities.

❐ **RLOGIN Server:** Provides similar capabilities to the Telnet server but using the Rlogin protocol.

❐ **Wide Area Information Search Server:** Real-time conversations via the TCP/IP Talk or Ntalk protocols.

❐ **Hypertext Transport Protocol Server:** HTTP is the network service used to provide the World Wide Web. Using the HTTPD Server from the Windows NT 3.5 Resource Kit, you can provide a full World Wide Web service.

Using a combination of the standard software with commercial and public domain applications, Windows NT can access most services found on a UNIX network.

Using the Telnet Client

Windows NT 3.5 includes a Telnet client. It can be used either by launching from the Program Manager or directly from a MS-DOS command window. When the Telnet application is run, a dumb terminal window is displayed. This Telnet session window is not connected to anything initially.

Select Connect→Remote System and a dialog box is displayed:

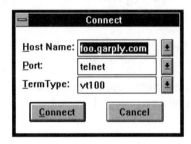

Connect dialog box.

Simply enter the nodename or Internet address of the host system. The two other fields in this dialog box are used to set the following characteristics.

❑ **Port:** Normally when you Telnet to another computer, you want to make a Telnet connection. Sometimes though, you want to connect to a different type of service, such as the Simple Mail Transfer Protocol (SMTP) or Network News Transport Protocol (NNTP) Service for debugging purposes.

❑ **Terminal Type:** Telnet is capable of emulating several different terminal types. If you are not sure which one to use, consult your system administrator.

You can also run Telnet from the command line and specify the host and port type as in the following example:

```
Telnet host.nowhere.com
```

This will connect to the SMTP port on the specified host. If you do not specify a port type, the default is Telnet.

If you have a machine that you will contact frequently, then use the following procedure to create a Program Manager icon for a Telnet connection to the specified machine:

1. Select the file *%SystemRoot%\system32\telnet.exe* in File Manager and drag it to a program group.

2. Highlight the new icon and select Program Manager→File→Properties.

3. Select the Command Line field and add the name of the host after the Telnet command. The field will look like the following: *telnet.exe host.no-where.com.*

4. Select the Description field and change it from Telnet to the host name.

Using this ability you can easily connect to any UNIX host.

Using the FTP Client

The built-in FTP client in Windows NT is a command line only utility. Many more fully featured Windows-based FTP clients are available from the public domain as well as commercial vendors.

The built-in client has the same syntax as its UNIX counterpart. The following figure shows a typical command session:

```
(C) Copyright 1985-1995 Microsoft Corp.

c:\nik>ftp foo.garply.com
Connected to foo.garply.com.
220 foo.garply.com FTP server (OSF/1 Version 5.60) ready.
User (foo.garply.com:(none)): nik
331 Password required for nik.
Password:
230 User nik logged in.
ftp> ls -C
200 PORT command successful.
150 Opening ASCII mode data connection for /bin/ls (165.113.188.20,1125).
.profile            n16e11b3.exe         t1
.rhosts             n32e11b3.exe         winvn_93_14_intel.zip
.sh_history         netscape-1.1b3.hqx   ws_ftp32.zip
eudor144.exe        psp30.zip            wsg-12.exe
ewan1052.zip        setshell.zip         wsping32.zip
html.zip            t                    wtalk121.zip
226 Transfer complete.
357 bytes received in 0.11 seconds (3.22 Kbytes/sec)
ftp> get eudor144.exe
200 PORT command successful.
150 Opening ASCII mode data connection for eudor144.exe (165.113.188.20,1126) (2
93763 bytes).
```

FTP session.

If you have Internet access, then the best use for the built-in client is to connect to an FTP site and *get ws_ftp* (see Appendix A).

Setting Up the FTP Server in Windows NT

Windows NT can also serve files to other machines using FTP. To set up Windows NT as an FTP server you'll have to install the FTP Server Service in the Networking Control Panel using the following procedure:

1. From the Main program group, execute the Control Panel.

2. From the Control Panel, execute the Network control panel.

3. Select the Add Software button. Windows NT will present a scrolling list of network software packages that can be installed. Select the TCP/IP Protocol and Related Components from the following list.

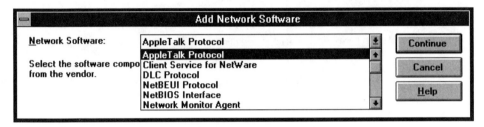

Add Network Software dialog box.

4. Windows NT will display a list of currently installed and available TCP/IP components as shown below.

5. Select FTP Server Service and then select Continue. Make sure you have your Windows NT distribution media available at this point. After installing the files Windows NT will run the configuration utility.

TCP/IP protocol and related components.

FTP Service dialog box.

The configuration dialog allows four parameters to be set:

1. **Maximum connections:** This is the number of active FTP connections that your server will allow.
2. **Idle Time-out (Mins):** The number of minutes to wait before automatically disconnecting an idle FTP connection.
3. **Home Directory:** When an incoming FTP connection is made, the contents of this directory will be the first thing the user sees. For maximum security and flexibility in assigning permission to incoming FTP connections, the FTP home directory should be on an NTFS partition.
4. **Allow Anonymous Connections:** When this is enabled, users can connect with the username *anonymous*. Anonymous connections will have the local privileges of the account specified in the Username field.

Once the FTP server has been installed you will see a new applet icon in control panel as shown below:

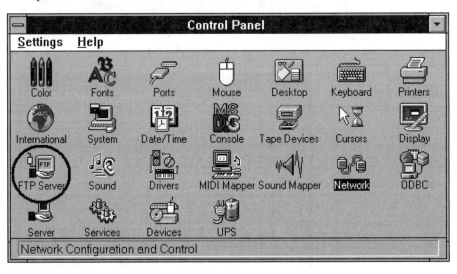

FTP Server applet in Control Panel.

Before any user connections will be accepted, you must use this applet to set permission on the drives on your machine. On startup, the FTP applet will display the following window:

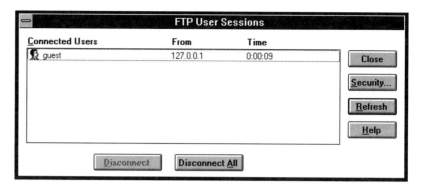

FTP Server applet display.

The Connected Users portions of the display show all the currently active FTP sessions. To allow users access to your drives, select the Security button, which displays the following dialog box.

FTP Server security dialog box.

This dialog box gives you the ability allow read and/or write access to drives on your system.

➥ **NOTE:** *In a secure environment, you should only allow FTP access to NTFS filesystems. NTFS allows much finer granularity in controlling access to your files than is possible with a DOS FAT filesystem.*

NFS Software Packages for Windows NT

Windows NT 3.5 does not include any support for the UNIX NFS protocol. Because NFS is widely used to share files between UNIX and other systems, it is important for Windows NT. Several companies have Windows NT NFS packages, including Intergraph, Beame & Whiteside, and Chameleon. For fuller details of these packages, see Appendix A.

✔ **TIP:** *NFS packages for DOS/Windows will not work with Windows NT.*

LAN Manager for UNIX

Adding NFS to a Windows NT node is only one way of allowing file sharing between Windows NT and UNIX nodes. The second alternative is to add Windows NT file sharing protocols to the UNIX node. Several UNIX systems have optional packages that provide Windows NT file sharing from a UNIX node. Contact the vendor of your UNIX system for more information.

For free connectivity, you can obtain a public domain UNIX package called SAMBA. SAMBA implements Windows NT style file sharing from a UNIX node. SAMBA has been compiled on most popular UNIX versions. For more information on SAMBA, see Appendix A.

Mail

With mail you have two options:

1. Implement a Microsoft mail to Simple Mail Transfer Protocol (SMTP) gateway. The software required for this solution is available from Microsoft.

2. Maintain existing UNIX mail system and add Post Office Protocol (POP3) support so that suitable mail readers can connect to and exchange mail with your UNIX mail system. Many UNIX versions include POP3 support. If your UNIX version doesn't, you can obtain source code for a POP3 daemon from several FTP sites. See Appendix A for more details.

Adding POP3 support will enable you to use a Windows mail reader such as Eudora from Qualcomm (see Appendix A).

Printing

Windows NT includes the ability to share printers with UNIX systems using the BSD LPD protocol. This allows your Windows NT nodes to use UNIX system printers and vice versa. When you install Windows NT it will install the client component of the LPD service. The client component enables you to connect to a printer queue on a UNIX node running the LPD service. This is covered in Chapter 5, "Printing."

Included, but not installed by default, is the server portion of the LPD service. If you want to make local printers available to UNIX clients you must install this service.

The first step is to install the LPD printer service. This is similar to the installation of the FTP server described previously.

1. From the Main program group, execute the Control Panel.

2. From the Control Panel, execute the Network control panel.

3. Select the Add Software button. Windows NT will present a scrolling list of network software packages that can be installed. Select TCP/IP Protocol and Related Components from the list as shown below:

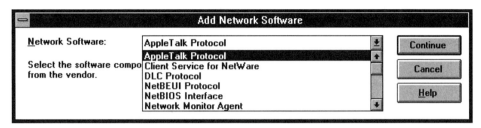

Add Network Software dialog box.

4. Windows NT will display a list of currently installed and available TCP/IP components, as shown below:

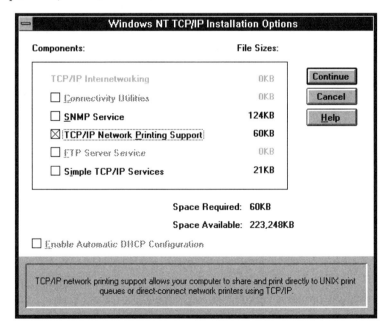

TCP/IP protocol and related components.

5. Select TCP/IP Network Printing Support and then select Continue. Make sure you have your Windows NT distribution media available at this point.

After installation is complete, you must reboot before continuing the configuration of the LPD service. After you've rebooted, run the Control Panel and select the services applet. The following dialog box will be displayed:

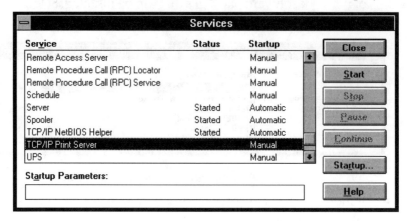

Service Control Panel applet.

Select the TCP/IP Print Server service and then select the Startup... button. The following dialog box will be displayed:

TCP/IP Print Server Startup dialog box.

Select the startup mode as Automatic. This will ensure that the service is started every time the machine boots. It must be running for the system to accept print jobs from UNIX systems.

Once the service is running, you must use a remote queue on any UNIX machine that will use this server, as you would for a printer in a UNIX system.

Case Study
UNIX-Windows NT Interoperability

Chapter 1 referred to Sequent's Windows NT-UNIX mixed environment. In creating this environment, Sequent faced many challenges. The solutions found by Sequent do not represent the only way of achieving a seamless interoperation, but they do represent a successful approach.

One of the most challenging tasks was to provide Microsoft Mail to the members of a workgroup while retaining the powerful alias and mail routing capabilities of the UNIX servers. The solution was to update the Microsoft alias database nightly via batch jobs run on the UNIX servers and the Microsoft Mail post offices. This prevented duplicate, and sometimes conflicting, aliases in the two systems.

The next problem to solve was accessing shared files throughout the company. Each client system had to be able to access Sequent Symmetry servers running Novell NetWare for UNIX. To make this task easier, Windows NT provides a Netware client capability, allowing users to continue to use the Netware servers. Netware was not the only file sharing system in use within Sequent; many servers and clients used the UNIX Network File Sharing system (NFS). To connect to this environment Sequent used an NFS client for Windows NT. This essential UNIX-Windows NT interoperability tool has been developed by several software vendors, so obtaining it was no problem.

With the problems of access to UNIX systems, electronic mail, and file sharing solved, only access to printing and network resources remained to be solved. Sequent had a well-developed network of printers, fax machines, and scanners all accessible from its old UNIX systems. The integration team knew it had to make these resources accessible to the entire organization. The problem of providing access to existing printer resources on the UNIX servers was solved by adding LAN Manager for UNIX to the UNIX servers. LAN Manager is the UNIX implementation of the network protocols found in

Windows NT, Windows for Workgroups, and OS/2. Now the UNIX servers could make their print resources available to the whole network. The devices now accessible to anybody on the Sequent network were also available to workers based at home or on the road via RAS.

While the first implementations of the subnetworks were challenging and took fine tuning, Mark Anastas, Senior Manager for Windows NT Systems at Sequent, now says that the integration effort was worth it. The cost savings from being able to use existing printers and cabling has saved the company thousands of dollars, as well as minimal loss of productivity as the new subnetworks were integrated into existing applications. "The main accomplishment of these initial efforts was to achieve that breakthrough where we now have a standard package that can be easily adopted and supported and is available to all groups in the company," Anastas said.

Because Sequent is a strong believer in using the products they sell, there is a strong bias to build future client/server products on the Windows NT operating system. There are plans for a contact management system for the sales force, and a decision support system for managers. Both of these applications use client-server technology where the necessary SQL database is stored on the WinServer servers. The company plans to continue pursuing development on the Windows NT platform because it provides the necessary tools for more effectively integrating tasks with mainstream office automation products like Microsoft Word and Microsoft Mail.

Summary

In this chapter you've had a brief overview of UNIX-Windows NT interoperability problems and solutions and reviewed a Windows NT and UNIX case study. You've learned how to use the Telnet client, the FTP client, and how to set up the FTP server service.

With these basic tools you can login to UNIX nodes on the network and also use FTP to transfer files between systems.

Managing a Windows NT Workplace

Introduction

Performance and compatibility claims are often the two most popular reasons for switching from one operating system to another. With Windows NT Workstation, how do you know you are really getting the performance you expect? And how can you troubleshoot problems with performance both locally and throughout a network? The intent of this chapter is to give you the necessary background to answer these questions and give you guidance in using the applets or tools available in Windows NT. These tools are found in the Administrative Tools group of Windows NT Workstation.

A Quick Tour of the Administrative Tools

Included in this file group are tools for managing the Windows NT workplace from a system administrator's perspective. Although these tools are excellent for completing administration-oriented tasks, you can also use these applets for first understanding the performance level of a Windows NT workstation, and then changing system parameters to increase performance.

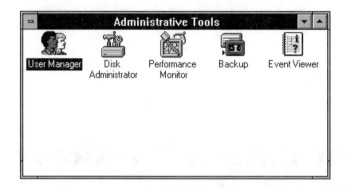

The Administrative Tools Group in Windows NT.

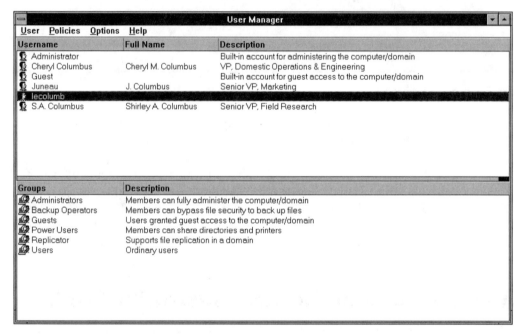

User Manager's main window.

Exploring User Manager

Windows NT sorts all users into three major categories within the context of the User Manager. These three categories determine which account and system maintenance functions are available to a given user. If, for example, you are a designer who has Power User status, you will be able to create and delete user accounts and groups. You can also control the members of the Power Users, Users, and Guest groups. In the case of a Project Manager who is working on the construction of a new building, being a member of the Power User group can actually make the task of managing others members of the same domain easier. Conversely, a new designer just joining the project needs to have either Guest or User status. The need for administrator privilege varies in terms of the size of the company, degree of control needed over the project, and the confidentiality of the resources being used. In short, administrator privilege is best left to the person now doing system administrator tasks with the current network. Here's a short description of each of these classes of users and examples of how members of a design team would be User Manager

The first applet in the Administrative Tools group is the User Manager, which is used for managing multiple accounts and providing security privileges for each account on a Windows NT workstation. Later in this chapter the User Manager will be explored, and you'll see how you can add new user accounts and monitor how resources are being used on your Windows NT workstation. You can use the auditing tools available in User Manager to see when various logins are used, and what resources are used as well. assigned:

❏ **Administrators:** Being a member of this group provides the highest level of control over system resources. Each individual workstation has an administrator login and can be used for completing system level modifications. When installing Windows NT, have the system administrator for your organization define a password on this account. By default, this type of account is installed during setup and is considered a built-in account, because once Windows NT is installed, this account exists.

❏ **Power Users:** Being a member of this group allows you to create or delete new user accounts, new user groups, and modify the members of a specific user group. A power user can also add and remove users from the Power Users, Users, and Guest groups. Project leaders are typically the most appropriate ones to be members of this group, as are assistant managers and others who need to manage entire groups of people. It's a good idea to be a member of the Power Users group on your own Windows NT workstation as well.

❏ **Users:** This group status allows you to create or modify groups and enter other account names into a group. Typically when a system administrator gets a new system up and running, all of the members of a given workgroup or domain are members of the Users group. Your system administrator typically changes the Initial User account, which is a built-in account delivered during Windows NT Setup, to a User account. This also makes it possible to change the password and protect the resources on each Windows NT workstation after installation.

❑ **Guest:** This type of user account is created during setup and is provided for the temporary user or a contractor who is going to be on a project for only a short period of time. The Guest account takes on all privileges as granted from the system administrator's definition of this account for the entire domain. The system administrator can redefine the rights of the Guest accounts on the network either remotely or by using the administrator login at the specific workstation being used. The Guest account does not have a password, but can be assigned one by the system administrator.

Understanding Event Viewer

Troubleshooting system performance bottlenecks is achieved using Event Viewer. You can also use this Microsoft-supplied utility to detect when a processor or program has failed and get an audit trail of the given event to understand why. An *event* is any significant occurrence in the system or in an application that requires users to be notified. Certain events, such as feedback from the Uninterruptable Power Supply or the Print Manager, are sent directly to the screen for your immediate attention; others are entered into a log file that is accessible via the Event Viewer.

As you would guess, the Event Viewer is a great way to figure out which processes or subsystem is having trouble, because there are short descriptions for each event. Each time Windows NT is started, the Event Viewer starts up and begins a new log. Using the options in the Event Viewer, you can manage multiple log files for the system you are using or for an entire series of systems you are responsible for. There are options from the pulldown menu that are used for formatting and printing event log reports. You can use the mouse to double-click on any event to obtain more information. This is particularly useful when troubleshooting a problem.

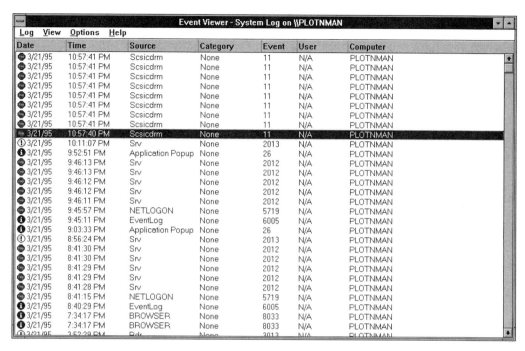

The Event Viewer in action.

Using the Disk Administrator

In any printer, file server, workstation, minicomputer, or mainframe computer, disk resources are the heart of all functionality. With a disk resource being reliably managed, an entire network can stay up and running. To ensure reliable disk resources on Windows NT workstations and servers, Microsoft has included the Disk Administrator program within the Administrative Tools group. An example of the Disk Administrator main window is shown in the following figure.

Disk Administrator main window.

Using the Disk Administrator, you can partition disk space, create and delete volume sets, extend volumes and volume sets, and create or delete stripe sets. Although partitioning of an internal hard disk is done during an initial Windows NT setup, modifications to the disk partitions can be completed using the Disk Administrator application.

In addition to being able to manage disk partitions, the Disk Administrator can be used for these tasks:

❑   Gain information about the available free space of a given partition and define drive-letter assignments, volume labels, and the filesystem type.

❑   Make and change drive letter assignments.

❑   Create, change, and delete volume sets.

❑   Create, change, and delete stripe sets without parity.

The Windows NT Server platform offers another option, Stripe Set with Parity. This is more commonly known as RAID level 5. RAID 5 groups drives together and presents them to Windows NT Workstation as a single device. When data is written to this "logical" device, Windows NT also writes error correcting information. If any drive in the stripe fails, Windows NT can recreate the data in realtime using data and error correction information from the remaining drives. This allows a server to continue to function and provide assess to all data even when a disk drive fails. In the past a failed disk drive would bring the system down and the data would have to be restored from backup.

How Performance Monitor Works

Just as a runner will complete an initial time around a 440-yard track to see her or his best time in a quarter mile, the Performance Monitor is used to get a baseline measurement of your system performance. With the baseline in place, you can devise steps to take that will increase your Windows NT workstation's performance. The Performance Monitor consists of a series of counters, which are in essence variables that capture a specific performance attribute of the Windows NT operating system. An example of the Performance Monitor in action is shown in the following figure.

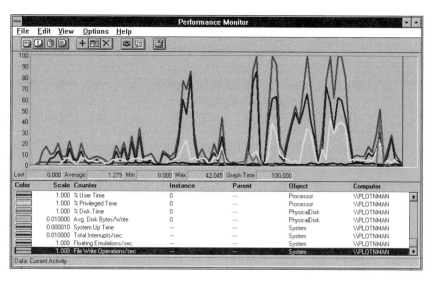

Performance Monitor in action.

Using the Performance Monitor, you can monitor both the performance of the local workstation and other Windows NT–based workstations located throughout the network. With trust relationships established within Windows NT Server, you can measure the performance of workstations and servers that are members of other domains as well.

Monitoring Network Activity Using Performance Monitor

The Performance Monitor can view the behavior of many aspects of the system, including processors, memory, cache, threads, and processes. Each of these measure is known of as an *object*. For each object, there is an associated set of counters or variables that provide information on such performance elements as disk usage, queue lengths, delays, in addition to the utilization of system memory and its actual speed. You can configure a customized set of counters for the specific workstation and network you are managing or using through the options in Performance Monitor.

With Performance Monitor you can accomplish the following tasks:

❏   View performance data from any other workstation you have Administrator login privileges to on the network.

❑   Display and dynamically change charts reflecting the current activity of key performance variables.

❑   Periodically update counter values based on a predetermined frequency. You can, for example, have specific system variables queried for status every few seconds or minutes.

❑   Export data from charts, logs, alert logs, and reports to spreadsheets or database programs for further analysis and presentation.

❑   Add system alerts that list an event in the Alert Log and, optionally, notify you by reverting to Alert View or issuing a network alert.

❑   Run a predefined program every time or just the first time a counter value goes over or under a user-defined value.

❑   Create log files containing data about various objects and events occurring on other Windows NT–based workstations and servers located throughout the network.

❑   View current activity reports or create reports from existing log files showing the system's performance level.

❑   Save individual charts, Alert Logs, report settings, or the entire workspace definition into a file that can be used later.

Using the features of Performance Monitor, the relative level of performance for your workstation can be checked and steps taken to increase overall performance. The Windows NT Performance Monitor uses a series of counters that measure the performance of key system variables over time. Within the Performance Monitor, there are four separate views, each of which can be used for analyzing system performance.

Let's take, for example, a situation where the Windows NT workstation you are using is a design seat for AutoCAD Release 13 for Windows NT, in addition to being a file server for certain tasks in the network. In addition, there are Windows for Workgroups–based PC computers that are connected to your Windows NT workstations as clients. In all, there are up to nine different workstations or PCs that can access and use resources on your system. What is this doing to the performance of AutoCAD when all possible users are sharing files from your system? You can get a graphical representation of this by using the Chart View included in Performance Monitor. Selecting counters that show the impact of these share points is captured in % Processor Time and % User Time from the Processor Object. If you are familiar with the WinMeter in Windows for Workgroups, you'll find the Performance Monitor easy to understand and use. The following figure shows the Performance Monitor's Chart View, with selected counters shown. Keep in mind that Performance Monitor's Chart View is dynamic and changes to reflect the ongoing changes in the system's performance on a real-time basis.

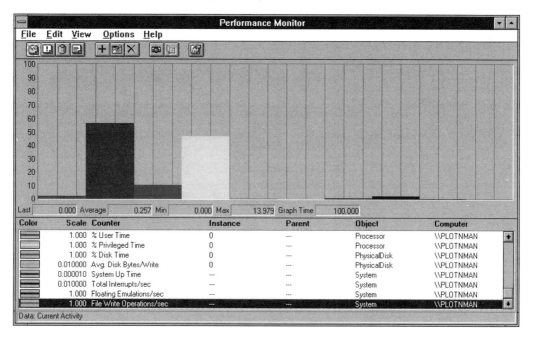

Chart View provides real-time feedback on system performance.

What are objects and counters? An *object* is really a set of variables, with each *counter* being a specific variable associated with an object's group. For example, one specific object is the processor. The processor has counters for tracking the values for % Processor Time, Interrupts/Second, in addition to several others. The Memory object has variables for tracking the Available Bytes, Pages/Second (a measure of how quickly your workstation is completing virtual memory swaps from the disk to RAM and back), and the number of Page Faults/Second that occur. There are additional objects and counters not mentioned here, but described within the Add to Chart dialog box. A small help file appears below the Add to Chart dialog box, explaining what the function of each object and associated counter is.

In the case of a Windows NT workstation being used for both CAD-oriented tasks and printing and file server tasks for a small workgroup, the objects that would be used to monitor performance are the Processor object and Server objects, with the Memory and Physical Disk objects also being useful for analyzing how the load on the workstation is affecting overall system performance. Within each of these objects, there are counters that capture the performance of the object itself over time. The following figure shows how the Add to Chart dialog box can be used to identify which object and associated counters are tracked.

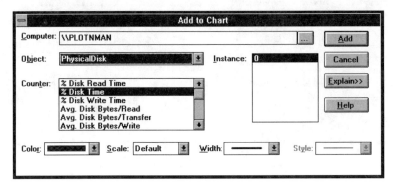

Adding objects and counters to the Chart View.

Notice that for each Object, a corresponding series of Counters are shown. The color of the lines representing each counter vary, so that the entire series of variables being tracked are easily distinguished on screen. In the example of a workstation being both a design seat, printer, and file server, the Page/Sec value for the Memory Object shows that there is a great deal of virtual paging occurring, which could slow down the performance of AutoCAD running in the foreground. In addition, the % Usage for the Paging File is consistently running at 60% or higher. The % Usage for Physical Disk along with % Disk Time show that the workstation's hard disk is being used over 40% of the time, making it difficult for AutoCAD to retrieve reference files, or X-REFs.

Over time, these values fluctuate in Chart View, depending on the relative network traffic and the level of activity in the foreground CAD application. Because the Chart View shows these figures as they fluctuate and you want to record the actual values, you can switch to the Report View. The following figure shows an example of the Report View within Performance Monitor.

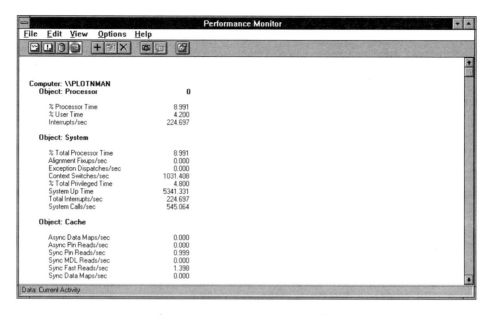

Performance Monitor's Report View.

Using the Report View, you can isolate just what the values are for each of the objects and their associated counters. This is the baseline you can use for gauging the effects of your efforts to increase system responsiveness. For the looks of the report in the previously shown figure, both the memory and hard disk are being used heavily, and the processor is also being taken up at least 30% of the time.

A first step to increase performance is to move the most commonly used files from the Windows NT workstation being profiled to another one. If the time is convenient and no one is using the share point for the files, stop sharing the files and then print out the Report View again. Notice that the counters associated with the Physical Disk drop significantly. The CAD applications aren't slowing down the system as much as the role the NT workstation is playing as a file server. From this simple change, you can see that it's a good idea to get a centralized file server if you want to increase the performance of this specific workstation. But what if you don't have the budget to do that? You allocated so much for workstations, and this is it for the next two or three years. You can look for ways to increase disk performance by adding a peripheral expansion module, replace the existing hard disk with another one with higher capacity, or both. With the expansion module, you could take the commonly used files and move them to another Windows NT workstation that is not currently being used as a design seat.

After moving the files to an expansion module or another workstation, use the Alert View to see if the problem of high disk usage persists. Included in Performance Monitor is the option of having an alert displayed once a specific counter for an object meets or exceeds a given value. This is accomplished using the Add to Alert dialog box.

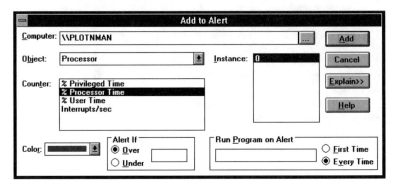

The Add to Alert dialog box in Performance Monitor.

Notice along the top of the Add to Alert dialog box, the name of the workstation is shown in the Computer: entry. With administrator status you could also log onto various workstations throughout the network, checking the performance status of each through Performance Monitor.

The Alert View shows occurrences of objects and counters and their associated values. Specifically, a counter's variable value is recorded in the Alert View if the system performance generates a value higher than the minimum threshold as defined in the Add to Alert dialog box. Why is this important? Let's say you are managing an entire network of CAD users and want to know when the object called Server registers a value for the counter Bytes Transmitted/second to see when the server load is highlighted. As users access shared files over the network, the Bytes Transmitted/second begins inching up, until the counter's value exceeds the figure as set in the Add to Alert dialog box. At that point, you'll be able to allocate additional resources, including additional disk space if needed, to alleviate a network slowdown. The following figure shows the Alert View within Performance Monitor.

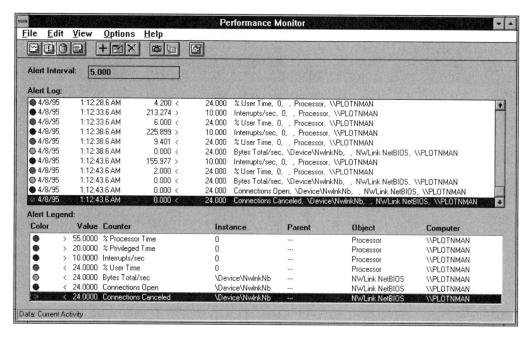

Monitor Alert View.

The Monitor Alert View makes it possible to track the various activities and performance of a Windows NT workstation, even an entire network on an "exception" reporting basis. Instead of having to monitor every aspect of a system, the Monitor Alert View shows only those events with counters that exceed specific values. The Monitor Alert View makes it possible to view those counters that exceed predetermined values as set in the Add to Alert dialog box earlier.

In the case of a CAD administrator who is busily supporting a workgroup of 40 to 50 designers, the Monitor Alert View makes it possible to get a message when one of the workstations exceeds the counter value for a given object. In other words, using the tools in Performance Monitor, system and CAD administrators can streamline their workloads and free up more time for proactive projects because the reactive aspects of their job can be more under control.

Saving and Reusing Settings in Performance Monitor

Often you will want to look at the same set of system performance counters. If you simply start the Performance Monitor, you'll get the default set each time. To overcome the default settings, follow these steps.

1. Start Performance Monitor and use the mechanisms described earlier to customize the view of system performance that you want.

2. From the File menu, select Save Chart Setting As and save the setting to a file with a *.pmc* extension.

3. Select the *.pmc* file in File Manager and then select Associate from the File menu in File Manager. Link the *.pmc* extension to the Performance Monitor, which is located at *%SystemRoot%\system32\perfmon.exe*.

You can now launch the Performance Monitor by selecting any *.pmc* file and have the view automatically show only those performance counters you want to see.

Using Backup

Using this tool, you can back up files, directories, or entire disks. Because Backup uses pulldown menus and is similar to Windows, completing backups using the utility is easy. This applet or utility does assume that a tape backup system is attached to your Windows NT workstation and up and running. The following figure shows the Backup main window.

Using Backup To Save Files

Preventing anxiety attacks generated from lost files, crashed hard disks, or bits blown to smithereens from an errant lightning bolt is the major benefit of Backup. This utility relies on the availability of a streaming tape backup system for getting files copied from the hard disk to the tape drive. Since Windows NT Workstation uses the NTFS, FAT, or HPFS filesystems for organizing data, the Backup utility supports each of these types of filesystems. In fact, you can configure Backup to write the data being copied to tape in any of the filesystems supported. With Backup, you can back up disk files to tape, restore tape files to disk, or periodically write files that have recently been created using any of the applications you have on a Windows NT workstation.

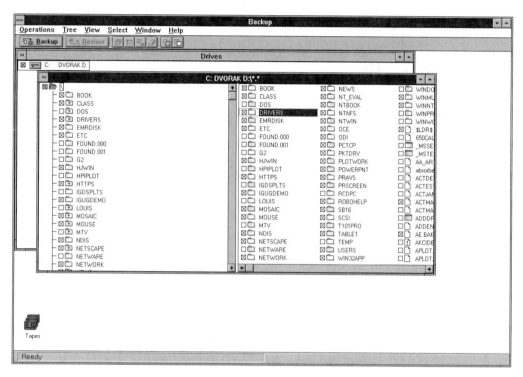

Backup's main window.

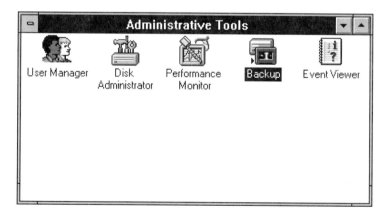

Backup is a member of the Administrative Tools Group.

Using Backup: Key Features

Instead of having to purchase a separate backup utility for getting files saved from Windows NT, Microsoft provides the Backup utility as part of the Administrative Tools group. The features of Backup include the following:

❑ Make multiple copies of the same image to tape or make multiple tapes of the same data set.

❑ Append data to the beginning or end of an existing data set that already has been written to a tape.

❑ Use a batch file that works very similarity to a UNIX-based shell script for invoking Backup and complete daily backups of an entire disk volume or only those files that have changed.

❑ Write data sets to multiple tapes, so the limitation of one tape's size doesn't limit the amount of data that can be stored.

❑ Using the graphical interface included in Backup, it's possible to select files for saving or restoring by volume, directory, or individual filename. Individual specifications of each file are also available, including current size and the date of the last modification.

❑ Backup can be configured to complete a verification pass, ensuring that the data has been reliably backed up to tape or reliably restored to a hard disk.

Using Backup

The Windows NT File Manager and Backup share a common appearance. Both use a series of icons to represent subdirectories and individual files. The one major difference is that Backup provides a small rectangular box next to each subdirectory and file, which is used for designating which items are to be copied to tape.

Notice how there are individual windows in Backup, each representing a different disk volume of the hard disk. The primary window in Backup shows the available disk volumes, with a window overlaying it, showing the subdirectories and files of an individual disk volume. In the previously shown figure, specific files have been selected for backup and are designated with a small "x" in the rectangular box to their left. Once all the files that are going to be backed up are selected, the Backup Information dialog box appears.

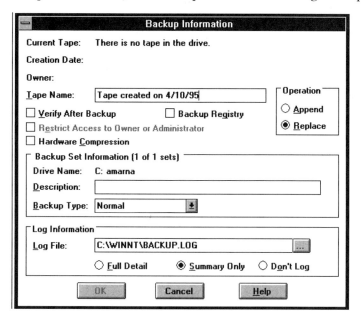

Backup Information dialog box.

Using the options in the Backup Information dialog box, you can specify a name for the tape, verify that the files have been reliably backed up, copy the registry from a Windows NT workstation to the tape (this is a good idea), restrict access to the Owner or Administrator of the tape, and specify if the backup is normal, copy, incremental, differential, or daily.

Once the Backup Information dialog box is ready, clicking once on OK begins the process of searching the hard disk for the files designated and placing them on tape. During the backup, a Backup Status dialog box is shown.

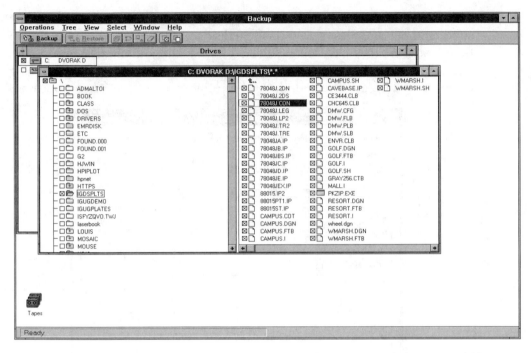

The Backup Status dialog box being used to save a subdirectory of files.

The elapsed time is recorded in the upper right corner and is also shown in the Summary portion of the dialog box. Once copying is complete, clicking on OK closes this dialog box and shows the Backup main window.

Security Issues

Integral to the Windows NT subsystem planning and design is security. Because the Windows NT operating system can track the performance of objects (as seen in the Performance Monitor), the security aspects of this operating system also make it possible to track the use of objects by individual accounts. In the case of a CAD administrator who is supporting an entire project consisting of individual groups of engineers, draftspersons, and architects, having the ability to secure specific system resources is critical.

Take, for example, a government subcontractor that is given the responsibility of creating a new military jet. While everyone on the project needs to see the schedule, only the electrical engineers with security clearances really need to know what the government expects in terms of electrical wiring and communication systems. An administrator working on this project could organize all the files associated with electrical wiring and communication systems, placing them into a secured directory on a Windows NT server, granting access only to the group that needs them. In short, the administrator has the ability to manage who gets to use which resources (printers, plotters, and files). Windows NT is unlike either Microsoft Windows or Windows for Workgroups in that neither of these operating environments provide for this level of security.

⇨ **NOTE:** *Using DOS FAT or HPFS filesystems, your security is very limited. Where security is a real issue, you should store important or sensitive files on an NTFS filesystem.*

Using the Security Log

The Administrative Tool's User Manager has options for specifying security for a given group of users or for individual user's accounts. Individual user accounts and groups can be monitored using Event Viewer. In the case of the CAD administrator who has set permissions on a specific series of files, the Event Viewer, and specifically the Security Log, show which users have accessed the resource, which users without access privileges have tried to access the resource, and which attempts have been successful. In the following figure of the Security Log in Event Viewer, notice that each event is entered into the Log in chronological order, making it possible to see any patterns of use as well.

If the CAD administrator in this instance sees that there is a high usage rate from users who have been given access privileges to the subdirectory, then adding another file server may be the best bet. If, on the other hand, there is a high level of unsuccessful logins, then the CAD administrator can speak with each account member who is trying to log into the files and let them know the area is restricted. Possibly someone has forgotten the password to access the shared subdirectory. In any case, the CAD administrator can see on an account basis who is trying to access restricted data.

Windows NT and Viruses

The spread of computer virus software in the IBM PC world has been a serious problem for companies for several years. A virus is a very nasty piece of software that can totally destroy data on your disk and render your system unbootable. Windows NT Workstation is not as prone to virus attach as MS-DOS, but you need to be aware of the following points:

❑ Viruses are often spread through executing infected programs. It does not matter if the infected program is on a Windows NT or UNIX server, a DOS client can still catch the virus when it runs the program. So while your system may not be affected, you can become the computer equivalent of Typhoid Mary and spread the virus to susceptible nodes on your network.

❑ Systems that boot DOS as well as Windows NT Workstation can catch the viruses that corrupt the Master Boot Record of the hard disk.

To minimize the chance of getting a virus on a Windows NT system, you should follow these steps, at a minimum.

1. Disable the ability to boot from a floppy drive. This is usually done in the system BIOS. This will prevent your system from catching many types of viruses that are spread when the system is booted from a DOS floppy.

2. Scan shared directories for viruses on a regular basis. This can be done by mounting the Windows NT drive on a DOS system and running a virus scan program.

3. Discourage other users from bringing floppies in from outside sources or connecting to badly maintained bulletin board services.

The need for virus protection in Windows NT Workstation has been recognized, and virus scanners that run under Windows NT are becoming available. For a reference to companies providing Windows NT virus scanners, see Appendix A.

Summary

This chapter provides you with a tour of the utilities available for managing a Windows NT workplace. Rather than providing you a comprehensive manual of point-and-click instructions on how to complete tasks using each of the applets and utilities in the Administrative Tools group, this chapter focuses on showing you the capabilities of each item included.

The Performance Monitor captures the performance of objects and their associated counters, so a baseline of system and network performance can be quickly created. Performance of a Windows NT system is dynamic, and the Performance Monitor is configurable to capture the interrelationships of one system performance variable relative to another.

The User Manager is self-descriptive in that all the functions included within this applet pertain to setting up, managing, granting permissions to, and deleting user accounts from a specific Windows NT workstation. Adding individual users to a group is also possible in User Manager.

Backup is a utility that is similar to File Manager in Windows and is used for taking files from a hard disk and getting them written to a hard disk drive and vice versa. The configuration options in this utility are comprehensive and can be easily customized, depending on what you are interested in accomplishing during a backup session.

The security aspects of Windows NT include the ability to set permissions on individual objects or resources (including printers, plotters, and file servers) and then monitor the level of activity on these objects using the Security Log in Event Viewer. Both authorized use and attempts at unauthorized use of a resource are reported in the Security Log.

Using Windows for Workgroups

Introduction

In the time between the introduction of Windows 3.1 and Windows NT, Microsoft introduced Windows for Workgroups. In the world of Microsoft Windows, connectivity between various computers located throughout an organization is difficult and frequently requires third-party software to ensure that accurate connections can be made. This major drawback of Microsoft Windows is alleviated in Windows for Workgroups. Included in Workgroups is the ability to share files, printers, and applications through File Manager with other members of the network.

The advantage that Windows for Workgroups has with regard to networking makes this graphical interface easily integrated into a Windows NT environment. Both Windows for Workgroups and Windows NT share a common network protocol—NETBEUI—which makes communication between each other possible, even transparent, so that a person using Windows for Workgroups will be able to use printers, files, or even applications located on a Windows NT workstation or server. In previous chapters of this book, the aspects of sharing resources and data through Windows NT is explored. In this chapter, the role of Windows for Workgroups relative to Windows NT and the complementary role of Windows for Workgroups in a distributed computing environment are explored.

What's New in Windows for Workgroups?

In Windows for Workgroups 3.11, there are additional features, ensuring that resource and information sharing can occur between various Windows for Workgroups–compatible systems. The following sections include some new features in Windows for Workgroups 3.11:

Network Access

What really differentiates Windows for Workgroups from Windows 3.1 is the ability Workgroups has for sharing information with Windows NT–based workstations, Novell NetWare–based servers, and Banyan VINES–based networks. In fact, if you are just beginning to plan a network for your office or school, you'll find that Windows for Workgroups is a great addition for PCs that you want to configure as Pro/ENGINEER or AutoCAD client seats to a centralized file or print server.

Network Efficiency

In the latest release of Windows for Workgroups, a new 32-bit network device driver makes file transfers and overall network performance significantly faster compared with previous versions.

Tools For Sharing Files and Printers

Members of a design team typically need to share files across a network when completing a project. Using the Connect Network Drive command in Workgroup's File Manager, designers and drafts people working on a project can easily share files. In fact, designers working in Windows NT will be able to share files with Workgroup-based systems as if both systems are Windows NT–based. The following figure shows the Connect Network Drive dialog box that is used within Windows for Workgroups.

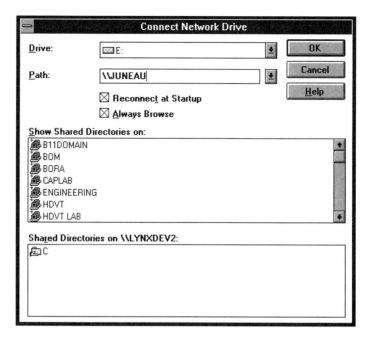

Windows for Workgroup's Connect Network Drive dialog box.

The person initiating the disk share can have the entire disk drive in a shared or accessible state or share only a single subdirectory.

Using the NETBEUI protocol also makes it possible for printer queues on Windows NT workstations and servers to be directly accessible for Windows for Workgroups–based client systems. Using the Connect To Printer command within Print Manager, it's possible to create a "pipe" queue from a Windows for Workgroups client directly to a Windows NT workstation or server. In the case of a designer needing to produce a plot, the options in Workgroup's Print Manager make it possible to use any of the printer queues directly located on any of the NT workstations located throughout the network of which the Workgroups system is a member.

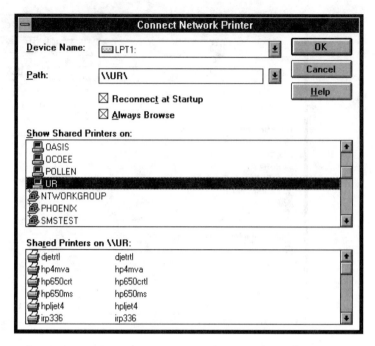

Using the Connect To Printer command in Windows for Workgroups.

Getting and Sending Messages Using Microsoft Mail

In the middle of completing a project, design files, data files, and messages need to be shared across buildings, cities, or even continents. Instead of putting the files and a note into a Federal Express envelope, or putting the files onto a bulletin board and having the other person take the time to retrieve the files, electronic mail can accomplish both the task of communicating and sending data at the same time. Included in Windows for Workgroups is Microsoft Mail. Messages created using this application can be sent to any other Windows for Workgroups–based computer or Windows NT workstation on the same network. Companies that have standardized on Microsoft Mail have found that few if any memos get typed, printed, copied, and distributed anymore. This means communication becomes instantaneous, with little lag time between when you send a design, drawing, or data file and the time when the person you are writing to receives it.

The following figure shows an example of a Microsoft Mail message with a MicroStation design file and Excel spreadsheet embedded within the message itself as an attachment. As you can see, messages can be easily integrated into the same message that is sending the data files. This greatly increases the speed at which project members can communicate and therefore complete a project. Once a company or university upgrades to electronic mail (called email) there is no going back to the conventional method of writing out memos then having someone else type, copy, and distribute them.

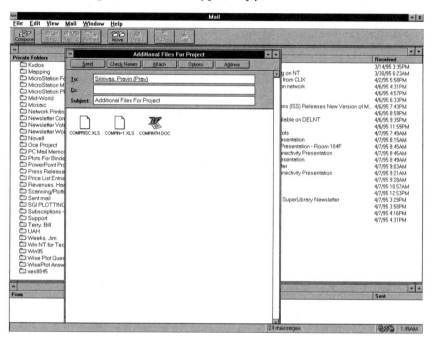

What a Microsoft Mail message looks like.

Fundamentals of Microsoft Mail in Windows for Workgroups

After Windows for Workgroups has been installed on an Intel-based PC, the following steps show how easy Microsoft Mail can be initiated and used. This can be accomplished by any experienced CAD system administrator or by a designer, draftsman, or engineer who is comfortable with the series of dialog boxes Windows-based applications use for getting configured.

To begin with, each Microsoft Mail "client" or member of a network must first become known to an existing post office, or create one of their own. If you think about it, it's just the same way many actual postal systems operate. When you move into a new house, you ascertain the street number and then fill out the appropriate form with the local post office. When you first click on the Microsoft Mail icon, you're prompted for the Workgroup Post Office (WGPO). You can either join an existing one or create your own. To receive and send mail, you'll need to join an existing WGPO, where the system administrator has already configured the entire post office for the workgroup. If unsure what this value is, consult your system administrator. Once online, you will be able to send and receive messages from all other members of the workgroup, making it possible to resolve design issues entirely through email, without having to stop development to meet and discuss an issue.

Understanding the Windows for Workgroups Network

Technical professionals have relied on networking tools for sharing data since the first computer systems were sold for the purpose of design and drafting. Many of the application programs that were used, and continue to be used today, rely on the client/server model of computing, where client systems throughout the network use both the computing and processing resources located on a centralized server. This client/server relationship is effective for centralized file management and especially for production plotting requirements in a thriving business.

The second approach to networking computers has become more pervasive as computers have spread throughout businesses that would otherwise have not tried automating processes. Companies such as Artisoft, Banyan, and Novell have pioneered the use of a network model that treats each system on the network at the same level of importance in terms of gaining access to resources. This model is called "peer-to-peer" networking because each computer on the network is a peer or equal to another. This approach to networking makes sense for smaller workgroups, where the overhead associated with having a centralized server would actually slow the response time, and therefore the efficiency of the network.

So, Microsoft, in creating Windows for Workgroups, decided that since many workers are already clustered by functional area and are interested in sharing data among the various computers that have the capability of acting as peers to one another, included peer-to-peer protocol support in Windows for Workgroups. The technical term for this protocol is *NETBEUI*. NETBEUI uses a LAN Manager to see every other Windows for Workgroups and even Windows NT workstations as fellow peers on a network. The following figure shows an example of how a peer-to-peer network running Microsoft Windows NT and Windows for Workgroups systems works.

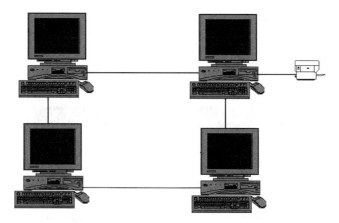

How a Windows for Workgroups network works.

As with any network, each of the computers that make up a Windows for Workgroups network requires a network adapter card within one of the computer's spare slots, along with cable linking one computer to another. Making sure these components are first in place makes it possible for Windows for Workgroups to be installed and configured to communicate with others on the network.

Logging onto a Workgroup

To see how the login process works for Windows for Workgroups, let's take a group of engineers and designers given the task of designing a new cruise ship. The designers are located throughout several buildings, sharing design files and data about the various subsystems located throughout the ship being defined. One group has the structural designs, whereas another is working with the electrical lines for both navigational and catering portions of the ship. Another design team is working on the 110-volt power lines that will be used throughout cabins that have outlets for hair dryers, curling irons, and other appliances people bring on board. Another group is working with the mechanical aspects of the ship, specifically what the engine displacement will be relative to the hull, and the location of the main power plant for driving the engine. With all these groups working in conjunction, there is the overwhelming need to share information and design files across functional boundaries.

As a new designer is added to the mechanical group, a PC is loaded with Windows for Workgroups and MicroStation Version 5 for Windows. The system administrator sets up the PC, giving the designer the opportunity to specify the password to use. The following figure shows the Windows for Workgroups login dialog box.

The Windows for Workgroups login dialog box.

The designer joining the mechanical group types in a password, and because the PC comes with Windows for Workgroups, the new designer now becomes a member of the Mechanical workgroup. The identity of this specific PC has already been defined, since each PC that is member of a workgroup has a specific identity. The identity for each system that is a member of a network is defined through the use of a computer name. This is similar to Windows NT Workstation, with the exception being that the former uses both a computer name and an Ethernet ID address for each workstation.

With the designer up and running, the system administrator gets the latest member of the Mechanical group logged into Microsoft Mail by first double-clicking on the Microsoft Mail icon located in the Network group of Windows for Workgroups.

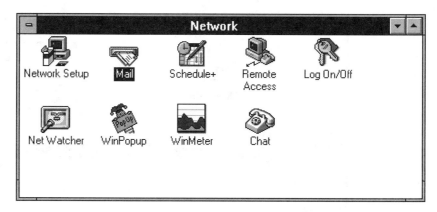

Microsoft Mail is located in the Network File Group.

Double-clicking on this icon, the system administrator launches Microsoft Mail. The Welcome to Mail dialog box appears, asking the system administrator whether a new post office should be created, or if an existing one will be connected to.

Welcome to Mail dialog box.

Since a WGPO already exists for the Mechanical Design Group, the system administrator clicks on the first option, Connect to an existing post office. The Connect to Post office dialog box appears and is used for specifying the network path to the existing Workgroup post office.

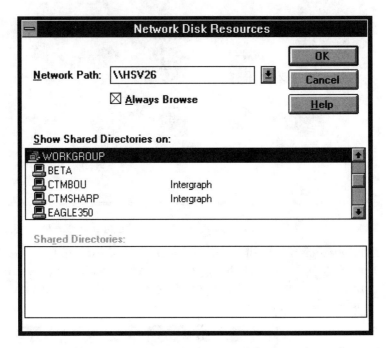

Connect to Post office dialog box, which is used for specifying the path to an existing Post office

With the path entered and making sure the new Workgroups PC is connected to the existing post office, the designer is ready to enter a password for the new Microsoft Mail account. With this password specified, the designer is ready to send and receive mail. Since the task of creating a ship is so large, there is a Global Address Book available to everyone involved in the project so that mail can be easily sent to each member of each workgroup. Upon logging in to Microsoft Mail, the designer sees that status reports from each functional area have been posted to the PC that he has been assigned. These status reports also include attachments. Microsoft Mail differentiates between Microsoft Mail messages with attachments and those without attachments by including a paper clip along the left side of the message's icon in the Inbox.

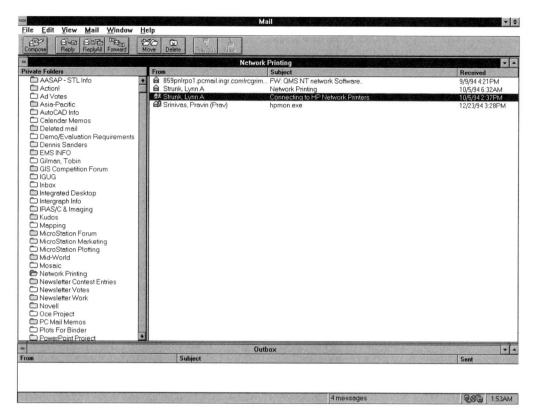

Microsoft Mail's main screen showing the accumulated Status Reports posted to all members of the project over the last three months.

Double-clicking on any of the messages shows the contents, including an icon along the lower portion of the message showing the attached file. Many of the status reports from other groups and from the Project Manager's Office are in Microsoft Word 6.0 for Windows. Double-clicking on the Word icon opens the Project Manager's Monthly Report that was posted two weeks previous to the designer's joining the group.

With Workgroup for Windows PC up and running with Microsoft Mail logged into the central post office, the designer is now capable of communicating with others, and most importantly, able to stay current with the developments being made during the project.

A Note on Passwords

When a password is not specified for a PC running Workgroups, it is assumed that all resources are available to everyone on the network. The entire contents of the hard disk and any printers attached to the PC are available using the Connect to Drive command. In the case of the designer using the Windows for Workgroups PC for contributing designs to the Mechanical Group, only a specific series of files need to be shared. To ensure that only the files that need to be shared are, and that no one else can log onto the PC, the designer decided to enter a new password. To do this, access the Network series of dialog boxes through the Network icon located in the Control Panel. The following figure shows the Network icon located in the Windows for Workgroups Control Panel group of applets.

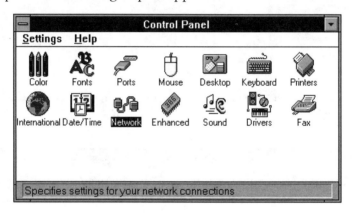

The Network Icon is used for changing passwords.

The designer double-clicks on the Password option in the Network dialog box and then changes the password. The designer confirms the password, and then clicks once on OK to close the dialog box. Now with Windows for Workgroups enabled with a password, only the designer will be able to gain access to its contents.

Optimizing Performance

As the project continues, design and drawing files grow in size and complexity. The attachments being sent over the network are growing, and sometimes network performance is affected by the number and size of messages being sent from one group to another. As with any project, in the closing stages, there is an acute need for rapid, accurate information sharing to ensure the entire project comes together according to the project schedule.

The cruise ship is taking shape on the dry dock. Work is now at a feverish pace as the designers, engineers, and draftsmen are trying to get their portions of the project completed on or before schedule. The system administrator needs to increase the Windows for Workgroup's PC performance to keep up with the larger files and accelerated pace. Instead of relying on the 16-bit access for files and disk drives that was originally provided in the first release of Windows for Workgroups, the system administrator decides to upgrade only the Workgroup-based PC systems to 32-bit applications and disk access. The system administrator sends out email to the Workgroup-based members of each team, giving them the instructions for getting their Workgroup-based PCs upgraded from 16-bit to 32-bit disk and file access.

The designer double-clicks on the 386 Enhanced icon located in the Control Panel.

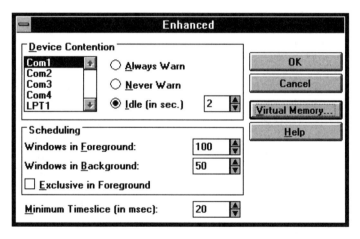

386 Enhanced dialog box.

The Enhanced dialog box appears and provides the designer with the opportunity of specifying a preference for device contention (or which output port gets precedence) and the scheduling of tasks in background or foreground memory. Clicking once on the Virtual Memory... button, the designer gets to the Virtual Memory dialog box, which is where both disk and file access can be changed from the default 16-bit mode to 32-bit.

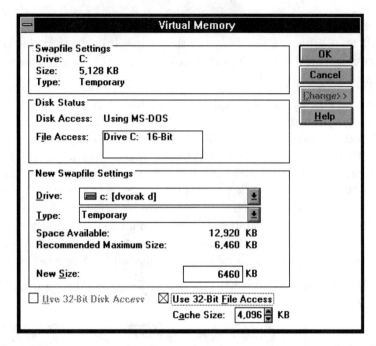

Disk and file access can be changed in the Virtual Memory dialog box.

Clicking once on the Change button, the Virtual Memory dialog box expands to show additional options for configuring Windows for Workgroups. Included in the expanded portion of the dialog box are the options of setting 32-bit Disk Access and File Access. Clicking once on each of these options, the designer ensures that the PC being used will now access both the disk drive and the network using 32-bit addressing, making it possible to retrieve the larger files that have been generated during the project. After selecting these two options, an interim dialog box is shown, asking the designer to confirm that the settings are to be changed. Clicking on Yes, the next dialog box asks if Windows should be restarted for the changes to take effect. Pressing Enter in response to this dialog box reboots the PC and has the 32-bit disk and file sharing options activated. With 32-bit addressing now in place, performance will increase.

Other Network Applications in Windows for Workgroups

Chat

As the designer becomes more familiar with the Windows for Workgroups environment, several other applets within the workgroup are used during designing and building the cruise ship. The first is Chat. Located in the Accessories file group, members of the design team can share messages interactively. This is typically used for cross-functional meetings with other groups located across the campus of buildings. Unlike Mail, Chat is interactive in that others you are conversing with can see what you type as you are typing it. Chat is simple to understand and use. The following figure shows an example of a Chat session in progress with regard to the ship's design.

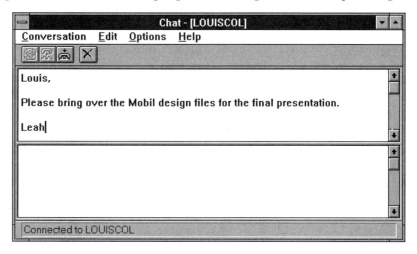

Chat Sessions are interactive and used for contacting others in the workgroup.

NetWatcher

As the designer works through the completion of how the mechanical components of the ship's engine will work in conjunction with other systems on the ship, it becomes necessary to share entire sets of drawings and files. Rather than opening up a file currently in use by another member of the design team, the designer can check to see which resources are being used by others using the NetWatcher applet. This applet makes it possible to view resources specific to the Windows for Workgroups PC that are being used by others throughout the network. This can be useful, especially if a design file is about to be modified or another series of Excel spreadsheets is in use locally.

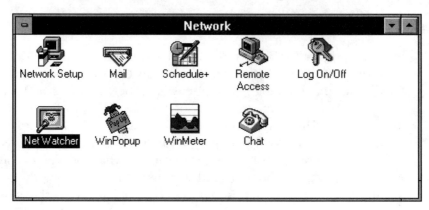

NetWatcher shows which resources are being used by group members

The series of icons along the top of the NetWatcher screen make it possible to display the properties of a specific connection, disconnect someone from using a resource, close a file, and log all activity viable by NetWatcher into an Event Log. Within the main window of the Event Watcher is a list of the resources currently being used. The eyeglasses that appear next to specific filenames designate the associated file is read-only. Before completing major modifications to existing design files, the designer checks the status of the resources that are available through the shared subdirectories on the system.

WinMeter

Another useful applet included in Windows for Workgroups is WinMeter. This applet or utility monitors the percentage of CPU time (or processing time) being used for processes you are working on relative to the CPU time being taken by others from your Workgroups-based PC. The percentage of the Applications portion of the WinMeter shows the percentage CPU utilization by local tasks, whereas the percentage of Server shows the percentage of CPU time being used by others throughout the network.

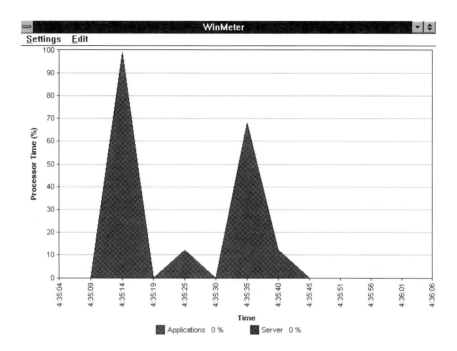

*The WinMeter shows CPU use during the completion
of the ship building project.*

Using the options in the Networks icon, which is described in an earlier section of this chapter, you can change the percentage utilization attributable to both local and distributed applications. WinMeter is a useful tool for measuring the amount of CPU time allocated for tasks being completed locally relative to those being completed on a network-wide basis, with the PC being used by the designer acting as a server-based CPU component.

Just as is the case with Windows NT, Windows for Workgroups includes a utility for being able to schedule appointments with others who are also members of the project team. Take the case of the cruise ship construction; each member of every design team has either Windows for Workgroups or Windows NT Workstation running on their systems. Because of this, when cross-functional meetings are scheduled to track the progress of a given series of subtasks, Schedule+ is used for getting everyone together. Schedule+ is actually a network-based application that is used for scheduling meetings automatically.

In Schedule+, the Project Manager responsible for the entire ship's construction opens up the Windows for Workgroups system, then uses Schedule+ for inviting all the team leaders to a cross-functional meeting. By typing their names into Schedule+ and then specifying a date and time, Windows for Workgroups sends email to each person mentioned as attendees, first checking each person's schedule to see if the time is available, and then sending them email that their schedule appears to be open for the meeting date and time. Each team leader can then respond to the mail message generated from Schedule+ and either accept the schedule meeting time or reject it. All meetings held on a cross-functional basis and from within each of the individual teams are scheduled without confirming dates and times with telephone calls. Schedule+ uses a format that looks just like a daily dairy, although views of months can be selected as well. Notice how meetings that have been successfully booked are designated with "shaking hands" in the left side of the meeting entry.

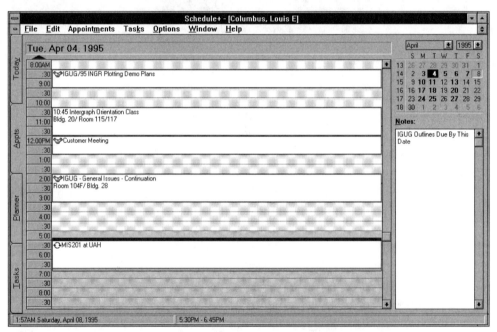

Daily View using Schedule+ to schedule meetings.

The company given the task of building the cruise ship has completely standardized on Windows NT Workstation and Windows for Workgroups, making sure that each team member can both send and receive mail and participate in meetings scheduled using Schedule+.

Summary

For technical professionals standardizing on Windows NT, the Windows for Workgroups operating environment provides members of workgroups the opportunity to share mail messages, files of all types, printers, plotters, and even schedule meetings using Schedule+. Due to NETBEUI, the peer-to-peer networking protocol present in both Windows NT and Windows for Workgroups, systems configured with either of these operating systems can actively share resources with one another.

In the context of the example of a cruise ship being designed and built, using Windows for Workgroups allows the system administrator to work with an operating environment that can easily hook into a Windows NT network. In addition, the cruise ship development project may eventually require laptop computers directly on the ship itself to check designs and complete design reviews. Having Ethernet lines through the ship's design would make it possible for laptop computers to have instant access to any design file. Many ships built today actually have complete networks integrated into the basic design. These networks are used for tracking the charges of passengers in various shops and bars on board. In addition, these networks receive email from a ship's main office, giving both the ship's navigational staff and cruise entertainment managers up-to-date information on excursions and the availability of special events for passengers in ports not yet reached. Windows for Workgroups provides this flexibility, so that the design of a cruise ship, and later its functioning, can be met using the features of this operating environment.

Tools and Utilities for Windows NT Workstation

Introduction

Windows NT is becoming a popular platform for developers of all types of software from public domain to shareware to a full suite of commercial applications for just about everything. This appendix will guide you through some of the best public domain, shareware, and commercial applications that will be useful in making your system fully productive and capable of speaking just about any network protocol including most popular UNIX TCP/IP services as well as DECNET, Banyan Vines, and Netware. The appendix consists of four sections:

1. **Public domain software:** Packages available for free include many 32-bit applications as well as some indispensable 16-bit applications that function in Windows NT.
2. **Shareware:** Shareware packages are packages you can obtain for a free evaluation; if you like them, pay for them, otherwise delete them.
3. **Commercial packages:** Concentrates mostly on UNIX interoperability tools as well support for other nonnative networking protocols such as Banyan Vines and DECNET.
4. **World Wide Web Resource Pointers:** Useful sites on the net to point your WWW browser at.

The information has been gathered from two main sources: The Microsoft maintained 32-bit application catalog and through surfing the net. If a MIPS or Alpha version is known to exist we'll mention that as well.

> ✔ **TIP:** *For public domain and shareware applications, if no specific FTP site is found, you can usually find the product at several sites, notably:*
>
> *ftp.oakland.edu*
> *ftp.cica.indiana.edu*
> *wuarchive.wustl.edu*
>
> *All the FTP site names given will accept "anonymous" as the user name and an email address as the password.*

Some sites are starting to specialize in collecting applications for the non-Intel NT platforms. Alpha users should make a point of visiting *ftp.garply.com*; check the directory */pub/pc/nt/alpha*. The *ftp.garply* site also maintains an archive of Intel NT apps maintained by one of the authors: Nik Simpson. This can be found in the directory */pub/pc/nt/intel*.

Public Domain Packages

Winvn: 32-bit version of popular NNTP based news reader for the USENET news network.

> Latest version always available from *ftp.ksc.nasa.gov*, and the directory is */pub/winvn/nt*.
>
> This is available in Intel, Alpha, and MIPS formats.

ws_ftp32: Simple, powerful, and fully 32-bit GUI-based FTP client. Ideal replacement for the command line client in Windows NT.

> Found on many FTP sites, the latest version is always available from the author John A. Junod, the site is *ftp.gordon.army.mil*, and the directory is */winsock/ws_ftp*.

Only available for the Intel platform; MIPS and Alpha users can use the 16-bit Windows 3.1 version.

Eudora 1.4.4: Still a 16-bit Windows 3.1 application, it provides a POP3 based mail client that can send and receive file attachments using the Multimedia Internet Message Exchange (MIME) standard. This version of Eudora is a slightly less functional version of the commercial product available from Qaulcomm.

> Latest version is always found on *ftp.qualcomm.com* in directory */quest/windows/eudora/1.4*.

Wintalk: Implements a complete UNIX style talk program with support for the "talk" and "ntalk" protocols. Has a simple Windows GUI interface.

Latest version found on *ftp.elf.com*; directory is */pub/wintalk*. Currently, this is a 16-bit program and should run on Alpha and MIPS platforms.

Winrsh: Implements the UNIX Remote Shell or "rsh" application. Simple GUI-based application; lets you run commands on a remote UNIX host.

Available from many FTP sites including those mentioned in the introduction.

This is available as a 16-bit version that can run on Alpha and MIPS as well as a 32-bit version for the Intel NT platform.

ws_ping32: Another excellent utility from the author of the *ws_ftp* program. The *ws_ping* application is actually several UNIX TCP/IP clients in one package. It implements **nslookup**, **ping**, and **traceroute.**

Found on many FTP sites, the latest version is always available from the author John A. Junod, the site is *ftp.gordon.army.mil*, the directory is */winsock/ ws_ping.*

No 32-bit Alpha or MIPS versions, but the 16-bit version found in the same directory on *ftp.gordon.army.mil.*

ws_gopher: Gopher is a UNIX-based Information server. Gopher clients are available for many systems. This is one of several available for Windows. Currently it is a 16-bit application so should run on any Windows NT platform.

Found on many FTP sites, the latest version is always available from *dewey.tis.inel.gov*, the directory is */pub/ws_gopher.*

Ewan: Windows NT comes with a simple Telnet client. If you want more functionality, then take a look at ewan. This has many more features than the built-in client. Currently only available as a 16-bit application, it should run on any Windows NT platform.

Found on many FTP sites, the official download site for the US is *fpt.best.com,* and the directory is */pub/bryanw/pc/winsock.*

WinWAIS: Provides a Windows-based interface to information stored on Wide Area Information Service (WAIS) servers. This is a 16-bit application and should run on any Windows NT platform.

Found on *ridgisd.er.usgs.gov,* the directory is */software/wais.*

Mosaic: This is a WWW browser application. Mosaic is available as part of several commercial packages, or as free version (fewer features than the commercial versions).

Latest version found on many including those mentioned in the introduction. You can be sure of getting the very latest versions from *ftp.ncsa.uiuc.edu* in directory */Mosaic/Windows*.

Mosaic is a fully 32-bit application available for Intel, Alpha, and MIPS platforms.

Windows NT 3.5 Resource Kit: The NT resource kit is an indispensable part of any serious Windows NT environment. You can purchase the resource kit on a CD along with several volumes of excellent information. If you just want the utilities, you can get the resource kit via FTP.

You can be sure of getting the very latest versions from *ftp.microsoft.com* in directory */bussys/winnt/winnt-public/reskit/nt35*.

The resource kit contains many tools and utilities, including servers for Gopher, HTTP (World Wide Web), DNS, and WAIS.

NNS: Windows NT News Server provides full USENET news server capabilities on Windows NT.

You can get this from *ftp.wa.com* in directory */pub/local/ntnews*.

NNS is a very good implementation of the News server service.

SAMBA: This is not an NT application. It is a UNIX application that adds Windows NT style file and sharing services to a UNIX node. Many different UNIX varieties are supported.

The Samba suite is available via anonymous FTP from *nimbus.anu.edu.au*. The latest and released version of the suite is in the directory */pub/tridge/samba*.

POPPER: This is another UNIX application. If your UNIX systems do not support the POP protocol, then you can obtain the source to a POP daemon from *ftp.qualcomm.com*. The software is pretty simple an requires little porting effort.

➡ *NOTE: This list of public domain or freeware applications is by no means exhaustive. If you have access to the Internet, then you should make a point of visiting one or more of the FTP sites mentioned in the introduction; these are vast repositories of public domain and shareware applications.*

Shareware Packages

Shareware is basically a "try before you buy" scheme. The software is free to obtain and evaluate. If you like the software, you should send money to the author. You'll find details of how to pay for a particular shareware application in its documentation or on-line help.

Dezktop: Currently, none of the vendors who provide "Program Manager" replacements for Windows 3.1 have Windows NT products; this includes such popular packages as Norton Desktop. If prefer the type of interface provided by Norton Desktop, then Dezktop may meet your needs.

> Found on *budman.cmdl.noaa.gov,* directory is */RMWNTUG/software/general.* This site is the home of the Rocky Mountain Windows NT User group (RMWNTUG)

Cost for this package is $15.

Ataman telnetd: Allows remote Telnet clients to get a Telnet command line connection to your Windows NT system. This allows a certain amount of remote administration from a UNIX or other Telnet capable system. For details of what can easily be done from the command line try typing "net help" from in a command window on your system.

> Found on *budman.cmdl.noaa.gov,* and the directory is */RMWNTUG/software/winsock.*

WinZipNT: The full 32-bit ZIP archiver with a Windows GUI. Lets you create and manipulate compressed ZIP archives.

> Found on *budman.cmdl.noaa.gov,* and the directory is */RMWNTUG/software/general.*

Paint Shop Pro: Supports many different image formats including TIFF, GIF, JPEG, Photo CD, and many more. If you have a need to manipulate raster image files, then this 16-bit application is an excellent and inexpensive choice.

> The evaluation copy can be found on many FTP sites, including *ftp.winternet.com,* the directory is */users/jasc/.* If you cannot find it on the net, contact the vendor directly at:

JASC, Inc.
10901 Red Circle Drive, Suite 340
Minnetonka, MN 55343 USA

MPEGPLAY: A 32-bit MPEG viewer. The free version will not load an MPEG file larger than 1MB (pretty limited). The full version costs $25.

The evaluation copy is available from many FTP sites. You can always find it at *ftp.ncsa.uiuc.edu* in directory */Mosaic/Windows/Viewers*.

Commercial Packages

This purpose of this section is to identify packages that can offer NFS and other network protocols to help integrate Windows NT into a heterogeneous environment.

NFS Packages

PROGRESS Software Corporation

NFSware for Windows NT, a 32-bit, multithreaded Network File System (NFS) server. Allows re-export of remote Windows NT filesystems to UNIX nodes.

Retail Price: Starts at $295.00
Contact: Beth Hennessy
Phone: 800-722-7770
Fax: 508-879-0042
RISC Versions: Yes

NetManage Inc.

Chameleon32/NFS provides a complete suite of TCP/IP applications for Windows NT including the first NFS client/server for Windows NT. Applications include Telnet, TN3270, TN5250, Scripting, FTP (client and server), TFTP, LPR/LPD, NFS (client-server), SMTP Mail with MIME, News Reader, Ping, Finger, Who ISS, Gopher, and Bind.

Retail Price: $695.00
Contact: Inside Sales
Phone: 408-973-7171
Fax: 408-257-6405

RISC Versions: Yes
International Sales: 408-973-7171

Intergraph Corporation

DiskShareNFS Server for Windows NT

Intergraph's DiskShare software is a robust Network File System (NFS) server product that enables UNIX users to share filesystems with systems based on Windows NT and Windows NT Server operating systems. Continuing its leadership role in development for Windows NT, Intergraph is the first vendor in the market to supply a kernel implementation of an NFS server that allows UNIX systems to access Windows NT Workstation and Windows NT Server as they would a UNIX-based NFS server. DiskShare supports the following Windows NT filesystems: File Allocation Table (FAT); High-Performance File System (HPFS); New Technology File System (NTFS); and Compact Disk File System (CDFS).

PC-NFS Client for Windows NT

PC-NFS for Windows NT is the standard for connecting Windows NT–based systems to Network File System (NFS) servers on a network. Based on the TCP/IP and Open Network Computing/Network File System (ONC/NFS) standards, PC-NFS for Windows NT provides a single solution to integrate Windows NT–based client systems into multivendor client/server networks. This means that Windows NT users can share files and network resources, such as printers and plotters, with multivendor networks including UNIX systems, mainframe hosts, and other systems. And TCP/IP networking standards give PC-NFS the power to provide a fully scalable networking platform, giving both local and wide area connectivity to countless PCs.

Retail Price: Call for pricing
Contact: Customer Service
Phone: 800-345-4856
Fax: 205-730-2108

RISC Versions: Call for availability

International Sales:
United States: 800-345-4856
Asia/Pacific: 852-8661966
Canada: 403-250-6100
Europe: 31-2503-66333
Middle East: 971-4-367555
Other areas: 205-730-2700

Consensys

Portage NFS

Portage NFS is the networking component of Portage, the complete integration of UNIX SVR4 with Windows NT and Windows Chicago. Portage NFS provides full peer-to-peer filesystem connectivity between Windows NT or Windows 95–based system and any UNIX or other NFS-capable computer. The portage NDK provides a complete environment for creating or porting UNIX networking programs to Windows NT or Chicago. It includes a full implementation of the UNIX sockets API, the complete set of Portage SVR4 system calls, plus all the Portage UNIX SVR4 development tools. Complete UNIX compatibility, including long, case-sensitive filenames, and symbolic links are supported.

Retail Price: Call for pricing
Contact: Vas Rajevski
Phone: 905-940-2900
Fax: 905-940-2903

RISC Versions: Yes

International Sales:
Europe and Africa: Phone: 44-734-833241; Fax: 44-734-835-391
Asia and South America: 905-940-2900

Distinct Corp.

Distinct TCP/IP Tools/NFS

Complete TCP/IP application suite for Telnet (VT100-VT220, TN3270), FTP, TFTP, E-mail, News Gopher, NFS, LPR/LPD, Finger, Whois, and others. Distinct TCP/IP Tools for Windows includes the smallest and fastest Windows Sockets, multiple Telnet sessions, drag and drop file transfer, email, TFTP, Ping, Network Monitor, network printer driver for transparent remote printing (LPR/LPD), Finger, Whois, SNMP agent, and more. Supports Packet, NDIS, and ODI drivers concurrently with SLIP or PPP.

Retail Price: Call for pricing
Contact: Inside Sales
Phone: 408-366-8933
Fax: 408-366-0153

RISC Versions: Call for availability

Beame & Whiteside

BW-Connect™ NFS Server for Windows NT, Version 1.0

BW-Connect NFS Server for Windows NT/Windows NT Server is a server implementation of the Network File System (NFS) that runs on top of the native TCP/IP stack that is included in Windows NT. BW-Connect NFS Server grants/denies access to local Windows NT disk, CD-ROM, and print resources based on a user-defined EXPORTS file. It allows remote users to browse the BW-Connect NFS Server for resources that have been exported. UNIX symbolic links, long filenames, "Holey" file support, and logging of mount/un-mount requests are all supported. BW-Connect NFS Server provides a graphical screen that displays server statistics such as NFS reads/writes, mount requests, lock requests, and PCNFSD requests.

Retail Price: $449.00
Contact: Inside Sales
Phone: 919-831-8989
Fax: 919-831-8990

RISC Versions: Yes

Banyan Vines

Banyan have recently announced a full 32-bit Banyan client for Windows NT. The Banyan client supports all the features of the Banyan network such as the "Street Talk" naming service, as well as integrating with the NT login process and File manager.

For more information contact Banyan directly at:

Banyan Systems Inc.
120 Flanders Road
Westboro, MA 01581 USA
Telephone: 508-898-1000
Fax: 508-898-1755

Netware

Novell recently announced a full 32-bit Windows NT client that integrates with the services provide by the Netware 4.x release, including the NDS naming service. The built-in client in Windows NT only supports the features of the

Netware 3.x releases. For more information on this product contact Novell dealer.

Beame and Whiteside

BW-MultiConnect™ for Windows NT/Windows NTBW-MultiConnect is a Novell NetWare 3.x file server emulator for Windows NT that makes a machine running Windows NT look like a NetWare file server to Novell client workstations. It provides existing NetWare users with seamless access to Windows NT–based files and printers. BW-MultiConnect comprises of a high-performance IPX device driver stack and a loadable network driver that provides file server functions. The network system administrator specifies that file and print resources on the Windows NT–based machine are to be exported to NetWare clients. All software resides on the Windows NT–based machine; no additional client workstation software is necessary. Supports Ethernet or Token-Ring hardware, all standard frame types, bidirectional printing, and symmetric multiprocessors. A programmer's API library is provided.

Retail Price: Call for pricing
Contact: Inside Sales
Phone: 919-831-8989
Fax: 919-831-8990

RISC Versions: Yes

DECNET

Digital Equipment Corporation

PATHWORKS for Windows NT

PATHWORKS for Windows NT software, available on Alpha AXP, Intel, and MIPS platforms, enables Windows NT Workstation users to share information and network resources, in local and wide area networks, with other PATH-WORKS clients (Microsoft Windows, MS-DOS, OS/2, and Macintosh users) and to access other PATHWORKS servers (PATHWORKS for OpenVMS, ULTRIX, SCO UNIX, and OS/2 servers). Additionally, any PATHWORKS client based on LAN Manager can use a Windows NT Server as a PATHWORKS network server.

Retail Price: Call for pricing
Contact: Abe Litman
Phone: 508-497-7817
Fax: 508-635-8724

RISC Versions: Yes

X11 Server Software

AGE Logic Inc.

XoftWare/32 for Windows NT brings full 32-bit X11R5 server performance to PCs running the Microsoft Windows NT operating system. With XoftWare/32 for Windows NT, users can concurrently access and display Windows, Windows NT, and network-based UNIX applications on the same PC. AGE also offers the most comprehensive line of PC X servers available for the Windows NT operating system. Versions are currently available for both Intel- and MIPS-based PCs. Versions designed for the PowerPC and DEC Alpha PC platforms will be available the first quarter of 1995.

Retail Price: $495.00
Contact: Inside Sales
Phone: 619-455-8600
Fax: 619-597-6030

RISC Versions: Yes
Dennis McNamara, Director, International Sales: 619-550-3128

Control Data Inc.

Vista-eXceed/NT

This product fully utilizes the multitasking of the Windows NT operating system, permitting the concurrent execution and interaction of X clients and MS-DOS, Windows, and Windows NT–based applications across the network. Features include full X11 Release 5 compliance, two windowing modes, X protocol tracer, and copy and paste of both text and images between X Window, Windows NT, Windows, and MS-DOS environments.

Retail Price: Call for pricing
Contact: Customer Service

Phone: 301-808-4281
Fax: 301-808-4288

RISC Versions: Call for availability

DataFocus Inc.

NuTCRACKER X/OE

The NuTCRACKER X/OE contains a 32-bit X Server based on X11R5 and the NuTCRACKER dynamic-link libraries (DLLs). It is designed to be an operating environment that turns your PC into an X Window System graphics terminal running under Windows NT. This serves as the run-time for applications ported using the NuTCRACKER X/SDK.

Retail Price: Introductory: $295 (Reg. list $495)
Contact: NuTCRACKER Sales
Phone: 1-800-637-8034
Fax: 703-818-1532

RISC Versions: Call for availability

Hummingbird Communications, Ltd.

eXceed/NT

eXceed/NT provides a high degree of integration between Windows NT and X Window System hosts (such as UNIX and VMS), offering end users concurrent access to X Window clients and applications for Windows NT. eXceed/NT fully uses the multitasking Windows NT operating system, permitting the concurrent execution and interaction of X clients and MS-DOS, Windows, and Windows NT–based applications across the network. eXceed/NT provides two windowing modes and allows users to switch window modes on the fly. eXceed/NT is fully X11R5 compliant, offers unlimited font size, and provides hundreds of fonts in Windows NT format. Supports up to 64 X Window client connections. eXceed/NT supports the Windows Sockets compliant TCP/IP transport provided in the Windows NT operating system.

Retail Price: Call for pricing
Contact: Hummingbird Sales Dept.
Phone: 905-470-1203
Fax: 905-470-1207

RISC Versions: Yes

International Sales:
Europe: 41-22-733-1858
United Kingdom: 44-532-467-253

Intergraph Corporation

eXalt

This is a full 32-bit X server for Windows NT. Product highlights include:

❏ 32-bit implementation for maximum processing power

❏ Open communication through compatibility with industry standards

❏ Choice of window managers, startup modes, and installation levels for administrative

❏ Flexibility and control

❏ Simple, dialog box-driven installation and configuration procedures

❏ Seamless integration between the X and Microsoft Windows environments

❏ Extensive font support: Intergraph's Font Server, *.PCF*, and *.BDF* formats

❏ Digitizer support

For more information on this product:

Retail Price: Call for pricing
Contact: Customer Service
Phone: 800-345-4856
Fax: 205-730-2108

RISC Versions: Call for availability

International Sales:
United States: 800-345-4856
Asia/Pacific: 852-8661966
Canada: 403-250-6100
Europe: 31-2503-66333
Middle East: 971-4-367555
Other areas: 205-730-2700

UNIX Shells and Porting Tools

Hamilton Laboratories

Hamilton C shell

Hamilton C shell recreates the original Berkeley UNIX C shell and utilities, adding numerous enhancements. Features history, full-screen command line editing, filename and command completion, user-defined and built-in procedures (even a print), aliases, expressions, local variables, command substitution, and improved wild carding. Outstanding scripting capabilities. Unlimited command line size. Extensively multithreaded. More than 130 commands, including chmod, cp, cron, cut, diff, fgrep, grep, head, kill, more, mv, printf, rm, sed, strings, tail, tar (supports tapes), touch, tr, uniq, and wc. Designed from scratch. Carefully follows all Win32 conventions. Fanatical quality. Shipping for Intel (including Windows Chicago), MIPS, Alpha, and PowerPC.

Retail Price: $350.00 ($395.00 international)
Contact: Doug Hamilton
13 Old Farm Road
Wayland, MA 01778-3117 USA
Phone: 508-358-5715
Fax: 508-358-1113

RISC Versions: Yes

Mortice Kern Systems, Inc.

MKS Toolkit

MKS Toolkit, winner of a 1993 Jolt Cola Product Excellence Award, provides 190+ powerful UNIX utilities for PC platforms, including vi, awk, uucp, make, and kornshell. Many of these utilities were once only available on UNIX systems, but now MKS has made them available on contemporary operating systems such as OS/2, MS-DOS, Windows, and Windows NT.

Retail Price: $299.00
Contact: Michelle Lyon
Phone: 519-883-4362
Fax: 519-884-8861

RISC Versions: Yes

Consensys

Portage

Portage is a complete integration of UNIX SVR4 with Windows NT and Windows Chicago, including more than 150 standard UNIX utilities, the Korn shell, and the C shell. Developed from the original USL UNIX source code, Portage is not merely UNIX-like, it is a complete licensed implementation of the UNIX operating system for Win32. In addition, Portage provides a Windows interface to manage multiple UNIX shells with a dialog box for every command, the ability to run UNIX commands from the Windows command prompt and Windows NT commands from UNIXC shells, and complete on-line manual pages in Windows Help format. Portage is available for Intel systems as well as the major RISC architectures such as Alpha AXP, MIPS, and PowerPC. Full Spec. 1170 conformance is scheduled for Q4 1994.

Retail Price: $695.00
Contact: Bob Ripley
Phone: 905-940-2900
Fax: 905-940-2903

RISC Versions: Yes

International Sales:
Europe: Phone: 44-734-833-241; Fax: 44-734-835-391
International (General): Phone: 905-940-2900; Fax: 905-940-2903

Portage SDK

The Portage Software Development Kit includes more than 20 standard UNIX SVR4 software development tools, the full curses library, along with the complete Portage run-time libraries that implement more than 500 UNIX SVR4 system calls and library functions. These are the same tools and libraries that were used to compile the UNIX SVR4 source code to produce all the UNIX utilities included in Portage. Whether you're porting existing UNIX software to Windows NT or writing new code that needs to run both UNIX and Windows NT, the Portage SDK can save you months of hard work. The Portage SDK allows you to combine Win32 and UNIX APTs to develop true native Win32 programs.

Retail Price: Call for pricing
Contact: Vas Rajevski

Phone: 905-940-2900
Fax: 905-940-2903

RISC Versions: Yes

International Sales:
Europe and Africa: Phone: 44-734-833241; Fax: 44-734-835-391
Asia and South America: 905-940-2900

DataFocus Inc.

NuTCRACKER™ SDK

NuTCRACKER SDK is the fastest and most cost-effective way to port any UNIX applications to Windows NT Workstation or Windows 95. Using NuT-CRACKER, developers can create native Win32 applications from their UNIX C or C++ source code. This way, organizations can preserve their investment in UNIX developers and applications while reducing porting time and costs by more than 60%.

Retail Price and Contact: See following product information.

NuTCRACKER X/SDK

NuTCRACKERs X/SDK is the fastest and most cost-effective way to port any UNIX application X/Motif, character-based, or daemon to Windows NT. NuTCRACKER X/SDK provides UNIX tools, UNIX libraries, and an X Server, all written to Windows NT. Developers simply compile their C or C++ source code and link it against NuTCRACKER DLLs, creating native Win32 applications and reducing porting time by 60%.

Retail Price: Call for pricing
Contact: NuTCRACKER Sales
Phone: 800-637-8034
Fax: 703-818-1532

RISC Versions: Yes

International Sales: Mark Funt at 908-583-7766

Interesting World Wide Web Sites

If you have access to the Internet, there is a wealth of information on Windows NT available to you using a browser like Mosaic. The following is a list of sites that may be of interest to you:

http://budman.cmdl.noaa.gov/RMWNTUG/RMWNTUG.HTM"

Home page for the Rocky Mountain Windows NT Usergroup

http://www.bhs.com/winnt/resources.html

Links to many Windows NT–related sites; this is one of the best and most complete Windows NT sites around. Lots of software, advice, and reference service for Windows NT Consultants and service providers.

http://www.luc.edu/tbaltru/faq/

Everything you ever wanted to know about connecting Windows NT systems to the Internet.

http://emwac.ed.ac.uk/mirrors/gowinnt/Advsys/winnt/winnt-publi c/NTFAQ.TXT

Part of a joint project between Microsoft and several academic sites in Europe. Many question and answers about Windows NT at this site.

http://www.microsoft.com/pages/bussys/ntw/ntw10000.htm

Microsoft Windows NT home page.

ftp://ftp.microsoft.com/developr/drg/Catalogs/win32cat.exe

Always has the latest addition of the Win32 application catalog. Much of the information in this appendix was obtained from that catalog.

http://bongo.cc.utexas.edu/neuroses/cwsapps.html

Home page of the Consumate Winsock Application list. This is a "must see" site; excellent collection of Winsock applications and a lot else besides.

http://www.ksc.nasa.gov/software/winvn/winvn.html

Home page for the Winvn newsreader. Get all the latest information about winvn here.

http://www.garply.com/tech/comp/sw/pc/nt/alpha.html

Best selection of software for Alpha-based Windows NT systems.

http://venus.earthlink.net:80/execsoft/

Executive Software Home page. Offers a tool to defragment NTFS file systems.

http://www.microsft.com

Home page for Microsoft.

http://www.intergraph.com

Home page for Intergraph Corporation. Has 1 month evaluation copies of Intergraph NFS and X11 products.

gopher://ftp.cica.indiana.edu:70/11/pc/win3/nt

Download archive of all Windows NT related software stored on the CICA site.

http://www.imagi.net/rmarty/nt.html

Home page for the Interior Alaska Windows NT User Group. Excellent site; many links to Windows NT related information.

http://www.mcs.net/sculptor/NTFAX-FAQ.HTML

Everything you ever wanted to know about FAX solutions for Windows NT.

Quick Reference to Keyboard Shortcuts

Getting around in Windows NT using the keyboard is easy using the keyboard shortcuts briefly described here. Consider this to be a quick reference resource you can use for getting access to menus and commands quickly.

For Getting Help

Press F1	Switches you to the Help window.
Press TAB, ENTER	Move to and view the next term, definition, or file.

Keyboard Shortcuts in File Manager

+ (keypad)	Expand the directory tree one level.
* (keypad)	Expand a directory branch one location.
CTRL+*	Expand branch to all levels available.
- (keypad)	Collapse a directory one level.
F5 (Function key)	Refresh the screen.

Keystroke Shortcuts for Moving Around in a Window or Dialog Box

Arrow keys	Scroll up or down one line, or left or right one item.
PAGE UP	Scroll up one window.

PAGE DOWN	Scroll down one window.
CTRL+PAGE UP	Scroll left one window.
CTRL+PAGE DOWN	Scroll right one window.

Moving and Selecting a Window or Dialog Box

TAB	Move to an item in the dialog box and select it.
Arrow keys	Move left, right, up, or down in a window or dialog box.
HOME	Move to the beginning of a line.
END	Move to the end of a line.
PAGE UP or PAGE DOWN	Move up or down one window.
CTRL+PAGE UP	Move left one window.
CTRL+PAGE DOWN	Move right one window.
SHIFT+arrow keys	Extend the selection left, right, up, or down.
SHIFT+HOME	Extends the selection to the beginning of the line.
SHIFT+END	Extends the selection to the end of the line.
SHIFT+PAGE UP	Extends the selection to the preceding window, or one window up.
SHIFT+PAGE DOWN	Extends the selection down one window.
CTRL+SHIFT+PAGE UP	Extends the selection left one window.
CTRL+SHIFT+PAGE DOWN	Extends the selection right one window.

Keyboard Shortcuts for Working with a Window

ALT or F10 (function key)	Select the menu bar.
ENTER	Carry out an action or command.
ESC	Cancel a command or action.
ALT+ENTER	Toggle on full-screen display for non-Windows applications running within the Command Prompt.
ALT+SPACEBAR	Select an application's Control menu.
ALT or hyphen (-)	Select the Control menu in the document window.

CTRL+ESC	Display the Task List.
ALT+TAB	Make the next active application active.
ALT+F4	Quit the current application.

For Working with Multiple Document Windows

CTRL+F7	Move a selected window.
CTRL+F8	Size an active window.
CTRL+F10	Maximize an active window.
CTRL+F9	Minimize an active window.
CTRL+F5	Restore an active window.
CTRL+F4	Close an active window.
CTRL+F6	Move or switch to the next window.
F6	Move to the next pane of the active window.
SHIFT+F6	Move the previous window's pane.

Index

More
OnWord Press Titles

Pro/ENGINEER and Pro/JR. Books

INSIDE Pro/ENGINEER
Book $49.95 Includes Disk

Pro/ENGINEER Quick Reference, 2d ed.
Book $24.95

Pro/ENGINEER Exercise Book
Book $39.95 Includes Disk

Thinking Pro/ENGINEER
Book $49.95

INSIDE Pro/JR.
Book $49.95

Interleaf Books

INSIDE Interleaf
Book $49.95 Includes Disk

Adventurer's Guide to Interleaf Lisp
Book $49.95 Includes Disk

The Interleaf Exercise Book
Book $39.95 Includes Disk

The Interleaf Quick Reference
Book $24.95

Interleaf Tips and Tricks
Book $49.95 Includes Disk

MicroStation Books

INSIDE MicroStation 5X, 3d ed.
Book $34.95 Includes Disk

MicroStation Reference Guide 5.X
Book $18.95

MicroStation Exercise Book 5.X
Book $34.95
Optional Instructor's Guide $14.95

MicroStation 5.X Delta Book
Book $19.95

MicroStation for AutoCAD Users , 2d ed.
Book $34.95

Adventures in MicroStation 3D
Book 49.95 Includes Disk

MicroStation Productivity Book
Book $39.95
Optional Disk $49.95

MicroStation Bible
Book $49.95
Optional Disks $49.95

Build Cell
Software $69.95

101 MDL Commands
Book $49.95
Optional Executable Disk $101.00
Optional Source Disks (6) $259.95

101 User Commands
Book $49.95
Optional Disk $101.00

Bill Steinbock's Pocket MDL Programmer's Guide
Book $24.95

Managing and Networking MicroStation
Book $29.95
Optional Disk $29.95

The MicroStation Database Book
Book $29.95
Optional Disk $29.95

INSIDE I/RAS B
Book $24.95 Includes Disk

The CLIX Workstation User's Guide
Book $34.95 Includes Disk

SunSoft Solaris Series

The SunSoft Solaris 2.* User's Guide
Book $29.95 Includes Disk

SunSoft Solaris 2.* for Managers and Administrators
Book $34.95

The SunSoft Solaris 2.* Quick Reference
Book $18.95

Five Steps to SunSoft Solaris 2.*
Book $24.95 Includes Disk

One Minute SunSoft Solaris Manager
Book $14.95

SunSoft Solaris 2.* for Windows Users
Book $24.95

The Hewlett Packard HP-UX Series

The HP-UX User's Guide
Book $29.95 Includes Disk

The HP-UX Quick Reference
Book $18.95

Five Steps to HP-UX
Book $24.95 Includes Disk

One Minute HP-UX Manager
Book $14.95

CAD Management

One Minute CAD Manager
Book $14.95

Manager's Guide to Computer-Aided Engineering
Book $49.95

Other CAD

CAD and the Practice of Architecture: ASG Solutions
Book $39.95 Includes Disk

INSIDE CADVANCE
Book $34.95 Includes Disk

Using Drafix Windows CAD
Book $34.95 Includes Disk

Fallingwater in 3D Studio: A Case Study and Tutorial
Book $39.95 Includes Disk

Geographic Information Systems/ESRI

The GIS Book, 3d ed.
Book $34.95

INSIDE ARC/INFO
Book $74.95 Includes CD

ARC/INFO Quick Reference
Book $24.95

ArcView Developer's Guide
Book $49.95

INSIDE ArcView
Book $39.95 Includes CD

DTP/CAD Clip Art

1001 DTP/CAD Symbols Clip Art
Library: Architectural
Book $29.95

DISK FORMATS:
MicroStation
DGN Disk $175.00
Book/Disk $195.00

AutoCAD
DWG Disk $175.00
Book/Disk $195.00

CAD/DTP
DXF Disk $195.00
Book/Disk $225.00

OnWord Press Distribution

End Users/User Groups/Corporate Sales

OnWord Press books are available worldwide to end users, user groups, and corporate accounts from your local bookseller or computer/software dealer, or from HMP Direct: call 1-800-223-6397 or 505-473-5454; fax 505-471-4424; write to High Mountain Press Direct/Softstore, 2530 Camino Entrada, Santa Fe, NM 87505-8435, or e-mail to ORDERS @BOOKSTORE.HMP.COM.

Wholesale, Including Overseas Distribution

High Mountain Press distributes OnWord Press books internationally. For terms call 1-800-4-ONWORD or 505-473-5454; fax to 505-471-4424; e-mail to ORDERS @ IPG.HMP. COM; or write to High Mountain Press/IPG, 2530 Camino Entrada, Santa Fe, NM 87505-8435, USA. Outside North America, call 505-471-4243.

Comments and Corrections

Your comments can help us make better products. If you find an error in our products, or have any other comments, positive or negative, we'd like to know! Please write to us at the address below or contact our e-mail address: READERS@HMP.COM.